TROUT AND SALMON RIVERS OF IRELAND

An Angler's Guide

Peter O'Reilly

MERLIN UNWIN BOOKS

First published in Great Britain by Merlin Unwin Books, 1991
Reprinted 1991
Second edition 1993

MERLIN UNWIN BOOKS
21 Corve Street
Ludlow,
Shropshire
SY8 1DA
England

British Library Cataloguing in Publication Data

O'Reilly, Peter
    Trout and salmon rivers of Ireland:
    an angler's guide.
    I. Title
    799.1755

ISBN 1–873674–09–0

Designed and typeset by Kingfisher Design Services
Maps drawn by Ken Smith
Printed in Great Britain by Cambridge University Press

Dedication
TO MY MOTHER

Contents

Introduction to the Second Edition and Acknowledgements

I did not think when I completed the first edition of this work in 1991 that a revised edition would be required so quickly. But time never stands still and in the wonderful world of nature, change is constantly taking place.

Nature, left to follow its natural course, can vary quite a bit from the norm but nearly always it seems to be able to maintain itself. Natural disasters occur from time to time and nearly always right themselves again. The eco-system of the salmonid species is very fragile, yet salmon and trout have survived for thousands of years. They have many enemies in the wild but they always survive. Man appears to be the greatest predator of all and has caused the most harm and the fastest decline in stocks over the centuries.

A time-span of two years is very short in the life history of salmon and trout. However, even in that short a time, the influence of man can be great for better or worse.

I am glad to be able to report that in Ireland, from my observation of salmon and trout stocks in rivers, the overall position has probably shown a slight improvement. There has been a greater awareness of the environment in recent times on the part of Government and industry in general and this reflects itself in improved water quality. Furthermore a lot of river rehabilitation schemes have been carried out by Fisheries Boards, repairing the damage caused by arterial drainage schemes.

The runs of salmon in 1992, and the rod catch on some rivers in particular, showed a vast improvement on previous years. In particular, certain rivers in the south of Ireland had an unprecedented late run of salmon.

The sea-trout situation is still best described as very fragile. Certain fisheries, once again, experienced great fishing in the 1992 season with vastly improved runs of sea-trout. Even some of the worst affected fisheries in Connemara and the West of Ireland showed a slight improvement, but sport was still well short of that enjoyed up to the early 1980s.

Brown trout river fishing has, in my experience, held its own quite well in the past few years and, personally, I have experienced some of the best brown trout sport of my life in latter years.

Changes in fisheries administration are ongoing and of most immediate interest to anglers are licences, permits and the like.

I am not aware of any major changes in the Foyle Area or Northern Ireland. The Republic of Ireland is a different story. There have been numerous changes in respect of licences following the protracted 'rod licence dispute' regarding brown trout and coarse fishing. A licence is also required for salmon and sea-trout fishing. Licences are now available in many forms: annual, nationwide or district, even one-day tourist licences. The price of permits on waters managed by the Regional Fisheries Boards was once uniform throughout the country, but now it varies by region.

Legislation was enacted in 1992 setting up eight fisheries co-operative development societies. The purpose of the societies is to assist the development of brown trout and coarse fishing by providing funds and offering anglers and others the opportunity of contributing towards development works. The societies work closely with the Regional Fisheries Boards and issue share certificates to anglers, clubs, etc. Annual share certificates cost IR£12. A 21-day certificate costs IR£5 and a 3-day tourist certificate costs IR£3.

When the Management Committees were elected at the end of 1992, the members of the Northern Fisheries Development Society and of the Upper Shannon Fisheries Development Society decided that a share certificate would be required to fish in those areas. Persons under 18 years of age, or 66 and over, unemployed people who receive social welfare assistance and people in receipt of invalidity pensions do not have to hold share certificates in order to fish.

Fishing tackle is very much a personal choice. I offer the following advice only by way of a guideline. When fly fishing for salmon on big rivers in spring or autumn, a 14-16 foot double-handed rod is desirable. A single-handed rod is adequate in low water conditions for summer grilse. For spinning, worm and shrimp fishing, 10-12 foot rods are my preference. Leader strength can vary – depending on water height and the average size of salmon – from 6 to 18 lb breaking strain. Sinking or sink-tip lines are necessary for spring fishing. Floating and sink-tip lines are more commonly used when salmon fishing in summer conditions. Summer sea-trout can be fished for with a single-handed rod and floating line. A sink-tip may sometimes be required. Very fine leaders may be necessary.

Biting midges can prove downright nasty on warm, still summer days. Be sure to take along a good insect repellant.

For successful salmon fishing an intimate knowledge of the river and the lies of the fish is essential. This can only come with experience and the latter is gained either by repeated visits over many years to the same fishery or by hiring a local gillie or guide. All the better fisheries can provide gillies if given adequate notice.

A word of advice on wild brown trout fishing here: A 9-10 ft rod rated AFTM 4-5 is ideal. The leader should have 2-4 lb breaking strain. tippets. More trout are hooked on the finer tippets but equally, more are lost in heavy weed situations. Chest waders and a wading staff are essential for fishing some of the bigger rivers.

In certain rivers, the trout stocks are very plentiful and completely wild. It should be remembered that wild brown trout are not easily caught. They are extremely shy and cautious. It is, therefore, very easy to put them off the feed. Clumsy bankside behaviour and poor fly presentation will dramatically reduce the chances of success, especially with the bigger trout. Fish the faster glides and riffles during the day. Here the trout have less time to examine your fly. Leave the quieter water till dusk or until a big hatch of fly puts the trout in a feeding frenzy and they become a little less cautious. Very often, there is no shortage of feeding fish. Getting them to take is the problem. Stay away from stretches near bridges and easily accessible places. Trout can be very sensitive to angling pressure. Better fishing and less cautious trout can often be found by the angler who is prepared to walk some distance and explore the unfrequented places.

The trout angling season runs from early March to 30 September. The peak angling periods are from 1 May to mid-June. The fishing at this time can be good right through the day. Throughout the summer, the best fishing is mainly at dusk. Come September, and the fishing reverts to daytime fishing with trout moving well to the fly at dusk, especially early in the month.

Compiling the information for this book has been a source of both joy and satisfaction: joy at discovering the existence of so many wonderful rivers and satisfaction at being able to record the details of them for another generation of fly fishers. Of necessity, I had to rely heavily on others to help me in my research. I received the utmost encouragement, kindness and assistance wherever I went. Without this, the book could not have been written.

I gratefully acknowledge the help given to me by the staffs of the Central and Regional Fisheries Boards. Michael Breathnach, Chief Officer of the Central Board was at once encouraging and accommodating at the idea of the project. The contributions of my colleague, Martin O'Grady, and former colleague Ken Whelan, now Director of the Salmon Research Trust, added an invaluable dimension to what I was trying to achieve.

A special word of appreciation is due to Ms Phil Kelly, Fisheries Division, Department of Agriculture for Northern Ireland, and to W.G.

Crawford, Secretary of the Foyle Fisheries Commission and his staff for their most valued assistance. I acknowledge too the information and hospitality received from Tommy McCutcheon, the tackle dealer and fly casting instructor from Sandy Row, Belfast.

Now that the task is complete, my thanks go to my publisher, Merlin Unwin, for his patient, persistent encouragement at those times when I was tempted to give up altogether.

How can I forget my wife Rose for her support and patience? She has always been able to find the missing questionnaire and the lost file. Her help has been indispensable. At last, hopefully, our young son Patrick's patience will be rewarded and I will be free to take him fishing.

A special word of thanks ito all those anglers who graciously endured my questioning and for so much useful information given so unselfishly.

I gratefully acknowledge the diligence and courtesy of my typist, Miss Bridie Fleming and the photographic skills of my friend, James Carney and his staff at Flower Hill, Navan.

I hope, in this second edition, to have picked up the changes that have taken place in Irish river fishing over the past two years: new riparian owners, new permit issuers, changed telephone numbers and addresses, up-to-date catch records and so on. If there are any mistakes, the fault is mine, and if brought to my attention, they will certainly be put right in the next reprinting.

So, welcome to this new edition of *Rivers of Ireland*. Once more, fellow anglers, go quietly on your way by river and stream, being always mindful of the privilege it is to be there; and never sully the image of our sport, nor damage in any way that which we hold in trust for those who will come after us.

Peter O'Reilly
Ballybatter House
Boyne Hill
Navan
Co. Meath
Ireland

March 1993

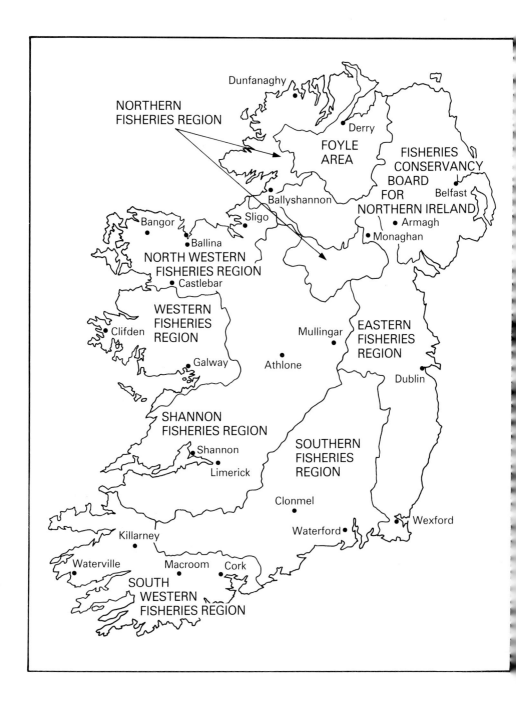

The fishery regions of Ireland

·1· Foyle Area

The Foyle area comprises all rivers entering the sea and Lough Foyle between Malin Head in Co. Donegal and Downhill in Co. Derry. It covers areas in both the Republic of Ireland and Northern Ireland. The conservation, improvement and protection of its fisheries is administered by the Foyle Fisheries Commission, a statutory body set up under the 1952 Foyle Fisheries Act. The Commission office is at 8 Victoria Road, Derry, BT47 2AB, *(telephone* 505 42100). The nature of the terrain ensures that salmon and trout are the predominant species.

The Foyle area has its own peculiar angling regulations, the chief one being that a rod licence is required to fish for both brown trout and salmon (this includes anglers under 18 years of age).

CULDAFF RIVER   C 51 48

The Culdaff River (10½ miles long and with a catchment of 25 square miles) drains north east Inishowen in Co. Donegal into Culdaff Bay. It is a deep, sluggish river, flows partly through bogland and is overgrown in places. Access is difficult and local knowledge is essential.

It can hold a very good stock of sea-trout in July and especially in August. The salmon come with the first flood in August. The river holds fair numbers of brown trout to 1 lb. There is a sea-trout draft-net fishery at the mouth.

The best sea-trout fishing is in the tidal water at Culdaff and – later in the season – up at Glenelly. There is good salmon fishing from about a mile above Gorey to a point 1 mile below Gorey. Note especially Bocan, where there are some good holding pools. Poaching is a big problem.

Permission

The fishing is with the landowners' permission. For information on the local angling club, contact:

Mr Bernard McGuinness
Culdaff
Co. Donegal

RIVER FOYLE   H 34 99

Season

River Foyle and all tributaries except River Finn 1 April to 20 October. There is a stipulation that the season can be curtailed by 10 days to 10 October, in certain circumstances.

The ownership of the fisheries is very fragmented. Some waters are in public ownership, some are private, while others are leased to clubs or syndicates. In some cases, the owners do not exercise their rights and the fishing is regarded as free.

The River Foyle with its extensive system of tributaries drains a scenic mountainous catchment of some 1,130 square miles, in the counties of Derry, Donegal and Tyrone, into Lough Foyle. It is primarily regarded as a salmon and sea-trout system. The total commercial catch for the Foyle area between the years 1979 and 1987 ranged from a peak of 83,252 fish in 1983 to a low of 18,483 in 1987. It would appear from the figures available that the River Foyle has the potential to be one of the top salmon producing rivers in the country.

The River Foyle to Lifford Bridge consists of 20 miles of tidal water. Angling is confined to a stretch reaching from a point about half a mile above Lifford Bridge and a one mile stretch downstream of the bridge. The river here is wide and shallow. It is tidal and fishes best when the tide is out and with low water conditions obtaining upstream in the tributaries. A rise of 6 inches on the River Finn or River Mourne can put it out of order.

The salmon fishing can be fair to good, depending on water levels. It is reported to produce about 20 spring fish and 100 grilse annually. The spring fishing is from March to May and the grilse run from the end of May to the end of July. There is no autumn run.

The sea-trout fishing can be exceptionally good in a short stretch half a mile either side of Lifford Bridge. It fishes best at night.

Permission

The fishery is managed by the Foyle Fisheries Commission (FFC). Permits available from:

FFC
8 Victoria Road
Derry

Mr Robert Cunningham
10-12 Bridge Street
Strabane, Co. Tyrone

Wm. Diver
The Variety Shop, 5 Castle Place
Strabane, Co. Tyrone

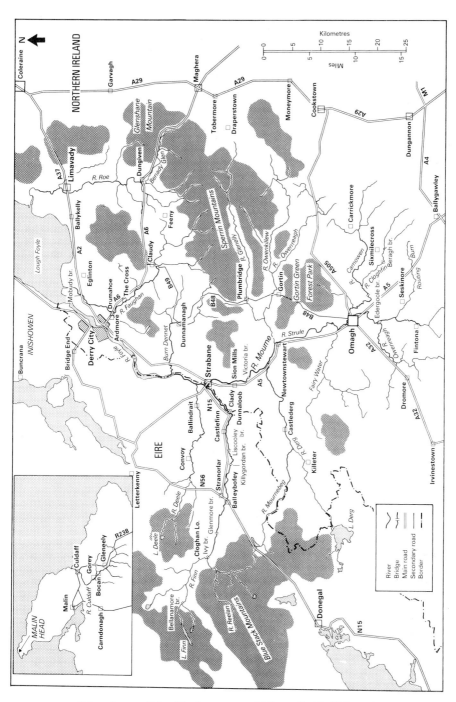

The rivers of the Foyle area and River Culdaff (inset)

RIVER DEELE   H 30 99

The River Deele comes down from Lough Deele in Co. Donegal, through
Convoy and Ballindrait, and enters the Foyle downstream of Strabane.
Its lower reaches are deep and slow-flowing and it is really only fished for
trout in the vicinity of Convoy, where there is a two-mile stretch of fast
flowing water. It holds a fair stock of brown trout ranging from $\frac{1}{2}$ to $1\frac{1}{2}$
lb. It often produces a few sea-trout in August and September. The
fishing is regarded as free.

BURN DENNET   C 40 04

The River Dennet rises in the Sperrin Mountains and flows west through
Dunnamanagh to the Foyle, downstream of Ballymagorry. Downstream
of Dunnamanagh it flows through rich agricultural land, while above the
countryside changes from rough pasture to mountain. The river has a
good stock of wild brown trout and can give excellent sea-trout fishing
from mid-June onwards. A few salmon move upstream in August and
September. The fishing is regarded as free with the permission of
riparian owners.

RIVER FINN   H 26 95

Season

All species: 1 March to 15 September.

The River Finn rises in Lough Finn in Co. Donegal and flows east
through a deep mountain valley to Ballybofey. From Ballybofey
downstream, the valley widens through Killygordan, Castlefinn and
Clady to the Foyle at Lifford. The Finn is 40 miles long and, together
with its tributary, the Reelan River, drains a catchment of 195 square
miles. The upper reaches of the Reelan and the River Finn are fast and
spaty downstream to Ballybofey and can give excellent sport with the fly
when conditions are right. From Ballybofey downstream the river
becomes deep and less spaty, though there is a mile of nice fly water at
Killygordon. Further downstream it becomes a big, deep, wide, slow
flowing river. Spring tides back it up $1\frac{1}{2}$ miles above Castlefinn and neap
tides back it up nearly to Clady.
    In the late 1950s the Foyle Fisheries Commission bought out and
suppressed two draft nets in the tidal section of the river. The
commercial netting on the Foyle does not begin till 21 June and this gives

spring fish a great opportunity to get into the Finn.

In all, there is more than 25 miles of salmon fishing on the river from Flushtown right up to Bellanamore Bridge and on part of the Reelan too. There is good sea-trout fishing at Liscooley and Killygordan and from Ballybofey to Bellanamore Bridge.

The fishing rights are fragmented and are either exercised by the owners or leased to angling clubs.

The Finn Fishery (River Finn)

The Finn Fishery is the first fishery above the tide. It is in public ownership and managed by the Foyle Fisheries Commission.

The fishery consists of approximately 6 miles of double-bank fishing extending from Liscooley Bridge to Flushtown Bridge. The river is deep and lazy here, 40–50 yards wide, but with enough of a push to fish a fly in high water.

It is predominantly a spring salmon fishery and the fishing can be very good in March, April and May. It produces an average of 200 fish per season and a few locals can take between 10 and 25 fish each.

The grilse tend to run through and the fishing is not usually as good as is the spring fishing. Most of the spring fish are taken either on spinner (brown & gold and blue & silver Devon minnows) or on worm.

The sea-trout fishing is just fair and the best of it is to be had above Clady Bridge, at Dunnaloob Chapel and at Castlefinn Bridge.

Permits

The FFC
8 Victoria Road
Derry
Telephone 0504 42100

Mr Kenneth Rule
Killygordon
Co. Donegal

McElhinney's Stores
Ballybofey
Co. Donegal

R. Cunningham
Bridge Street
Strabane
Co. Tyrone

D. Campbell
Main Street
Newtownstewart
Co. Tyrone

Wm. Diver
The Variety Shop
5 Castle Place
Strabane
Co. Tyrone

Finn Angling Club Water (River Finn)

Glebe Angling Club Water

Finn Angling Club has approximately 15 miles of fragmented fishing on both banks between Liscooley Bridge and Stranorlar. Glebe Angling Club has 9 or 10 linear miles on both banks in the same area.

This is mainly slow, deep water with the occasional stream. The banks are reasonably good and there are stiles and footbridges.

This is primarily a spring salmon fishery and it is very good in the months of March, April and May. Club members probably take in excess of 300 salmon annually. It is fairly heavily fished but not crowded.

The grilse fishing can be good in June and July and is not as heavily fished as is the spring run.

Permits (daily and weekly)

> Mr Michael Housten (Finn Angling Club)
> 5 Mount Carmel View
> Strabane
> Co. Tyrone
> *Telephone* 0504 883921

> Mr D. Floyd (Glebe Angling Club)
> 28 Melmount Villas
> Strabane
> Co. Tyrone
> *Telephone* 0504 883981

Ballybofey, Stranorlar and District Angling Club (River Finn)

This club has about 8 linear miles of double bank fishing (some single bank too) stretching from a point a short distance below Stranorlar up to a point about a mile downstream of Glenmore Bridge.

The character of the river begins to change here and it becomes more streamy with glides and pools. The spring salmon fishing is good, though not perhaps as good as the downstream fisheries (best from mid-April to mid-June). The grilse tend to run through to the upper reaches and the sea-trout fishing is quite good from the end of June, through July and August. The banks are well developed and the fishing not crowded.

Permits and information from

> Mr Brian McDermott
> Ardmiran
> Stranorlar, Co. Donegal

Cloghan Lodge and Glenmore Fishery

The top of the River Finn and its tributary, the Reelan River is controlled by Cloghan Lodge Hotel and the Glenmore Estate. Part of the fishery is in joint ownership for about 75 per cent of the river.

Permits for the Cloghan Lodge Hotel fishing from

> Cloghan Lodge Hotel
> Cloghan
> Ballybofey, Co. Donegal
> *Telephone* 074 33003/33016

This is true spate water set against a background of exceedingly beautiful mountainous Donegal countryside. The Finn rises in Lough Finn and the Reelan originates deep in the Blue Stack Mountains. Both are characterized by a very steep gradient which gives the river a marvellous character for the fly when it is in spate. It holds a share of spring fish from Glenmore to the Ivy Bridge from March to May, but it is as a grilse fishery that it really shines. The grilse run peaks in mid-June – depending on water – and there are fish up to Bellanamore Bridge and beyond and on the Reelan by July. It can get a very good run of autumn fish from mid-August. The season closes on 15 September The sea-trout run is also very good, but they are usually taken as a by-product of the salmon fishing. Fly fishers swear by the Reelan for grilse when it is in order.

Favourite flies are Garry Dog, Yellow Goat, Red Shrimp, General Practitioner, Hairy Mary and Thunder and Lightning.

Sion Mills Angling Club (River Mourne)

The River Mourne extends from Strabane to is confluence with the River Derg. It is a big, wide (over 100 yards in places) fast-flowing river. The salmon fishing can be very good from the end of May onwards and it gets an excellent run of sea-trout from the end of June. Sion Mills Angling Club manage the fishing rights for the Department of Agriculture on an extensive stretch of the river from Strabane to a point upstream of Victoria Bridge.

Permission

There are restrictions on the fishing in certain areas. Day permits are available from:

Mr Timothy McKee
Mourne Bar
Victoria Bridge, Co. Tyrone
Telephone Sion Mills 58243

Mr Mark Gough
6 New Street
Sion Mills, Co. Tyrone

RIVER MOURNE

RIVER STRULE

There are extensive private fisheries for salmon and sea-trout on the River Mourne and on its headwaters, the River Strule, extending upstream towards Newtownstewart.

Omagh Angler's Association Fishings

Omagh Anglers Association has extensive fishing on the River Strule, the Drumragh River, the Camowen River, and Owenkillew River.

Day permits are available from

C. A. Anderson
Lower Market Street
Omagh, Co. Tyrone

J. Graham
Ulster Cottages
Newtownstewart, Co. Tyrone

D. Campbell
Main Street
Newtownstewart, Co. Tyrone

The River Strule is an extension of the River Mourne from the confluence of the River Derg upstream to the town of Omagh. The Omagh Anglers' Association fishing extends downstream from Omagh to a point a short distance downstream of Newtownstewart. The wild brown trout are small, but 1 lb brown trout are stocked annually.

The salmon fishing can be quite good, depending on water conditions.

The grilse run up from the end of June or early July and it gets a run of summer salmon up to 17 lb. The Strule and Mourne have a reputation for good-quality, big, well proportioned fish.

The Drumragh River flows north to join the Strule at Omagh. Omagh Anglers' Association. has the greater part of the fishing up to Edergoole Bridge. It is stocked annually with brown trout.

The Camowen River flows westwards from Carrickmore to Omagh. The association has the fishing on the greater part of it up to Drumduff Bridge. It is stocked with brown trout and the salmon fishing can be good – given water – from mid-August to the end of the season.

The Owenkillew River flows westwards through Gortin to join the Strule at Newtownstewart. It is a spate river and can give prime sea-trout and salmon fishing — sea-trout from the end of June and salmon from mid-July. Omagh Anglers' Association has some fishing on the lower reaches.

The Blackiston-Houston Estate lets day tickets on stretches of the Owenkillew and Owenreagh River. This is spate river fishing for salmon and sea-trout in lovely countryside and can be quite good with a flood from July to October.

Day permits from

Mr Vic Betteridge	Mr John J. Patterson
Gortin, Co. Tyrone	Gortin, Co. Tyrone
Telephone Gortin 48346	*Telephone* Gortin 48207

GLENELLY RIVER   H 48 91

The Glenelly River is a tributary of the Owenkillew. The fishing is private.

THE FAIRY WATER   H 40 75

The Fairy Water is primarily a coarse-fishing river.

RIVER DERG   H 28 84

The River Derg rises in Lough Derg in south east Donegal and flows eastwards through Killeter and Castlederg to join the Strule River downstream of Newtownstewart. The gradient is steep and the river fast-flowing upstream of Castlederg, while most of the water from there to the confluence is deeper and more slow-flowing.

Salmon can be fished up as far as Killeter. It does not get a spring run but gets a good run of grilse on every spate from early July to the end of the season. The sea-trout fishing is also very good, beginning at the end of June.

Permission

A lot of the water is private but Castlederg Angling Club lets day tickets. Apply to:

Mr Robert Harron
Castlederg, Co. Tyrone
Telephone 06626 71256

RIVER FAUGHAN   C 50 10

The Faughan rises on the northern slopes of the Sperrin Mountains and meanders westwards, towards Derry City, through a pretty valley of pastureland and woodland, past Claudy, Ballyartan and Ardmore. At Drumahoe, the bankside environment changes from rural to an urban setting and the river swings north. About two miles downstream, it emerges into a rural setting once more before discharging through an industrial estate into Lough Foyle, 3 miles north of Derry City.

The Faughan is truly one of Ireland's most prolific sea-trout rivers and has provided a rich source of angling recreation for generations of anglers from Derry City and the surrounding countryside.

The following table of rod catches from the Foyle Fisheries Commission Annual Report of 1987 tells only part of the story.

RIVER FAUGHAN ROD CATCH RETURNS 1982-90

Year	1982	1983	1984	1985	1986	1987	1988	1989	1990
% returns	17	7	15	10	8	4	5	6	4
Sea-trout	2188	5723	1425	2808	1864	1210	1003	648	660

Season

The season opens on 20 May (angling club regulation) and closes 20

October.

The first salmon appear in the tidal water around the end of June and the first flood takes them over Campsie Dam and up to Ardmore. The summer fishing can be fair to good on up past Ballyartan and Claudy – depending on water and the size of the run of fish.

The sea-trout begin showing in numbers in the tidal water in June and up as far as Lynch's Dam, below Mobouy Bridge. Thereafter, they quickly move up river and the fishing peaks in July. At the time of writing (after the 1990 season) individual anglers reported taking as many as 200 sea-trout in the stretch from Drumahoe downstream for the season.

The best fishing is either early in the morning or late at night. The fishing is fly-only from one hour after sunset to one hour before dawn and fly fishing, spinning or worm fishing by day. In 1990, work carried out at the weir at Ballyartan has caused anglers to complain that both salmon and sea-trout have difficulty in making their way upstream. Only time will tell if this is so.

Permission

The fishing is leased by the Faughan Anglers' Association. The association has a big membership and at peak times fishing space is at a premium and very crowded indeed. Club membership is closed presently, but day and weekly permits are available from:

The Fishery Manager
Faughan Anglers' Association Office
Carlisle Road
Derry
Telephone 080504/267781

RIVER ROE   C 67 23

Season

1 April to 20 October. The angling clubs suspend fishing until 20 May.

The River Roe's tributaries rise on the north eastern slopes of the Sperrin Mountains and on Glenshane Mountain and the river flows north through Dungiven and Limavady into Lough Foyle. It is a spate river, draining the Roe valley, a place of great natural beauty, and the fine salmon and sea-trout fishing complements the lovely surroundings. It is a spate river, characterized by nice streams and pools with some deeper, slow flowing water in the middle reaches.

A progressive angling club on the river bought out two of the three draft nets operating at the mouth and the fishing has improved greatly since then. Depending on water, salmon and sea-trout can be taken up as far as Aghanloo and into the Benady Glen upstream of Dungiven.

The river gets a good – even an excellent – run of grilse in July and a very good run of salmon in late September and early October. This run can be so good that anglers reserve their holidays to fish it then.

The originator of the Red Shrimp, James Curry, fished the river with his brother, Joe, as does the modern fly tyer, Robert McHaffie. The Red Shrimp and the Gold Shrimp are still firm favourites, used mostly in sizes 8 and 6 but up to size 2 at the back end.

The sea-trout fishing is fair to good from early July onwards. Silver flies, such as the Teal, Blue and Silver, are best early on and more sombre patterns, such as the Blue Zulu, later. It is fly only at night and fly, spinner or worm by day.

Permission

The Limavady and Dungiven Angling Clubs amalgamated in 1990 to form the Roe Anglers' Association and the association controls the greater part of the fishing. Carrickmore Angling Club have a short stretch and riparian owners reserve occasional short stretches. Day permits on club waters are available from:

Richard Douglas   S. J. Mitchell & Co
6 Irish Street   29 Main Street
Limavady   Limavady
Co. Derry.   Co. Derry.

Sean McCluskey
Main Street
Dungiven
Co. Derry.

The Department of Agriculture has a $1\frac{1}{4}$ mile stretch in the Roe Valley County Park, near Limavady, and can be fished with a Department of Agriculture game fishing permit (over-18 or under-18) and, of course, an FFC game fishing rod licence.

·2· Northern Ireland Conservancy Board Area

There is a wide variety of excellent game-fishing available to the game angler in Northern Ireland.

Since the Department of Agriculture was given responsibility for the acquisition and development of public angling waters in Northern Ireland under the Fisheries Act (N.I.) 1966, some sixty-four waters have been provided, including twelve stretches of game-fishing rivers with a total length of over 50 miles. Other rivers available to anglers holding department permits include the Rivers Roe, Mourne, Shimna and Bush, all of which are renowned trout and salmon rivers.

Copies of statutory angling regulations are available from the Government Bookshop, 80 Chichester Street, Belfast, BT1 4JY.

LICENCES AND PERMITS

Anglers are sometimes confused as to the difference between a licence and a permit. A licence is required by law for each fishing rod used by anyone over 18 years of age to fish anywhere in Northern Ireland (except for sea angling). Under the age of 18, a rod licence is required if fishing for salmon or sea-trout anywhere in Northern Ireland and for game fishing in the Foyle area. Licences are issued by either the Fisheries Conservancy Board (FCB) or the Foyle Fisheries Commission (FFC), depending on which area you are fishing.

The FCB and FFC are conservation bodies responsible for protecting fish stocks generally in Northern Ireland. Both bodies issue angling licences in their respective jurisdictions and on payment of an additional supplement, allow fishing by licence holders in each other's jurisdictions.

A permit is a separate document issued by the owner of a fishery which confers the right to fish in the owner's fishery. The owner may be a private individual, a company, an angling club or a government department.

The following licences are currently available from the FCB:

Game-fishing

 Season game-fishing rod licence
 15 day game-fishing rod licence
 Endorsement to FFC season game-fishing rod licence
 Note A game-fishing licence also covers coarse-fishing

The following licences are currently available from the FFC:

Game-fishing

 Season game-fishing rod licence
 14-day game-fishing rod licence
 Under 18 years of age game-fishing rod licence
 Endorsement to FCB season game-fishing rod licence

The following permits are currently available conferring the right to fish on Department of Agriculture (DOA) waters:

Game-fishing

 General season game-fishing permit
 Juvenile (under 18) season game-fishing permit
 15-day general game-fishing permit
 Daily general game-fishing permit
 Local season game-fishing permit

RIVER BANN

The River Bann rises in the Mourne Mountains, south east of Hilltown in Co. Down. It flows north to Lough Neagh, the biggest lough in these islands, and thence to the sea at Coleraine. It is 86 miles long and together with its tributaries and the Lough Neagh tributaries it discharges into the North Channel the waters from a vast 2,243 square mile catchment.

 Salmon are taken in big numbers on the Lower Bann and in lesser numbers on the Upper Bann and many of the tributaries. The river gets only very occasional spring fish. The fishing picks up from early May. Sea-trout run in big numbers to the weir at Carnroe and above to some tributaries. Brown trout are dispersed throughout the system and runs of Lough Neagh trout, locally referred to as dollaghan, add a special dimension to the late-season fishing. These trout achieve weights of 6 to 7 lb and better. They run up the inflowing rivers after a flood and are fished in the tributaries by tactics similar to sea-trout fishing. For daytime fishing, the three most popular flies are Connemara Black, Fiery Brown and Mallard and Claret, size 8 and 10. At night they are fished in the deep pools. Big flies – for example, a Wye Bug, size 4 or 6 – a sinking line and a slow retrieve are the most productive tactics.

LOWER BANN

The Lower Bann is mainly a slow, deep, navigable channel with some fast runs in the vicinity of weirs. It is a wide river – over 400 yards in places. The water usually has a good deal of colour due to the eutrophic nature of Lough Neagh. It fishes best in low-water conditions and anglers don't like to see a lot of water being let down from Lough Neagh.

The main salmon fishing stretches are at Culliff Rock (Movanagher), Carnroe, Portna and The Cutts at Coleraine.

The river gets only a small run of spring fish and little fishing is done before May. From 1 May, it is estimated that there are enough fish in the river to begin fishing and the peak of the run is from mid-June to mid-July and there are always fish in the river from then until the end of the season on 30 September.

As can be seen from the Carnroe rod-catch figures below, the quality of the fishing can be excellent. The summer run is very big and the Lower Bann carries fish up for at least fifteen tributaries of Lough Neagh.

Salmon fishing is available at four locations, Portna, Culiff Rock, Carnroe, and The Cutts. It is available on three days per week only (Friday, Saturday and Sunday) at Portna, Culiff Rock and Carnroe, whilst day permits are available for The Cutts. Carnroe is a prime beat. It can fish well to the fly when the water reads around 16 feet on the gauge. Lightly dressed flies with a hint of orange or red are said to be best. Size is very important; at $14\frac{1}{2}$ feet, use size 10 and 12; at $15\frac{1}{2}$ feet use size 10 and 8; and over 16 feet, use size 6 upwards.

CARNROE ROD CATCH 1990-92

	1-16 May	17-31 May	1-15 June	16-30 June	1-16 July	17-31 July	1-16 Aug	17-31 Aug	1-16 Sept	17-30 Sept	1-15 Oct
1990	7	10	64	77	131	115	77	42	75	93	20
1991	-	7	8	162	140	114	60	31	11	62	99
1992	2	5	46	159	291	181	260	141	23	147	38

The beats at Portna, Culiff Rock and Carnroe are let on half day shifts and the allocation is usually made in February. Day tickets are available at The Cutts after 1 May. Apply in both instances to:

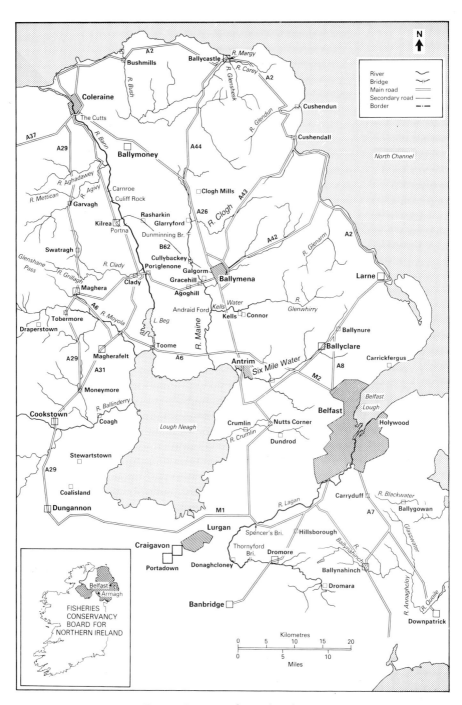

Lower Bann and Antrim rivers

Bann System Ltd
Dundarave
Bushmills, Co. Antrim BT57 8ST
Telephone 02657 31215

RIVER CLADY

The River Clady rises near Glenshane Pass in the Sperrin Mountains and flows east past Swatragh and Clady to join the Bann near Portglenone. It is a lovely little salmon river but the main run is quite late. Clady and District Angling Club leases all of the river and its tributary, the Grillagh River. Certain stretches are restricted to fly fishing only and no shrimp, float or maggot fishing is allowed.

Permits

Weirs
Clady Road
Portglenone, Co. Antrim

Boyle's
Gulladuff, Co. Derry

Moira's Shop
Portglenone
Co. Antrim

MOYOLA RIVER

The Moyola River rises deep in the Sperrin Mountains and flows east for 31 miles past Draperstown, Tobermore and Castledawson to Lough Neagh. Like many of the Lough Neagh rivers, it depends on water late in the season to get fish upstream. The Moyola is a good salmon and dollaghan river and also holds some nice resident brown trout. The Moyola and District Angling Club has fishing on the river and access to the river on the club water is by landowner's permission, except where public rights of way exist. The fishing methods are fly fishing, spinning and worm fishing. Maggots are not allowed.

Permits

Ewing's Confectionary Shop
41 Main Street
Castledawson
Co. Derry
Telephone 0648 68517

Mr Gilbert Crawford
Main Street
Moghera
Co. Derry
Telephone 0648 42369

H. Hueston's Tackle Shop
55 Main Street
Castledawson, Co. Derry
Telephone 0648 68282

BALLINDERRY RIVER   H 89 78

The Ballinderry River flows east from the Sperrin Mountains to Lough Neagh, through the towns of Cookstown and Coagh. It holds a good stock of resident brown trout with plenty of fish to 1 lb. In addition, it gets a very good run of dollaghan and a fair run of late-summer and autumn salmon. Much of the fishing is free, but with the permission of the riparian owners. Ballinderry Bridge Angling Club controls some of the fishing from Lough Neagh upstream to the village of Coagh.

Day tickets and season permits from

Mr W. McIvor
Croagh, Co. Tyrone.

RIVER BLACKWATER   H 88 60

Season

Salmon and Trout: 1 March to 31 October.

This is a big river by the time it reaches Lough Neagh. One branch rises near Clabby in Co. Tyrone and the other comes across the border from Co. Monaghan (see page 138). The northern branch flows past Clogher, Augher, Aughnacloy, Caledon and then northwards past Benburb, Blackwatertown and Moy.

The river has undergone arterial drainage in recent years but a lot of rehabilitation works have taken place.

There is a lot of nice streamy water from Clogher down to Benburb. The lower reaches, downstream of Blackwatertown are deep and sluggish.

Those upper reaches hold some great resident brown trout. The river gets a very good run of dollaghan and a fine run of big salmon in the months of September and October.

Augher and Clogher Angling Club controls fishing on the upper reaches and a Department of Agriculture game-fishing permit gives access to a stretch on the right bank upstream of Blackwatertown Bridge. There are a number of salmon lies down stream of The Island on this stretch.

CRUMLIN RIVER   J 15 85

This small spate stream gets a fair run of dollaghan in the month of October.

SIX MILE WATER   J 20 85

The Six Mile Water comes down from Ballynure and Ballyclare, and past Doagh, Templepatrick and Dunadry, before entering Lough Neagh west of Antrim town.

It is one of the finest brown trout rivers in Northern Ireland. It is well managed and stocked by Antrim and District Angling Club and the fishing is fly only till 1 September. It gets a good run of dollaghan and end-of-season salmon. There is no Sunday fishing.

Permits

Mr T. Wilson
Race View
Antrim

AGIVEY RIVER   H89 20

Season

1 March to 20 October (last 20 days reserved for club members only).

Permission

Mrs McCann
Agivey Road
Aghadoeey
Co. Derry

This is a spate river. It gets a great run of salmon and grilse. The first fish appear at the end of May. Fishing can be especially good in early July. It is worth fishing thereafter on every rising water till closing date. It has a fair stock of brown trout to 1lb. No shrimp, prawn of maggot fishing is allowed.

RIVER MAINE   J 08 09

The River Maine (34 miles long) flows south from Clogh Mills, in north Antrim, past Cullybackey, Ballymena and through the town of Randalstown to Lough Neagh. The Kells Water and its headwaters, the Glenwhirry River, are its most important tributaries.

The River Main holds a good stock of brown trout averaging ½ lb and gets a run of dollaghan and salmon from July. There is a lot of nice fishing on the entire system and the best approach to gaining fishing is through the clubs.

Maine Angling Club has about 4 miles of double bank fishing from a point a few hundred yards above Cullybackey to just above Dunminning Bridge. It has plenty of interesting streams and pools. It holds an excellent stock of resident brown trout, with dollaghan and salmon late in the season. The club issues twelve daily permits. There is no Sunday fishing.

Permits

> Mr R. Cotter
> Newsagent, Pottinger Street
> Cullbackey, Co. Antrim

Permits are on sale till 10 a.m. on bank and public holidays.

Gracehill, Galgorm and District Angling Club has some nice trout fishing with dollaghan and salmon when the water is right from late July. There is no Saturday or Sunday fishing and spinning is not allowed before 1 August.

Permits

> Galgorm PO, Galgorm
> Ballymena, Co. Antrim

Randalstown Angling Club has a long stretch of the Maine from Randalstown Road bridge upstream to Andraid Ford. It has good stocks of trout with dollaghan and salmon in season. No Sunday fishing. There is a bag limit of 4 fish and a 10-inch size limit. No maggot fishing.

Permits

> Mr Curtis Spence
> 32 New Street,
> Randalstown, Co. Antrim

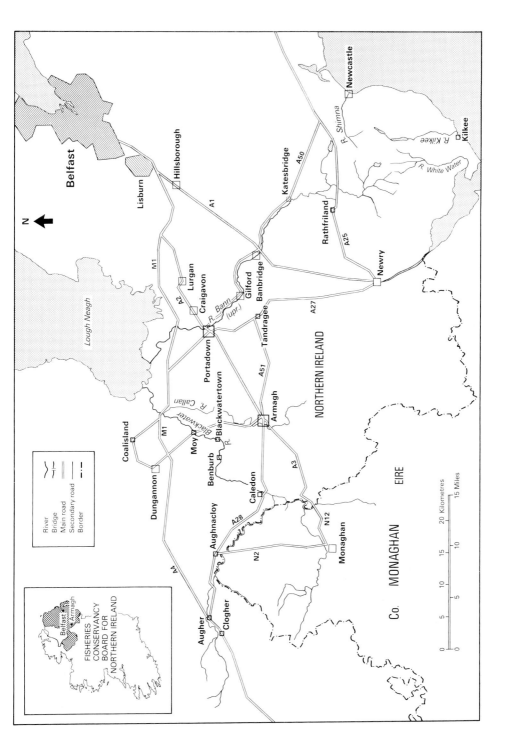

The Blackwater, Upper Bann and rivers of County Down

Kells and Connor Angling Club has fishing on the Kells Water and Glenwherry River. The upper reaches of the Kells Water and all of the Glenwherry River flow through rough pasture and are really spate water, but with some good pools. The Kells Water has some nice brown trout and can also hold fair numbers of escapee rainbows. Both rivers get a late run of dollaghan and salmon in September and October. Fly only to 31 July and then fly, spinning and worm fishing. No maggots and no Sunday fishing.

Permits

> Duncan's Filling Station
> Kells
> Co. Antrim

Flies

Useful trout flies on the River Maine and tributaries include Hare's Ear, Wickham's Fancy, Ginger Quill, Grey Duster, Greenwell's Glory, Mallard and Claret, Fiery Brown, Connemara Black and Ballinderry Black, Ballinderry Olive and Ballinderry Brown.

Flies for salmon: Black Doctor, Silver Doctor, Curry's Shrimps, Thunder and Lightning and Wye Bug.

THE UPPER BANN

Season

1 March to 31 October

The Upper Bann rises in the Mourne Mountains and flows north past Rathfriland, Katesbridge, Banbridge, Gilford and Portadown to Lough Neagh. It was a noted dollaghan, brown trout and late-run salmon river until the drainage scheme.

Thankfully, it has recovered well. It now gets a small run of dollaghan from July. It holds a good stock of small wild brown trout and the three clubs stock the river with takable brown trout annually. It can get a very good run of salmon from early July, depending on water conditions.

The best of the fishing is shared by three clubs, Gilford, Banbridge and Rathfriland.

Permits

Day permits on the Gilford Angling Club water are available at:

Moffatt's Newsagent
Main Street
Gilford, Co. Down

Banbridge Angling Club day tickets are available from:

Coburn's Ltd
Scarva Street
Banbridge, Co. Down
Telephone 08206 62207

The Anglers' Rest
Corbet
Katesbridge, Co. Down

Rathfriland Angling Club day tickets can be obtained from:

Mr W R Trimble
25 Downpatrick Street
Rathfriland, Co. Down

In the case of each of the above clubs, only a limited number of day tickets are available each day.

RIVER BUSH

Season

Game Fish: 1 March to 30 September

The River Bush flows north through Bushmills and into the sea at Portballintrae. The River Bush Fishery is run primarily as an experimental salmon river for the study of the biology and management of salmon. The Bush gets a small run of spring salmon from opening day and a good run of grilse from early July.

The letting of the fishing is divided into three sections:

1. The Private Stretch, where rods are sometimes available. Apply to Sir Patrick MacNaghten, Dundarne, Bushmills, Co. Antrim BT57 8ST, *(telephone* 02657 31215).

2. The River Bush day-ticket stretches available on Department of Agriculture game-fishing licences. A limited number of day tickets are available at the hatchery.

3. The unrestricted stretch (24 miles) — with the exception of the Lion Park — available on Department of Agriculture game-fishing permit.

MARGY, CAREY AND GLENSHESK (GLEN) RIVERS   D12 40

Season

1 March to 31 October.

The Margy ($\frac{1}{2}$ mile) and its tributaries, the Carey ($2\frac{1}{2}$ miles) and Glenshesk ($1\frac{1}{2}$ miles) flow into Ballycastle Bay. This is a noted sea-trout system in September and October and it also gets a small run of salmon.

The Margy is fly only between Bonamargy Bridge and the confluence of the Carey River. The remainder of the Margy is fly, spin and worm, as are the Carey and Glenshesk rivers.

The fishing on the Margy is almost entirely from the right bank by agreement with the riparian owner, Ballycastle Golf Club. Anglers should be alert to the golfers cry of 'Fore'. On certain golf competition days, fishing is restricted and notices are posted.

Permits

Department of Agriculture game-fishing permits.

GLENDUN RIVER   D 22 32

Season

1 June to 31 October.

The Glendun River drains one of the biggest of the Glens of Antrim into Cushendun Bay. It is very much a spate system that drains a mountain hinterland with clear, open banks. It gets a good run of small sea-trout and a small run of very good salmon. Fly fishing, spinning and worm fishing only.

Permits

Glens Angling Club tickets from:

Mrs M. McFettridge
116 Tromara Road
Castle Green
Cushendun
Co. Antrim

GLENARM RIVER   D 30 16

The fishing is private.

RIVER BLACKWATER (CARRYDUFF)   J 50 61

The River Blackwater comes down from Carryduff and flows into
Strangford Lough. The brown trout are very small and it gets a few sea-
trout in October.

QUOILE RIVER   J 46 46

The Ballynahinch River and the Glasswater River join to become the
Annaghcloy River and it becomes known as the Quoile River just west of
Downpatrick. The Quoile basin at the bottom of the river has brown
trout.

Permit

Department of Agriculture Game-fishing permit.

Further upstream, the fishing is controlled by Blackhead Angling Club.
The river here holds wild trout and the club stocks with brown trout.
There is some lovely fly water up at Kilmore.

RIVER LAGAN   J 12 55

Season

1 March to 30 September.

The Lagan rises on Slieve Croob, south of Dromara in Co. Down, and
flows on in a crescent-like course through Dromore, Donaghcloney, past
Lurgan and Lisburn to the tide at Belfast Lough.
  Under an agreement with the Department of Agriculture, Iveagh
Angling Club exercises the fishing rights on all stretches of the River
Lagan between Thorneyford Bridge, outside Dromore, to Spencer's
Bridge, Flatfield, Co. Down.
  This is a well stocked, well maintained and beautiful river to fish. It
offers some of the nicest brown trout fishing in Northern Ireland and
stretches at Donaghcloney and Blackscull can be especially

recommended.

Notices are posted at access points on all stretches indicating permitted methods and restrictions, where appropriate. Day tickets issued for Sunday fishing do not permit holders to fish those stretches signposted 'No Sunday Fishing'.

The stretch is approximately 7 miles long and it was here that Mr Percy Perry developed and tested his very effective and famous Perry's Black Midge. There is a six trout bag limit and part of the stretch is fly fishing only.

Permits

Mr Sidney Beckett
54 High Street
Lurgan, Co. Antrim

McCartan's Bar
Donaghcloney
Co. Armagh

Premier Angling
Queen Street
Lurgan
Co. Armagh

The Iveagh Angling Club makes available an unlimited number of day tickets to non-club members. In addition, 10 daily tickets are available per day, free of charge, to holders of Department annual game season permits on production of their adult or juvenile permit.

Sea-trout

In recent times, sea-trout have made a comeback in the river. They can be taken at Stranmillis Weir, in Belfast, usually on maggot or worm in the months of August and September.

Permit

Department of Agriculture annual game season permit.

SHIMNA RIVER   J 37 32

Season

1 March to 31 October.

The Shimna is a small spate river with good deep holding pools. It drains the northern slopes of the Mourne Mountains into the sea at Newcastle,

Co. Down. It gets a good late season run of salmon and sea-trout. The sea-trout are above average in size and the river holds the Irish freshwater rod caught sea-trout record – 16 lb 6 oz, caught in 1983.

Two and a half miles are under the control of the Department and can be fished with a Department of Agriculture game-fishing permit.

The rest of the river is controlled by Shimna Angling Club. The club makes four day permits and six weekly permits available. They can be obtained on a 'first come, first served' basis during business hours only from:

The Four Seasons
47 Main Street
Newcastle, Co. Down.

Note that Department permit holders are not entitled to fish Shimna Angling Club waters without the necessary club permit.

KILKEEL RIVER   J 31 04

WHITE WATER   J 27 03

Season

1 June to 31 October.

These two little spate rivers hold small brown trout and late season sea-trout and salmon.

Day tickets are restricted to six per day, there is no Sunday fishing and fishing within Mourne Park Demesne is excluded.

Tickets available from:

S. R. Nicholson   Graham's Sports Shop
Hardware Merchant   Kilkeel
The Square   Co. Down.
Kilkeel, Co. Down.

BALLINAMALLARD RIVER   H 21 53

Season

1 March to 30 September.

The Ballinamallard River flows into Lower Lough Erne between Kesh and Enniskillen. It holds trout, salmon, roach and pike. The trout predominate and a small number of salmon run from mid-July. Access is off the A35 Enniskillen to Irvinestown Road at Kilgortnaleague Bridge.

Permit

Department of Agriculture game-fishing permit.

A good start! New Year's Day on the Drowes

·3· Northern Fisheries Region

The Northern Fisheries Region extends from Malin Head in Co. Donegal – the most northerly point in the country – south along the western coast of Donegal to Dunlevy's Point in north Sligo. It stretches far into the north midlands and includes parts of Leitrim, much of Co. Cavan and part of Co. Monaghan. The headquarters of the Northern Regional Fisheries Board is at Station Road, Ballyshannon, Co. Donegal, (*telephone* 072 51435).

The Donegal rivers are mostly acid waters draining mountain, moor and bogland. Brown trout are very small but the sea-trout, grilse and, in many instances, spring salmon make up for lack of brownies. The River Drowes frequently produces the first salmon of the season on New Year's Day. Further inland, the Upper Erne and its tributaries are totally wild and for the most part unspoiled by arterial drainage schemes. These waters can give spectacular sport in certain areas for good quality wild brown trout.

TRAWBREAGA BAY   C 42 51

This is one of the few places in Ireland where you can fish for sea-trout in the sea. They are fished at Trawbreaga Bar mouth either from Doagh Island or from the Five Fingers Strand, 3 miles north of Malin. The best fishing is for an hour before and after both high and low-water. Sandeels and spinning silver Devons, silver eels or small spoons are the recommended fishing methods.

GLENNAGANNON RIVER   C 48 48

Permits

Mr Conn Smyth
134 Ard Colgan
Carndonagh
Co. Donegal

The Tourist Office
Carndonagh
Co. Donegal

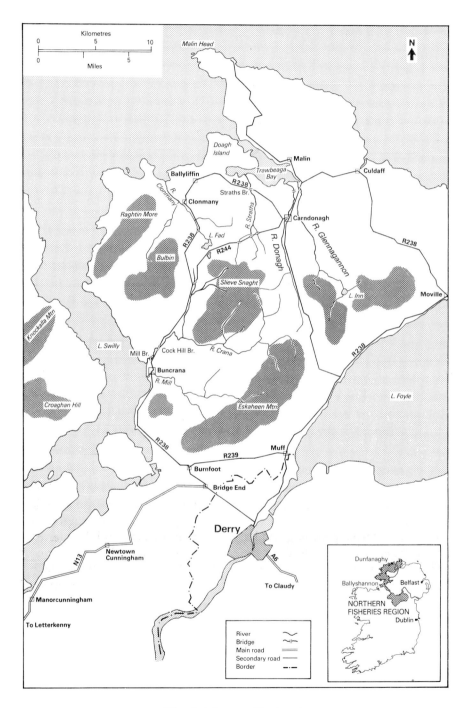

The Inishowen Peninsula

Season

Salmon: 2 February to 30 September.
Sea-trout: 2 February to 12 October.

This little river flows 10 miles from Lough Inn and drains a 14 square mile valley into Trawbreaga Bay. It is regarded as one of the better rivers for sea-trout and salmon on the Inishowen Peninsula. The sea-trout run in July and the salmon come in late August and September. The best of the fishing water is downstream of the Malin Road bridge – fishing off the left bank. On a spate, the local anglers fish both banks up to the village of Carndonagh. It can produce some big sea-trout – to 6½ lb – and all methods are allowed.

DONAGH RIVER   C 46 46

Season

Salmon: 2 February to 30 September.
Sea-trout: 2 February to 12 October.

Permits

Mr Conn Smyth
134 Ard Colgan
Carndonagh
Co. Donegal

The Tourist Office
Carndonagh
Co. Donegal

The Donagh River is 9 miles long and flows through Carndonagh into Trawbreaga Bay. It drains picturesque Glentogher and a 15 square mile catchment and holds sea-trout from July and grilse from mid-August. It suffers badly from poaching and has a pollution problem. It is best fished immediately after a spate from the village of Carndonagh downstream. There are some nice pools below Corvish Bridge. Access is off the Malin road and the Corvish road. For salmon, spin a 1¼ inch Devon minnow or a Mepps No. 2 or 3 or fish a worm. Recommended sea-trout patterns are Silver Doctor, Connemara Black, Zulu and Butcher.

STRATHS RIVER   C 43 47

Season

Sea-trout: 2 February to 12 October.

Permission

Free.

The Straths River enters the west side of Trawbreaga Bay. It drains a 9 square mile catchment and is fished for sea-trout. The bottom half-mile is regarded as best from June onwards but there are some deep pools up in the valley that hold fish too. It suffers from occasional bouts of pollution.

CLONMANY RIVER   C 35 47

Season

Salmon: 2 February to 30 September.
Sea-trout: 2 February to 12 October.

Permits

> Mr John (Danny) Doherty
> Clonmany
> Co. Donegal

The Clonmany River rises in Lough Fad and flows 7 miles through the village of Clonmany into Tullagh Bay. It gets a fair run of salmon and grilse and a few sea-trout. It is heavily poached. The fish run early – from June – and it is fished after a spate from the village to the sea.

CRANA RIVER   C 34 33

Season

Salmon: 1 March to 30 September.
Sea-trout: 1 March to 12 October.

Permits (weekly)

Mr Tom Sreenan
Westbrook
Buncrana
Co. Donegal

Mr Leo Burke
Westbrook
Buncrana
Co. Donegal

The fishing rights of the Crana River (including the netting rights) were purchased by the progressive Buncrana AA. in 1988. It is a 12-mile-long spate river which rises deep in the mountains of Inishowen and drains a 40 square mile catchment into Lough Swilly, just north of Buncrana. The countryside is wild and beautiful with mountain, rough pasture and some forestry in the upper reaches and the river is characterized by deep pools and a rocky gravel bed. It holds salmon and sea-trout from June.

Access is reasonably easy, involving no more than a half mile walk at the furthest point.

The salmon fishing peaks with the grilse run in July and can be very good when the water is right. It is estimated to have produced an average of 250 fish annually up to 1990. The figure for 1992 was 515 salmon. All fishing methods are allowed except 'bubble and fly' and there is no spinning allowed in low-water. The best of the fishing is in the 6 miles to the sea. A copper and silver spoon is favoured in a flood and the Fiery Brown, Wye Bug and various shrimp flies are also popular.

The first sea-trout begin running at the end of June and the run peaks at the end of July and through August. The best fishing is at night for half a mile from the Mill Bridge down to the estuary but they can also be taken up to Wilson's Pool and Cock Hill. Suggested fly patterns include Black Pennell, Bibio, Connemara Black, Watson's Fancy and Raymond, in sizes 10 and 12.

THE MILL RIVER   C 35 31

Season

Salmon: 2 February to 30 September.
Sea-trout: 2 February to 12 October.

Permission

Free.

The Mill River drains the mountains of southern Inishowen into Lough Swilly just south of Buncrana. It is about $8\frac{1}{2}$ miles long and its catchment is 18 square miles. There are impassable falls half a mile above the tide, so the river only holds occasional salmon, but it can be good for sea-trout fishing in its lower reaches from July onwards.

RIVER SWILLY   C 14 10

Season

Salmon: 2 February to 30 September.
Sea-trout: 2 February to 12 October.

Permit

Not required.

This is a substantial little spate river, nearly 26 miles long and draining 112 square miles of Donegal mountains and farmland into Lough Swilly at Letterkenny. It was the subject of arterial drainage works some twenty-five years ago and a spate runs off very fast. The estuary is fished from February to the end of July by some twenty loop nets, similar to the haaf nets used on the Solway – a right granted by royal charter.

The grilse run in good numbers from about the second week of June and the sea-trout come in August. There was a dramatic decline in the catch of both grilse and sea-trout in the 1991 and 1992 angling seasons. The banks are overgrown from Old Town upstream and the fishing is with worm, shrimp and spinner. It is fishable from Old Town for about 7 miles up as far as Breenagh Bridge but the best is said to be from Rashedoge to Conwall graveyard. Local anglers are estimated to take 30-40 fish each per season. A 24 lb fish was taken in 1989 and a 12 lb sea-trout in 1988. It is very unusual to meet a flyfisher on this river and the sea-trout are taken as a by-product of the salmon fishing.

RIVER LENNON (LEANNAN)   C 21 20

Season

Salmon: 1 January to 30 September.
Sea-trout: 1 January to 30 September.

Permits

The bottom half mile (or so) of the river downstream of Drummonahan Bridge at Rathmelton belongs to the Rathmelton Fishery Company and

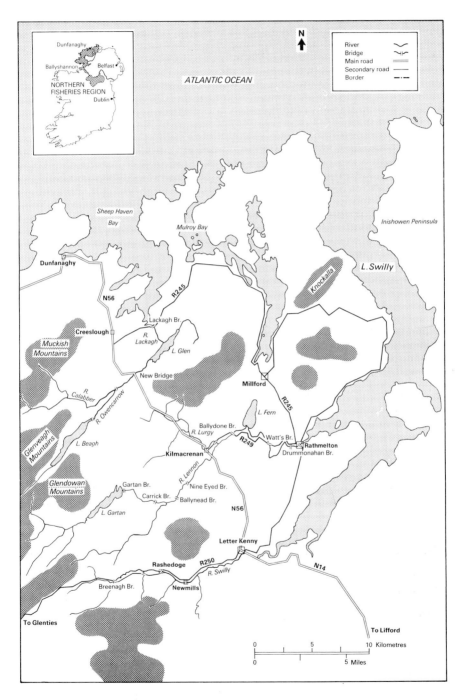

The rivers Swilly, Lennon and Lackagh

the fishing is not let. This stretch includes the renowned Watt's Pool. The rest of the river is free fishing.

The River Lennon drains the Glendown Mountains in mid-Donegal into Gartan Lough and flows through the village of Kilmacrenan to Lough Fern and on over a series of weirs to meet the tide at Lough Swilly just below Rathmelton. It is 29 miles long and drains 109 square miles, including numerous loughs. These loughs play a major role in maintaining good water levels for spring fishing. There are eight draft nets operating at the mouth, fish traps at Rathmelton and there are problems too from domestic and agricultural pollution.

Up until 1977 the River Lennon was regarded as one of the great Irish spring salmon rivers. A measure of its greatness was 70 fish taken by anglers up river on Easter Monday, 1975. An outbreak of UDN that year decimated the stocks in subsequent years and only in recent times has the disease shown signs of waning and the run begun to improve again.

Watt's Pool nearly always produces a fish on opening day – 1 January – and the stretch from Drumonahan Bridge above Watt's Pool up to Lough Fern tends to fish best in the cold weather of February and up to 17 March. This stretch is lazy and deep. Woodside, Lagmore, the Black Bridge and the Hawthorn Pool at the bottom of the Long Lane are all noted taking spots. Occasional fish are taken between Lough Fern and Gartan Lough at this time too but this stretch of nearly 8 miles comes into its own from April. There are noted lies at Ballydone Bridge, Coyle's Pool and Harkin's Pool at Kilmacrenan, below the Nine-Eyed Bridge, above and below Ballynead Bridge and above Carrick Bridge. Patrick Cullen, The Anglers' Haven, Kilmacrenan, Co. Donegal, (*telephone* 074 39015) always has a good knowledge of the most up-to-date state of the fishing in this area.

The Lennon spring fish are good fish, averaging about 9 lb, and the best fish recorded weighed 33 lb. In spring, spin a yellowbelly, blue and silver or brown and gold Devon. Favourite flies include the Hairy Mary, Badger and Shrimp Fly.

The grilse come into the Lennon in late June. They have to contend with the nets and traps till 25 June. It takes a good flood to get them over the weir at Rathmelton and once they get over that obstacle they seem to run as fast as they can for Gartan Lough. Because the grilse run through so quickly, the fishing is confined to the local anglers and such others as may be fortunate to be in the area at the time of a good July flood. Stocks of spring salmon and grilse declined mysteriously, almost to the point of extinction, in the 1992 season.

There is no sea-trout fishing available up the river. They only run as far as Watt's Pool on the Rathmelton Fishery Company stretch.

LACKAGH RIVER   C 10 30

OWENCARROW RIVER   C 05 26

Season

Salmon and Sea-trout: 1 January to 30 September.

Permits

Creeslough and District Angling Clubs issue permits for the left bank of the Lackagh above the tide to Glen Lough and on the Owencarrow River on the left bank from Glen Lough up to the confluence of the Calabber River. Permits available at Lafferty's Supermarket, Creeslough, Co. Donegal. Letterkenny and District Anglers' Association have fishing on the right bank of the Owencarrow River and tickets are available from Mr John Doherty, Derryscleagh, Glen Lough, Termon PO, Co. Donegal (*telephone* 074 38057).

The Lackagh is a short river of less than 2 miles and drains Glen Lough and a 51 square mile catchment into Sheep Haven Bay in Donegal. It is crystal-clear and flows through rough moorland. It is noted for its run of spring salmon, grilse and sea-trout.

The spring run commences in January and peaks in March and some fish continue to run till May. There is a fair run of grilse in June and July when the water is right as well as a small run of autumn fish in September. The sea-trout fishing can be very good from mid-July. They can enter the river freely at all times on the tides. The Lackagh spring salmon were noted for how freely they took a fly. This was best fished on a sinking line and a $1/_2$-inch Willie Gunn tube fly was as good as any. Nowadays, spinning is allowed and the river is heavily fished. There are only three pools, the Eel Weir, the Garden Pool and the Grilse Pool, which doesn't fish well for spring fish till April.

The grilse can be taken on either sink-tip or floating line and a Badger or Shrimp Fly work well.

The sea-trout respond best to a fly at night and useful patterns are Mallard and Claret, Donegal Blue, Peter Ross and Connemara Black, sizes 10 and 12.

The Owencarrow River links Lough Beagh and Glen Lough and is $4^1/_2$ miles long. It, too, gets runs of salmon, grilse and sea-trout. The lower section at Glen Lough is deep and slow and fishes best with a wind to break the surface, while further up there are occasional pools. The banks are undeveloped and overgrown and access is difficult and involves a lot of walking.

RAY RIVER   B 95 33

Season

Salmon: 2 February to 30 September.
Sea-Trout: 2 February to 12 October.

Permits

Permits are issued by Cloughaneely Angling Association and are available from:

> Sean Meehan, Newsagent or
> Michael Sweeney, Fishing Tackle Shop
> Falcarragh
> Co.Donegal.

The Ray (pronounced Rye) River drains Muckish and Agla Beg Mountains north to the Atlantic west of Horn Head.   It is just 8 miles long with a 21 square mile catchment of mountain and rough moorland from source to sea.   The bottom pools are tidal and fish can get up in low-water conditions.   The lower reaches, below Ray Bridge, are mostly flat and dead.   Upstream, it is rough and rocky and fishable only on a spate.   Favourite fishing areas are at the Tractor Bridge, the Pots and a couple of nice pools above.   On a high spate, it can be fished up for nearly 3 miles.   It is very heavily fished!

A few spring fish run in May and from mid-June to the end of the season fish run on every spate.   It is a remarkably prolific as well as a beautiful little river and produces an unusually big percentage of 10–12 lb fish.   The most popular fly is a Curry's Red Shrimp.   Natural shrimp is not allowed.

The sea-trout run from mid-July and are mainly fished at the estuary and below the Tractor Bridge.   The best fishing is at night with a Silver Spider, Peter Ross or Butcher.   Access is good by road and some stiles have been erected.

TULLAGHABEGLEY RIVER   B 93 30

Season

Salmon: 2 February to 30 September.
Sea-trout: 2 February to 12 October.

Permits

Permits are issued by Cloughaneely Angling Association and are available from:

Sean Meehan, Newsagent or
Michael Sweeney, Fishing Tackle Shop
Falcarragh, Co. Donegal

The Tullaghabegley River is much better known locally as the Baawan River and the Baawan Pool – just above the tide with its steep waterfall – is known far and wide and is a favourite haunt of worm fishers. It enters the sea just west of Falcarragh, a small, insignificant stream, just 9 miles long with a 13 square mile catchment, which includes Lough Altan and the north slope of Mount Errigal, but it is a very productive little salmon and sea-trout river. The Baawan Pool fishes practically all the time from June – for the fish can ride in on the tide – but on a spate there are four or five nice little pools above the main road bridge with a nice stretch above the old railway bridge and a lovely flat at Meendarragh. Fish a small Shrimp Fly, Black Pennell or a Donegal Blue. The Baawan Pool is very heavily fished and anglers stand shoulder to shoulder.

GLENNA RIVER B 91 30

Season

Salmon: 2 February to 30 September.
Sea-trout: 2 February to 12 October.

Permit

Not required.

The Glenna is only 6 miles long and drains half a dozen small hill loughs and a 10 square mile catchment. It enters the sea at Gortahork. It is alleged to have been greatly abused in the past with poison and 'blowing' (explosives). It still gets a very late run (September) of good sea-trout and big salmon of 8 and 9 lb.

RIVER CLADY B 81 23

RIVER CROLLY (GWEEDORE RIVER) B 83 20

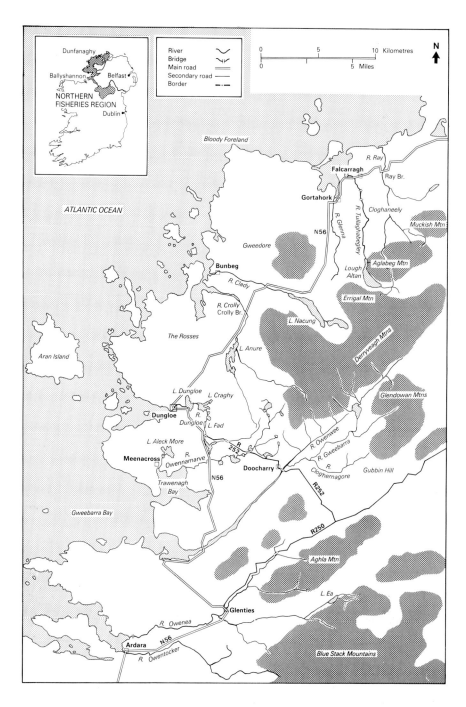

Ardara and Glenties, the Rosses, Gweedore and Cloughaneely

Season

Salmon: 2 February to 30 September.
Sea-trout: 2 February to 12 October.

Permits:

Mr C. Boner
Rosses Anglers' Association
The Bridge
Dungloe, Co. Donegal
Telephone 075 21163

The Manager
E S B power station
Meenacuing
Gweedore, Co. Donegal
Telephone 075 31033/31271

The Clady and the Crolly rivers have been joined in anglers' imaginations for generations for the excellence of their salmon and sea-trout fishing. Today, they are physically joined by a canal, a concrete umbilical cord, which channels the water from the top of the River Clady at its outflow from Lough Nacung and delivers it to a hydro-electric power station situated at the mouth of the Crolly. The hydro dam at the top of the Clady has a fish pass and the flow on the river is euphemistically described as a 'controlled flow'. In addition, a total of eighteen 'freshets' are let down per season to help get the fish up – two freshets in May, six in June, six in July, three in August and one in September. When the hydroelectric power station is generating the water from the Clady is discharged into the mouth of the Crolly in such quantities that it confuses the homing instincts of the Clady fish and draws them down the estuary to the mouth of the Crolly. There, the confused fish flounder and few make their way back to their own River Clady.

The Clady River, by all accounts, was one of the best little salmon rivers in Ireland. In spite of its 'controlled flow' and hydro dam, it still gets a fair run of fish and is estimated to produce an average of 300 fish to rod and line in the summer months. The rod fishery extends for a distance of about $3\frac{1}{2}$ miles from Ard Dun bridge, below the dam, to the sea at the fishing port of Bunbeg. It is a wild moorland river (catchment area 36 square miles), characterized by rocky granite outcrops, some deep pools and a deep gorge, and it flows through one of the most densely populated rural communities in western Europe. The main run of grilse is in June and Whit weekend can be an excellent time to take fish if the water is right. After that, there are good runs in July and some big fish run in late August and September. The best of the salmon fishing is regarded as being from Bunbeg Bridge down to the harbour. It is all fishable when in flood and should be approached from the left bank. Much of the fishing is done with worms but it is worth trying a fly in the Doctor's Pool, the Spinks, the Falls, Diver's Pool and especially the one below it.

The Clady gets only a fair run of sea-trout, which peaks at the end of August. The best of the fishing is in the evening from Bunbeg Bridge downstream, and sea-trout are taken in lesser numbers up to the bridge below the dam.

Fishing is not permitted between the dam and the bridge and natural shrimp may not be fished for salmon.

RIVER CROLLY

The River Crolly drains Lough Anure and a number of other loughs in its 23 square mile catchment. It is a narrow, rocky river with long, deep pools, waterfalls and rocky gorges. The surrounding countryside is wild and beautiful and very thickly populated. Much of it is narrow – 5 to 7 yards wide. A few spring fish run in March, April and May. The grilse begin to run in early June and fish enter the river, with a spate, right through to September. However, June sees the peak of the run and can give 8 or 9 fish a day. Access is easy, with a road all along the bank, but bankside conditions are rough, as is the case on the Clady.

There are some good lies between Crolly factory and a place upstream called 'The Flag'. There are three pools between Crolly Bridge and the sea, and downstream of Lough Anure is said to fish best in August–September.

Late June and July sees a fair run of sea-trout and the best fishing is from Crolly down to the estuary.

DUNGLOE RIVER   B 77 11

Season

Salmon: 2 February to 30 September.
Sea-trout: 2 February to 12 October.

Permits

    Mr C. Boner
    The Bridge
    Dungloe
    Co. Donegal

This small river drains several of the loughs in the Rosses area. It is fished for sea-trout in the summer months and the fishing is in three parts:

The first part stretches from Dungloe Lough to the sea has some good holding pools. There is good fishing on a spate below the town when the tide is filling. The stretch above the town from the hospital to Mulherns Pool, 50 yards below the lough, has some good holding pools for night fishing or for when the surface is rippled by the wind.

The second part of the river, between Dungloe Lough and Craghty Lough, is narrow but very deep. It is only about 600 yards long and can be fished downstream of the bridge.

The third part, the little stream above Lough Fad has some deep holes and it too can be fished up as far as the bridge.

ALECK MORE RIVER B 76 07

Permit

Mr C. Boner
Rosses Anglers' Association
The Bridge
Dungloe, Co. Donegal
Telephone 075 21163

This short river drains Lough Aleck More into Trawenagh Bay. It is very narrow, but fishable in parts. You can get sea-trout at the Bridge Pool at Meenacross in July and August when the tide is full.

OWENNAMARVE RIVER B 78 07

Permit

Mr C. Boner
Rosses Anglers' Association
The Bridge
Dungloe, Co. Donegal
Telephone 075 21163

The Owennamarve is a small, narrow river which drains about a dozen small lakes and an 8 square mile unspoiled, pollution-free catchment west into Trawenagh Bay, south of Dungloe. Its insignificant appearance belies its ability to provide a good day's sport with either salmon or sea-trout for those who know it. A few spring salmon enter it from March and it gets a heavy run of grilse from mid-June. All methods are allowed, but if conditions are right small flies – Shrimp Fly, Badger, Teal and Black – can get results. There are several good lies and a long pool about half a mile below the bridge on the N56 Dungloe–Glenties road is one of the favourites. There is another at the second falls about 500 yards above the same bridge.

The river gets a run of good spring sea-trout (2–4 lb) in May and the summer run peaks in mid-July. It can be fished at several points from the estuary up and the best fishing is at night or by day with a fresh west breeze to ripple the surface. Access is at the bridges. The banks are clear but uneven and the setting peaceful.

GWEEBARRA RIVER   B 88 05

Permit

Not required.

The Gweebarra drains Lough Barra and a lonely mountain valley with Crocknasharragh and Slievesnaght rising up to the north west and Crockastoller and the Glendown Mountains to the east. It flows into Gweebarra Bay and its estuary is all of 10 miles long, as narrow as a medium-sized river and heavily worked by ten draft nets in the salmon season up as far as Doocharry. The river itself is 20 miles long from its source and the upper reaches of its 60 square mile catchment are about as remote and beautiful as you will find anywhere. Being a free fishery, information is sparse on the rod fishery but the banks are sufficiently trodden to suggest that it is quite heavily fished in summer. It is a typical medium sized spate river with lovely long, deep pools and shallow rocky stretches in low-water. There are some nice pools above Doocharry. About a mile above Doocharry is the famous Mayo Pool at the confluence of the Cloghernagore River, which looks more like a small lough. Above this is the Falls Pool. These latter two pools are reached via a long, rough bog road off the Doocharry–Churchill road. This is virtually the end of the fishing unless one is prepared for a good two-mile mountain walk down the east side of Lough Barra, where there are three or four deep, slow pools below the outflow. It is much easier to reach them by boat on Lough Barra, if you have a boat!

The spring fish do not run till the end of April, the grilse run from late June and there is a run of big summer fish in August and September.

The Cloghernagore River joins the Gweebarra from the east at the Mayo Pool. It drains Lough Nanuroge and several other small lakes under the shadow of Gubbin Hill. This river has a long, lazy stretch 1½ miles long up in the hills and it holds salmon late in the season. It is reached via a winding 3-mile forest road off the R252 Doocharry–Fintown road.

The sea-trout arrive in the Gweebarra in July. It gets a fair run and they are fished in the estuary and in the pools in the vicinity of Doocharry.

Footnote: There are anglers who like to find their fishing easily accessible and convenient, and there are anglers who like to take to the hills and find solitude. The Gweebarra is for the latter. Sadly, on my visit in 1990, the whole hinterland showed signs of preparation for extensive forestry plantation and I wonder if I was not one of the last anglers to view this magnificently beautiful river catchment in its unspoiled natural state.

OWENEA RIVER   G 74 92

Season

Salmon: 1 March to 30 September.
Sea-trout: 1 April to 30 September.

Permits

The river is managed by the Northern Regional Fisheries Board. Permits are available from:

The Hatchery
Glenties, Co. Donegal

Kennedy's Filling Station
Glenties, Co. Donegal

Eddie Doherty's Public House
Ardara, Co. Donegal

The Owenea is one of Donegal's premier salmon and sea-trout rivers. It is a spate river, 16 miles long, and drains the mountains of mid-west Donegal and a 45 square mile catchment of moorland and some farmland into the sea one mile north of Ardara. In the first two miles up from the sea deep pools alternate with shallow rocky areas, while further up towards Glenties deep pools and short streams predominate. The salmon fishing extends beyond the town of Glenties to Meenachallow and the sea-trout for another 2 miles upstream. In all, there are about thirty named pools.

There is a run of spring salmon in April–May, ranging from 8 to 12 lb and the grilse begin to run early in June. July and August are the two best months, with September offering fair to good prospects of sport.

RIVER OWENEA ROD CATCH 1989-92

Year	1989	1990	1991	1992
Salmon	320	631	540	460
Sea-trout	2,723	200	180	455

This is as good a little river as is to be found anywhere and the fish take a fly very freely. All methods are allowed except on a 1½-mile stretch below Glenties from Ward's Pool to Archies Pool, which is fly-only. Favourite patterns are Jock Scott, Black Doctor, Fiery Brown, Lemon and Grey, Badger, and Shrimp flies.

The banks are reasonably well developed with stiles and footbridges. Access is at Owenea Bridge and via a number of long lanes off the R261 road and the N56 Ardara–Glenties road.

The sea-trout run in late July and give fantastic sport through August and into September.

Some of the best taking places are above and below Owenea Bridge and from the hatchery at Glenties down to the Mullindara Bends. The best fishing is in the evening and at night and many anglers prefer to fish small dark flies.

OWENTOCKER RIVER   G 74 90

Season

Salmon: 1 April to 30 September
Sea-trout: 1 April to 30 September.

Permits

The Hatchery
Glenties, Co. Donegal

Kennedy's Filling Station
Glenties, Co. Donegal

Maguire's Filling Station
Ardara, Co. Donegal

Eddie Doherty's Bar
Ardara, Co. Donegal

The Owentocker is an extremely spatey river. It is 12 miles long with an 18 square mile mountain catchment. It is rocky and shallow and has very few pools to hold fish. The banks are quite overgrown and what fishing there is is on the last 2 miles, where it flows through farmland. The Ness Pool under the falls is its best-known pool and gets a lot of attention from worm fishers when the grilse are running.

RIVERS BRACKEY AND DUOGH   G 72 90

Permit

Not required.

The Brackey and the Duogh are two little rivers that converge as they reach the tide at the top of Loughros Beg Bay, about one mile south of Ardara. They look so insignificant that you would pass them by unnoticed, yet they get a run of sea-trout and grilse in sufficient quantities to keep three draft nets operating at the mouth. The rod fishery is in three or four small tidal pools below where the two rivers join and on a short stretch – about 300 yards – of the Brackey. It holds grilse and sea-trout in July, August and September and is always worth a try if you are passing that way. It is ideal for fly with a wind on the pools, otherwise try a worm. Access is opposite Molloy's Factory on the N56 Ardara–Killybegs road.

OWENWEE RIVER   G57 80

THE GLEN RIVER   G 60 80

Permits

Enquiries about fishing to:

Donal Ward
Cumann Iascairi, Sliabh a'Liag
Ardcrin
Carrick
Co. Donegal   *Telephone* 073 39004

The Glen River drains the mountains of west Donegal, through the village of Carrick, and tumbles over a rocky cascade at its mouth into Donegal Bay. The upper reaches down from Meenaneary flow through a treeless moorland valley of smallholdings, whilst from Carrick downstream there is some bank cover. It gets a small run of salmon in May and the big run of grilse comes in early July. August sees the arrival of good summer fish up to about 12 lb. The fishing can be very good

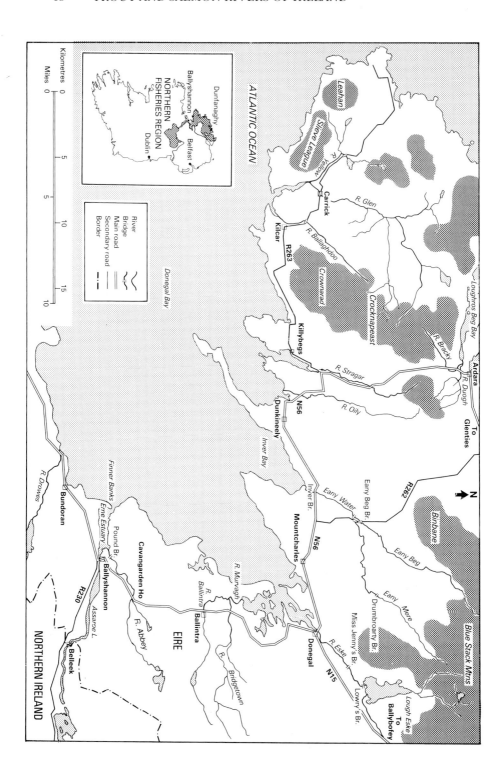

South-west Donegal

with fresh fish in the river and a falling spate. The best pools are in the first 3 miles up from the sea but there are fishable pools up for about 6 miles. Worming in the Salmon Leap pool at the sea is a favourite pastime and produces fish even in low-water. It is a lovely little river on which to fish a fly on falling water.

The Glen River used to get a great run of sea-trout but their numbers declined greatly in 1989.

The Owenwee, or Yellow, River shares the same estuary as the Glen River. Its catchment differs from the former in that it drains half a dozen lakes and their effect on the river is to maintain a better flow after a spate. It is fishable about 3 miles up and gets a good run of summer fish. It is always well worth fishing in August and September.

Access to both of these rivers is relatively easy, with roads running parallel to the banks in each case.

BALLAGHDOO RIVER   G 61 80

STRAGAR RIVER   G 72 80

OILY RIVER   G 74 80

The runs of salmon and sea-trout into these three rivers are so small that they are rarely if ever worth considering by the fisherman.

EANY WATER   G 82 79

Permits

	Northern Fisheries Board Office		
Kelly's Bar	Station Road		Doherty's Tackle Shop
Frosses P O	Ballyshannon		Main Street
Co. Donegal	Co. Donegal	*Tel.* 072 51435	Donegal Town

The Eany Water is about 15 ½ miles long and drains the southern slopes of the Blue Stock Mountains and a 46 square mile catchment which includes farmland, some moor and the remains of mature oak and beech woodland at Inver Bay - an offshoot of Donegal Bay. It is managed by the Northern Regional Fisheries Board. The Board ended the controversial draft net licence that permitted a draft net to operate in the river mouth. Fish can now negotiate the river unhindered.

The grilse begin running in June but the run doesn't really peak till the end of July and into August. It is a river that can fish well in September, with fish averaging about 7 lb. The fishing extends upstream from Inver Bridge to Drumbroarty Bridge on the Eany More Water, a distance of approximately 7 miles, and as far as Eany Beg Bridge on the smaller western tributary. This is a salmon river with a lot of potential, if the overfishing problem at the estuary can be overcome. Even under the present arrangement, it fishes well. It is a typical spate river with a gravel and flag bottom and numerous big holding pools. It colours quickly in a spate but clears just as quickly and the fishing can be very good indeed on falling water. The river twists and winds mainly through old pasture. It is possible to get a car fairly close to the water but walking the banks could be made much easier by the erection of stiles and footbridges. Fly fishing, worm and spinning are all practised but natural shrimp is prohibited. Useful fly patterns include Blue Charm, Silver Doctor, Shrimp Flies, Silver Blue, Thunder and Lightning and a Donegal Blue for the sea-trout. A Black Pennell also works well for sea-trout, as does a Connemara Black and a Teal, Blue and Silver – sizes 10 and 12.

The peak of the sea-trout fishing is in early July. It fishes best at dusk and good sea-trout pools include the Devil's Hole, the Carry, the Boat Hole, the Black Hole and Hughie's Pool.

RIVER ESKE   G 93 80

Permits

> C. Doherty
> Fishing Tackle Dealer
> Main Street
> Donegal

The River Eske is about 3½ miles long and drains Lough Eske and a 41 square mile catchment into Donegal Bay at Donegal Town.

There is a small run of grilse in June and the main run goes through in August and September. Fish continue to run in October and November. The banks are heavily overgrown and the river itself is lightly fished – most of the anglers concentrate on the lough. The main areas of interest for the salmon fisher are above the town, above and below Miss Jenny's Bridge and below Lowry's Bridge.

THE MURVAGH (BLACKWATER) RIVER   G 90 72

Permit

Not usually required.

The Murvagh River and its tributaries the Bridgetown River and the Ballintra River drain a 33 square mile catchment of farmland and numerous small loughs into Donegal Bay. The Murvagh holds salmon, sea-trout and brown trout. The end of July and the month of August see the peak of the salmon run and the main salmon angling areas are below Murvagh Bridge and in a couple of pools above the bridge. A few fish are also taken on the tributaries.

This is an excellent sea-trout system. The fish begin running at the end of June and the peak is in mid-July, if there is enough water.

The Bridgetown River is regarded as a better sea-trout river than the Ballintra and trout are taken for two miles up as far as Rath Mill.

This is a difficult, undeveloped river system with little or no provision made for anglers.

RIVER DROWES   G 80 58

Season (between Lough Melvin and the sea)

Salmon and Sea-trout: 1 January to 30 September
Brown trout: 15 February to 30 September

Permits

All of the left bank from Lough Melvin to Bundrowes Bridge and most of the right bank is owned by Thomas Gallagher, Edenville, Kinlough, Co. Leitrim, (*telephone* 072 41208)

Permits are available at

The Fishery Office
Lareen
Kinlough, Co. Leitrim
Telephone 072 41055

Barrett's Fishing Tackle Shop
Bundoran
Co. Donegal

The Drowes Bar
Bundrowes
Tullaghan, Co. Leitrim

Mr Jack Phillips
West End
Bundoran, Co. Donegal

Mr Patrick Bradley, Magheracar, Bundoran, Co. Donegal, issues permits for parts of the right bank.

The River Drowes is one of Ireland's premier spring and summer salmon fisheries. Sea-trout rarely enter it. It has a good stock of brown trout.

The spring salmon fishing opens on 1 January and rarely does a season pass without a fish being taken on opening day. The peak of the spring run is in April and in some seasons March can be quite good too. The fishing can be very good in May, and June sees the peak of the grilse run. In August and September anglers are mainly fishing over resident fish.

RIVER DROWES ROD CATCH 1987-92

	1987	1988	1989	1990	1991	1992	6-yr. av.
Salmon	728	650	1240	1228	860	1132	973

The Drowes is a delightful little salmon river, some 4½ miles long with a catchment of 103 square miles. It has 55 named pools. The upper section, down to the Four Masters Bridge, has a lovely series of streams and pools and is usually reserved for anglers staying at Mr Gallagher's holiday bungalows at Lareen. The middle section to Lennox's Bridge is mostly fast-flowing and fishes best in medium to low-water. The third section down to the tide has a mixture of stream, pool and deep, slow-water and a very prolific sea pool, which is always well worth fishing at high tide. It is especially productive on a spring tide. The commercial traps at the mouth have not been operated since 1979 and are now derelict.

There is no beat system and the number of rods per day is not limited.

All legitimate fishing methods are allowed and the fish take a fly from April. Silver Doctor, Curry's Red Shrimp, Silver Rat, Hairy Mary, Blue Charm, the Badger and the Garry Dog are some of the favourite patterns – fished as small as size 14 low-water double in summer.

The brown trout fishing is largely ignored but good sport can be had with Blue-Winged Olives and Sedges on summer evenings.

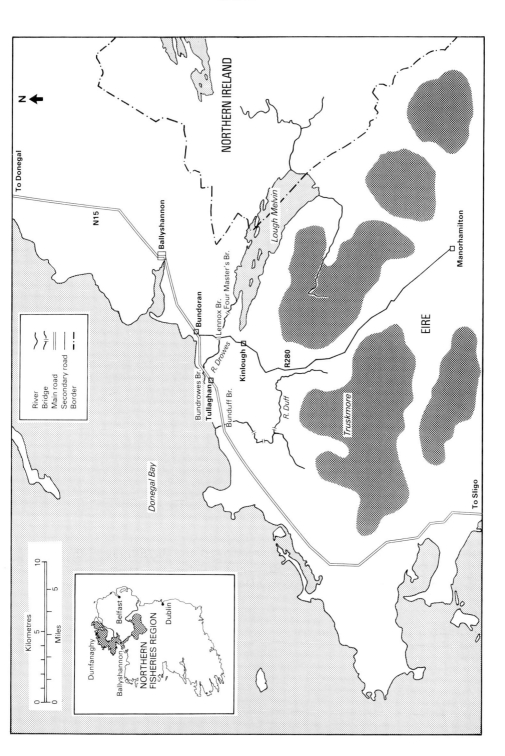

The rivers Duff and Drowes

RIVER DUFF (BUNDUFF RIVER)   G 75 57

Season

Salmon: 1 February to 30 September

Permits

> Mrs McGloin
> The Shop
> Bunduff Bridge
> Tullaghan
> Co. Leitrim

The Bunduff River drains into Donegal Bay just north of Mullaghmore. It is 14 miles long with a 36 square mile catchment on the borders of counties Sligo and Leitrim. It is a spate river which gets a very good run of grilse and summer salmon. The first fish come into the river at the end of May, the peak of the run is in July, and, with good water, it can fish through to September. Most of the fishing is done at the pool below the waterfall, where there is a two-fish daily bag limit. Fly, spinner, worm and shrimp are fished here but spinning is prohibited in low-water. Upstream of the waterfall the river can be fished – mostly with worms – to the second bridge. It is badly overgrown with bushes.

ABBEY RIVER   G 87 82

Permit

Not required.

The Abbey River drains into the Erne Estuary west of Ballyshannon. It is a narrow, fast-flowing stream on which a lot of pools were destroyed by a drainage scheme. Some pools have recovered. It is overgrown and difficult to fish in places.

It still gets a run of sea-trout, from $1/2$ to $2^1/2$ lb, and the best of the fishing is in July and August. It fishes best with worm after a flood and in a wet season and the best fishing is from Cavangarden House down to Crockacapal – a distance of about 3 miles. Flies get results too and local anglers favour Hare's Ear, Blae and Black, Mallard and Claret, Butcher, Blue Dun and Alder.

RIVER ERNE (AND TRIBUTARIES)   G 93 60

Season

Salmon, Sea-trout and Brown trout: 1 March to 30 September.

The River Erne rises in Beaghy Lough, 2 miles south of Stradone in Co. Cavan, and flows 64 miles through Lough Gowna, Lough Oughter, and Upper and Lower Lough Erne before meeting the sea at Ballyshannon. For 30 miles from Crossdoney in Co. Cavan to the town of Enniskillen it is difficult to distinguish the river as it winds its way through a thousand interconnected loughs or parts of loughs nestling among the drumlin hills of Co. Cavan and south Fermanagh.

It is a river that has seen many changes to its fish stocks in the last forty years.

The building of hydroelectric power stations at Cliff and Ballyshannon (work began in 1945 and the first power station was commissioned in 1950) caused the eight famous salmon beats from Belleek to Ballyshannon to be flooded and the mighty run of salmon into the Erne has now declined to such a tiny trickle as to be of little angling value except for the few fish that are occasionally caught below Cliff when the power station is generating.

Roach first appeared in the river in 1963 and there was a massive increase in the roach population in 1968. This increase could well have had an adverse effect on trout stocks, which went into decline at that time. Water pollution became a major problem in the 1970s and up to 1987. Since 1987 the pollution problem has been well controlled, the roach population has declined dramatically and trout stocks have made a welcome return and provide exceptionally good angling once more, both on the Erne itself and its tributaries.

ERNE ESTUARY

Permit

A special local licence is required to fish for sea-trout in the estuary and anglers with a valid salmon licence can get an extension to that licence for a small fee.

Agents

Mr Tom Waters
Drowes Bridge
Tullaghan, Co. Leitrim

Mr Jack Phillips
West End
Bundoran, Co. Donegal

Rogan's Fishing Tackle Shop
Bridge End
Ballyshannon
Co. Donegal

Imperial Hotel
Ballyshannon
Co. Donegal

Regional Fisheries Board Office
Station Road
Ballyshannon
Co. Donegal

The Erne Estuary is an important sea-trout fishery with fishing extending for two miles from the Mall Quay in Ballyshannon to the bar mouth. The season opens on 1 March but the fishing is best from May, through June and July, and it can be very good in August.

The sea-trout range from 1 - $1\frac{1}{2}$ lb, though a $32\frac{1}{2}$ lb sea-trout was taken in a draft net in the late 1940s. The best of the fishing is for two hours either side of low-water, except at Finner Banks and Ramsey Hole at the Old Castle, where you can fish all the time. Anglers have been known to take up to 60 sea-trout in a day here. The trout can be taken spinning Stucki spoons, Tobys or Mepps. Some prefer to fish the fly and Rogan's Gadget, the Needle Eye, Mallard and Claret, Teal, Blue and Silver, Gosling and Daddy are all used.

Access is at Abbey Road, on the north side, at the Mall Quay, Port na Mona or make the long walk across Tullan Strand from Bundoran at low-water.

ERNE SALMON FISHING

Permit

The ESB Shop
Castle Street
Ballyshannon
Co. Donegal

Salmon lie below the power station at Cliff in a stretch of water about $\frac{1}{4}$ mile long and 100 yards wide. The best fishing is when the station is generating from July through to September. All methods are allowed – spinning, shrimp, worm and fly. Access is off the Knather Road. Sadly, this is all that remains of the great Erne salmon fishery.

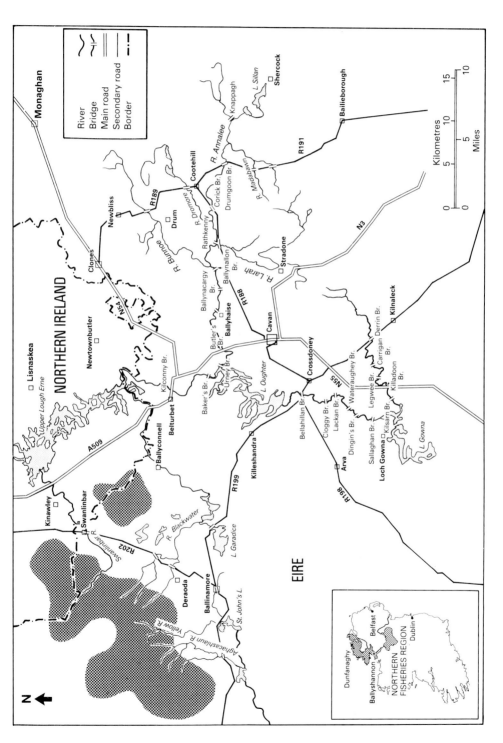

West Cavan rivers and the Erne system

THE ERNE - BELTURBET

Permits

> The Railway Bar
> The Diamond
> Belturbet
> Co. Cavan

Belturbet TAC have carried out extensive improvements to the river and there is three quarters of a mile of good trout fishing from Kilconny Bridge upstream. The fishing is for wild and stocked trout and over the years, the fishery has built a reputation sufficient to attract return visits from overseas visiting anglers. It is fly fishing only. There are other stretches that hold trout up river at Cornadara, Pogue's Ford and Baker's Bridge.

THE MIDDLE ERNE

By the Middle Erne I mean that part of the river between Sallaghan Bridge, near Loch Gowna, and Bellahillan Bridge, near Crossdoney. Trout stocks have made a marvellous recovery here since about 1985 and good numbers of fish to over 4 lb are to be found in all the streamy water along this 8-mile stretch. The best of the fishing is with wet fly from April to June. The water drops and is clouded with algae from the loughs in summer, but September fishing can be fair. The river flows through farmland and is completely undeveloped for anglers. Much of it is overgrown and quite difficult to fish.

THE UPPER ERNE

This is the stretch from the source down as far as Lough Gowna. A drainage scheme in 1989 destroyed many of the pools down to Carrigans (Bruskey) Bridge. The trout stocks are recovering below Carrigans and are in sufficient numbers, especially in spring, to provide sport as far as Legwee Bridge, Killardoon Bridge and Kilsarn Bridge. A natural river, well overgrown in places, with no provision made for anglers.

ANNALEE RIVER   H 45 12

The Annalee River rises near Lough Egish in Co. Monaghan and flows via Cootehill, Ballyhaise and through Butlersbridge to join the River Erne at Urney. It is 42 miles long. It was along its banks at Lurganboy, that I learned to fish, as a child. It was then an exceptionally good trout river and I'm glad to record that after years in decline, due to the introduction of roach and pollution, the trout are back and in some stretches they are as good as ever.

The river can be divided into two parts. Upstream of Cootehill the river, the fly life and the trout are recovering and the river holds some nice trout in places from Knappagh Bridge downstream.

The second part, from Cootehill to Butlersbridge has recovered well. There are big trout at Deredis, some nice stocks of trout at Butlersbridge, and big numbers of small trout and plenty of good trout in the middle reaches, with fair stocks up nearly to Cootehill. The roach have virtually disappeared and fly hatches are good with a fair hatch of mayfly in places. Local angling clubs have carried out a lot of bank development work in the vicinity of Ballyhaise and Bunnoe in Co. Cavan.

LARAGH RIVER   H 51 04

Permits

Mr Gerry O'Grady	Mr Felim Donohoe
Stradone	Clifferna
Co. Cavan	Stradone, Co. Cavan

The Laragh River flows down from Clifferna to join the Annalee River at Rathkenny. The fishing is managed by a very progressive Laragh Angling Club. They monitor pollution, stock the river and have had the banks developed through a social employment scheme. There are excellent stocks of trout up to 3 lb and good hatches of olives, sedges, black gnat and even some mayfly. The best fishing is in spring.

THE BUNNOE RIVER   H 51 13

Permits

Mr Patrick McCaul	Mr Seamus Hughes
Scotshouse	Lisboduff, Bunnoe
Co. Monaghan	Cootehill, Co. Cavan

This marvellous little trout river flows south from Newbliss to join the Annalee River near Lisboduff. There is an active angling club that keeps the banks well serviced with stiles and footbridges. The best of the fishing is up as far as Magheratemple near Drum. Part of it is fly-only.

WOODFORD RIVER   H 27 18

It is proposed to develop the Woodford River as a navigable canal. At present it holds trout at Ballyconnell, downstream of Corraquill, at Agherlare Bridge and at the confluence with Lough Erne.
Upstream of Ballyconnell there are trout from Coologe Lough down to Skelan Lock and there are small numbers of trout upstream and downstream of Garadice Lake.
   If the river is developed as a navigable canal it is unlikely that trout will survive, except in the stretch at Ballyconnell.

RIVER BLACKWATER (WEST CAVAN)   H 20 15

This little river drains Benbrack Mountain and a number of loughs into Ballymagauran Lough. It is undeveloped but holds trout to $1\frac{1}{2}$ lb. It is worth investigating upstream and downstream of Ballymagirril Bridge, as also is the stream that comes down from Derradda.

THE YELLOW RIVER   H 09 12

A small mountain river that drains into St John's Lake west of Ballinamore. The river banks are very high in places. It holds fair stocks of $\frac{1}{2}$ lb trout up to Pollanass Falls.

AGHACASHLAUN RIVER   H 03 10

The Aghacashlaun River flows down from Slieve Anierin into Lough Scur. It is very overgrown but is reported to hold fair stocks of trout to $1\frac{1}{4}$ lb.

SWANLINBAR RIVER   H 20 27

This is a spate river, flowing down from the Cuilcagh Mountains of west Cavan. It flows through Swanlinbar and thence across the border into

Northern Ireland and into upper Lough Erne. It is an important salmon spawning river but is also reported to hold brown trout to $2\frac{1}{2}$ lb. It is worth fishing from the border up for $1\frac{1}{2}$ miles above Swanlinbar.

Trout fishing on a good stretch of the Shiven (see page 229)

·4· North-Western Fisheries Region

The North-Western Fisheries Region stretches from Mullaghmore Point in Co. Sligo to Pidgeon Point near Westport, Co. Mayo. It covers part of Counties Leitrim, Sligo, Roscommon and all of north and west County Mayo. The headquarters of the North-Western Regional Fisheries Board is at Ardnaree House, Abbey Street, Ballina, Co. Mayo (*telephone* 096 22623).

Without a doubt, the River Moy is the primary river in the region. It is world-famous for its prolific runs of salmon. It is alleged that in the town of Ballina, when the grilse are running, the schools might as well close because all the children go fishing. But good salmon fishing is not confined to the Moy. From Ballycroy in the west to Sligo in the north and south to Newport there is a wealth of fishing. The brown trout angler too will find gems of rivers to occupy his passion. They are mainly to be found in the Moy tributaries and the Sligo area. The sea-trout have survived well and anyone who has fished the hauntingly beautiful rivers around Bangor and Ballycroy will understand the spell this lovely area can cast on the fisherman, drawing him back again and again.

GRANGE RIVER   G 65 49

Permission

Not required.

Season

Salmon: 1 February to 30 September.
Sea-trout: 1 February to 12 October.
Brown trout: 15 February to 12 October.

The Grange River is a small spate system that drains the northern slopes of Benbulbin and its hinterland through the village of Grange in north Sligo to the sea. It is primarily a sea-trout fishery. Most of the fishing is done in the estuary in July and August either by spinning or by fishing sand eel. The sea-trout run to about 2½ lb. The river itself is very overgrown. It produces occasional salmon to worm or spinner in a spate in August and September. The Chicken Pool, a short distance below the main road bridge, is a favourite fishing spot. Access is off the N15 at Grange and there is a small road that runs parallel to the river on the south bank.

DRUMCLIFF RIVER   G 68 42

Permission

> Harold Sibbery
> The Waterfall
> Glencar, Co. Leitrim

Season

Salmon: 1 February to 30 September.
Sea-trout: 1 Februray to 12 October.
Brown trout: 15 February to 12 October.

The Drumcliffe River is just over 4 miles long and drains Glencar Lake and a 26½ square-mile catchment into Drumcliffe Bay in Co. Sligo. The character of the banks and river varies greatly along its length. It is partly open and can be fished with fly but in places it is quite overgrown. The river itself has some nice streamy pools and a lot of deep, heavy water. Access is at the bridges.

This river gets a small run of spring salmon in January and February and the grilse run in June and July. It is estimated that anglers took about 200 salmon in 1990. Most are taken either by spinning or on worm. A by-law prohibits the use of any lure other than artificial fly, for any kind of fish, in the section of river downstream of Drumcliffe Bridge.

The river gets a good run of sea-trout. They start running in early July and the average size is quite big — probably close to 1½ lb. Fresh trout are reported to run in every month of the season.

GARAVOGUE RIVER   G 69 36

Permission

Free.

Season

(except between 600 yards upstream of New Bridge and the Lodge)

Salmon and sea-trout: 1 January to 30 September.
Brown trout: 15 February to 30 September.

From the Weir up to the Park Gates opens on 1 February for salmon fishing.

From the Weir down to the Silver Swan Hotel opens on 1 June for salmon, sea-trout and brown trout fishing.

The Garavogue River is about 3½ miles long. It drains Lough Gill and its tributaries through the town of Sligo, with a total catchment of 140 square miles, and carries a huge volume of water in spring. It produces occasional spring salmon and the grilse fishing can be good in June and July. Salmon, sea-trout and brown trout can be taken from the Silver Swan Hotel up to Bective. The best of the sea-trout fishing is downstream of Hyde (formerly Victoria Bridge).

RIVER BONET   G 80 31

Season

Salmon: 1 February to 30 September.
Brown trout: 15 February to 30 September.

The River Bonet is 28 miles long and rises in Glenade Lough in north Leitrim. It meanders south past Manorhamilton and the ancient village of Dromahair before entering Lough Gill. It can give excellent salmon fishing in spring, summer and autumn and its potential is not widely recognized. It also holds very good stocks of brown trout in certain well defined areas.

A drainage scheme was completed in the late 1980s by the Office of Public Works and, contrary to the normal opinion, many believe that it actually improved the river. The work was carried out as a flood relief exercise rather than a fully fledged arterial drainage scheme. It retained the bends and meanders, left adequate deep pools for salmon and increased shallow areas suitable for brown trout. Since the completion of the drainage works, the water tends to run off very quickly.

There are six distinct fisheries on the river:

(1)   Manorhamilton Angling Club Water

This comprises about 7 miles of single- and double-bank fishing, extending from a mile below Glenade Lough to just below Gortgarrigan Bridge. This fishery holds spring salmon from mid-March and the grilse start running in late June or early July. The fishing can be very good in July and every flood thereafter brings more fish up from Lough Gill, with the result that fishing can be very good in September if water conditions are right.

Access to the fishery is good and stiles and footbridges have been erected by the North-Western Regional Fisheries Board.

The best flies are said to be Silver Doctor, Hairy Mary, Green Peter and Jock Scott. A copper and silver spoon and a copper Toby do well, as does a bunch of worms. Natural shrimp is not allowed.

There is some good brown trout fishing on this stretch. A survey carried out by Dr Martin O'Grady of the Central Fisheries Board revealed that for about 2 miles from Glenade Lough downstream to Gortinar there are trout to 1 lb. The banks are overgrown.

There are very good stocks of trout to $1\frac{1}{4}$ lb from Lurganboy for $2\frac{1}{2}$ miles downstream to a Land Commission bridge below the confluence of the Shanvaus River. There are good stocks of trout to $\frac{3}{4}$ lb in the Owenmore River up to Manorhamilton. Daisy's Ford provides about 400 yards of good trout fishing.

Permits

Day permits on the above fishery are available from E. Flynn, The Post Office, Manorhamilton, Co. Leitrim; John McDonnell, 2 Church Street, Manorhamilton, Co. Leitrim, (*telephone* 072 55217); and Harold Sibbery, The Waterfall, Glencar, Co. Leitrim.

(2)   Dromahair Lodge Fishings

Dromahair Lodge has about 9 miles of fishing stretching down to Dromahair. The salmon fishing season is as for the Manorhamilton water above with, perhaps, even better spring salmon fishing in March-April.

There are good trout stocks from Gortgarrigan to Drumlease Glebe. Many of the shallows in this area are newly exposed and the fishing will improve as time goes on.

There is an arrangement whereby local anglers are allowed to fish this water. Otherwise the fishing is reserved and free to residents staying at Dromahair Lodge and Breffni Holiday Cottages, Dromahair, Co. Leitrim (*telephone* 071 64103).

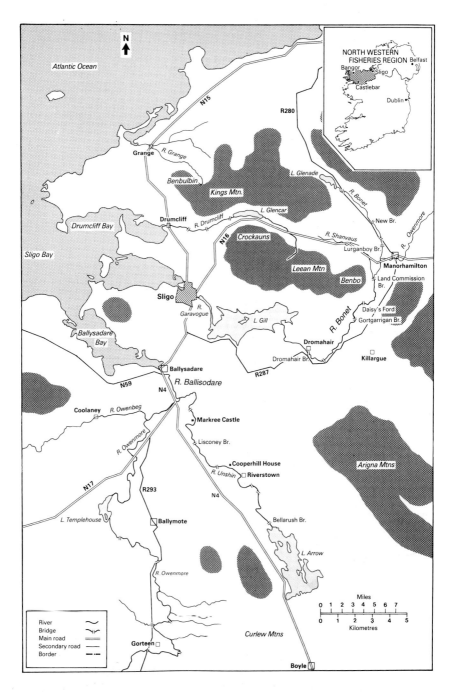

Grange, Drumcliff, Garavogue, Bonet, Ballisodare, Unshin
and Owenmore rivers

(3)   Stanford's Inn

Stanford's Inn, Dromahair, has $3/4$ mile of double-bank fishing with three good pools. There is good spring salmon fishing in April and June-July sees the peak of the grilse fishing. This is some of the best fishing on the river and the Island pool is reported to have produced over 90 fish in 1990. Worm, fly and spinning are allowed. Contact Mr Thomas McGowan, Stanford's Inn, Dromahair, Co. Leitrim, (*telephone* 071 64140).

Of the other three fisheries on the river, the Land Commission has $1/2$ a mile at Glebe House (contact the North Western Regional Fisheries Board), there is $1\frac{1}{2}$ miles of syndicate water downstream of Dromahair and Sligo AC has a stretch above the lough that is deep and not very productive.

Fly Hatches

The peak of the brown trout fishing is from late April to mid June and in late August and September. There are hatches of large dark olives, medium olives and a good mayfly hatch in some areas There are big numbers of blue-winged olives and sedges (small red and brown) are very important.

BALLISODARE RIVER   G 67 29

Season

Salmon and sea-trout: 1 February to 30 September
Brown trout: 15 February to 30 September

Permission

> Mr Charles Cooper
> Markree Castle
> Colloney, Co. Sligo
> *Telephone* 071 67800

The Ballisodare river is just 5 miles long and flows down from Collooney into Ballisodare Bay. With its tributaries, the Unshin River , the Owenmore River and the Owenbeg River, it drains a catchment of 252 square miles which includes Lough Arrow and Templehouse Lake.

The fishing rights for the migratory fish in the system were vested by an act of parliament in the Cooper family of Markree Castle in 1837. The Coopers then built fish passes at the impassable Ballisodare Falls and introduced salmon to the system.

An average of 900-1,000 salmon are taken annually in the pools at the bottom of the falls. Fly fishing only is the rule. There is a small run of spring salmon from April and June-July sees the peak of the grilse run.

The river above the Falls is wide, shallow and overgrown, with some nice pools. Mr Charles Cooper of Markree Castle has taken off the nets and developed the river as a rod fishery for guests at Markree Castle Hotel. Fishing is available on two beats: the first is the productive Falls Pools, the second is a two-mile stretch from Ballisodare to Collooney.

The river also holds a nice stock of brown trout averaging ³/₄ lb with some to 3 lb It has a mayfly hatch. The trout fishing starts in April and the best of it is in May and June.

RIVER UNSHIN   G 70 26

Permission

> Mr Charles Cooper
> Markree Castle
> Collooney, Co. Sligo
> *Telephone* 071 67800

The Unshin is a limestone river which drains Lough Arrow and flows north for 15 miles to join the Ballisodare River at Collooney. It is very overgrown downstream of Lough Arrow with a lot of deep water. Down at Markree Castle the banks are more open and it holds good stocks of trout from ³/₄ to 2 lb and recently a 7 lb brown trout was taken on a dry Sedge. The best of the fishing is from the end of April to mid-June. There is a prolonged mayfly hatch and the spent gnat fishing is especially good in the month of May.

OWENMORE RIVER   G 65 22

Permission

> Mr Charles Cooper
> Markree Castle
> Collooney, Co. Sligo
> *Telephone* 071 67800.

The Owenmore River rises near Gorteen in south Co. Sligo and flows through Templehouse Lake to join the Ballisodare at Collooney. It holds small trout and the banks are clear downstream of the confluence of the

Owenbeg River. There is also a fair stock of trout in a 2-mile stretch upstream of the bridge near Ardkeeran on the R293 Ballymote-Gorteen road. Further up river at Moydoo near Greyfield, there is a good stock of trout to 1 lb and some even to 3 lb.

EASKY RIVER   G 38 38

Season

Salmon and sea-trout: 1 February to 30 September.

Permission

There is a draft net fishery in the tidal section at the mouth. From the bridge in Easky village upstream to Fortland Falls, a distance of one mile approximately, is syndicate water and the rest of the river is controlled by a local angling association (Permits from Forde's Shop, Easky, Sligo).

The Easky is primarily a salmon river and gets an excellent run of grilse and summer salmon. It is 18 miles long and drains a 41 square mile catchment which includes Easky Lough and the northern slopes of the Ox Mountains. From the Workhouse Bridge on the N59 Sligo-Ballina road downstream, the river flows through deep limestone gorges and is difficult to fish, with high, overgrown banks. It has been opened up recently by the North Western Fisheries Board and stiles and footbridges have been provided. The character of the river changes upstream of the bridge and it flows through moorland with occasional streams, pools and deep stretches. On a spate, it can be fished up as far as Grants Griddle. Access is good with roads all along the right bank.

The grilse start running in late June and a prolific run of fish enters the river on every flood to the end of September. A conservative estimate puts the number taken annually on rod and line at 500 fish.

RIVER MOY   G 24 18

Season

Salmon: 1 February to 30 September.
Sea-trout: 1 February to 10 October.
Brown trout: 15 February to 10 October.

Permission

There are presently ten fisheries on the river which let fishing, extending from Bartragh Island in the estuary upstream to a point about 2 miles above the confluence of the Gweestion River, near Swinford. The character and location of these fisheries will be discussed later. The rest of the river, together with its tributaries and loughs, is free fishing.

The main channel is 62-miles-long and enters the sea at Ballina. With its tributaries, it drains a catchment of 806 square miles, stretching from the Ox Mountains in the east to Castlebar in the south and Loughs Conn, Cullin and the Nephin Beg range of mountains in north Mayo.

The Department of the Marine purchased the former Moy Fishery Company and operates draft nets in the tidal waters and salmon traps at the top of the tide in Ballina.

The Moy is probably the most prolific salmon river in the country. It would be impossible to obtain exact figures for rod catches, but the following table of reported rod-caught fish gives some idea of how many fish the river produces.

REPORTED RIVER MOY CATCH

	1988	1989	1990
Salmon	5,000	11,075	6,294

Compiled by the North Western Fisheries Board

A major arterial drainage scheme was carried out on the river between 1960 and 1970. The drainage works had a devastating effect on the natural character of the river and most of the famous old pools and famous fishing sites were destroyed. It is remarkable that the drainage works did not appear to have a long-term detrimental effect on the potential of the river to produce salmon. This has remained as good as ever. Regretably, the fish have to be fished for in aesthetically less pleasing surroundings. The banks are high and difficult, much of the river is wide, canal-like and featureless and the natural pool – stream sequence is missing. Nevertheless, it still holds enormous numbers of salmon and gives joy to thousands of anglers every season.

It is said that fresh salmon run the Moy every month of the year. Certainly, if conditions are right – mild weather and the water not too high – salmon can be taken from opening day, 1 February, at Ballina (behind the fish traps), Mount Falcon (Coolcronan), Cloongee (the Cross River), Armstrong's Fishery, at Pontoon Bridge (between Lough Conn and Lough Cullin and probably one of the best lies of all), on the Clydagh

River and the Manulla (Ballyvary) River. If conditions are not suitable, the fishing picks up as soon as they improve. A run of small spring fish, known as 'black Backs' runs in April and the peak of the spring fishing is between 1 and 20 April. The grilse begin running in early May, with the peak of the run being from about 20 May to 20 July.

Low water tends to prevent fish from running past the traps in Ballina in August, with the result that there is a big build-up of fish in the estuary. The first good flood in late August or September brings more fish up river and can give excellent back end fishing with plenty of fish of 7–9 lb.

The average weight of the spring fish is 9 lb and the best fish in the last ten years was 38 lb and was taken in 1983. The grilse range from about 3 to 7 lb and the sea-trout average $3/4$ lb.

All fishing methods are allowed on most of the fisheries, except natural shrimp. The latter bait is not allowed on a number of fisheries by popular demand, but there are others that still permit its use.

Popular artificial baits include the Stucki spoon, Swinford spoon, Devons and the Flying 'C'.

Most of the fisheries have stretches suitable for fly fishing. A wide range of flies is used, including some local patterns. The most popular are Silver Doctor, Black Doctor, Hairy Mary, Blue Charm, Blue Badger, Foxford Shrimp, Munro Killer, Thunder and Lightning, Logie, Dunkeld, Claret Shrimp, the Goat and the Moy Garry Dog.

The sea-trout fishing is mainly confined to the estuary, where it can be very good from April to September. Boats are available for hire from Mr J. Ruane, the Docks, Ballina, Co. Mayo. Up river, there is limited night fishing in July in the vicinity of Foxford.

THE FISHERIES:

---

1   THE MOY FISHERY, BALLINA, CO. MAYO.

Permits

> The Manager
> Moy Fishery Office
> Ridge Pool Road
> Ballina, Co. Mayo
> *Telephone* 096 21332

The Moy Fishery controls both banks downstream of the weir in Ballina (the left bank from a little distance above the weir). For angling purposes, it is divided into six sections.

The Ridge Pool

This is one of the most sought-after stretches of water in Ireland. It extends from the weir down to Ham Bridge and is a mere 300 yards long. Figures are not available for the annual catch over the years, but before a bag limit was imposed in 1990 it is known to have produced over a hundred fish to four rods for a day at the height of the grilse run.

The fishing is let by advance booking. It is let by the boat. There are two boats with two anglers and a gillie per boat. Fishing is from the boat or from the left bank only. Spinning and worming are allowed, but it is 'fly only' when West's Rock is showing. There is a bag limit of fourteen salmon per boat, six of which may be retained by the anglers. Fishing is from 6 a.m. to 9 p.m., but from 1 June to 31 July a second party of four anglers is accommodated between 6.15 p.m. and 10.15 p.m., depending on tide and light. The Ridge Pool is tidal and fish go off the take when the tide is in. Anglers vacate the pool at that time.

Being at the bottom of the river, the Ridge Pool and the other fisheries downstream are adversely affected by high water and flood. They all fish best in medium to low water. There are a number of favourite fly patterns and the more important ones are the Yellow Goshawk, Garry Dog, Doherty's Shrimp, Goshawk, Blue Badger, Hairy Mary, Thunder and Lightning and Silver Doctor. In low water, fine leaders and small flies (size 12 double and size 14 treble) are essential for success.

Between the Bridges

This fishery, situated at the cathedral, extends from Ham Bridge down to West's Bridge and is a little over 300 yards long. The fishing is free, but permission to fish must be obtained from the Moy Fishery Office. It produces a lot of fish every season. The best throws are immediately below Ham Bridge and at The Railings in a pool above the lower bridge. When fishing, it is best to wade. In high water, a draft net operates at this spot.

Beat 1, also known as The Wells

This beat is let on half-day tickets for a very modest sum. It is situated immediately downstream of West's Bridge and extends for 400 yards. It is limited to eight rods. There is a draft net site at Polnamonagh, half-way down, but the best fishing is downstream of the netting site. Here there is a nice stream in low water and it can be fished with body waders. The Wells produced 240 salmon in 1989.

Beat 2, also known as the Ash Tree Pool.

This beat is about 200 yards long. It is situated at the town park, immediately above the confluence of the Bunree River. The fishing is limited to two rods and is let with a boat and gillie. It is slack water and therefore fishes best with an upstream or downstream wind. All methods are allowed except natural shrimp. It fishes best in June and July, when it holds an awful lot of fish. Being tidal, it must be vacated for 3–4 hours every day. This beat produced 296 salmon in 1989.

Beat 3, also known as The Point

This beat extends from the confluence of the Bunree River to the end of the island – about 300 yards. It is let on a season ticket at a modest charge and day tickets are available too, with the result that it can get very crowded. The fishing starts in May and this beat produced 1,100 salmon in 1989. A high tide spoils the fishing for 5 hours and a low tide for about $3\frac{1}{2}$ hours. The best fishing is at the top of the beat. Use the same flies as for the Ridge Pool.

Evening sea-trout fishing can be good here in July and small silver-bodied flies give good results.

The Moy Estuary

Sea-trout are fished here. The permission of the Moy Fishery is required but there is no charge.

2 BALLINA SALMON ANGLERS' ASSOCIATION

Permits

Mr Billy Egan	North Western Regional Fisheries Board
Barrett Street	Ardnaree House
Ballina, Co. Mayo	Abbey Street
	Ballina, Co. Mayo
Moy Fishery Office	Local fishing tackle shops
Ridge Pool Road	
Ballina, Co. Mayo	

Ballina Salmon Anglers' Association has over 3 miles of double-bank fishing, extending upstream from the weir in Ballina (with the exception of a short stretch on the left bank) to the confluence of the Corroy River. The best of the fishing is on the mile-long stretch, known locally as 'the canal', from Rahan's House down to the weir. It fishes well with fly, worm or spinner and gives excellent sport when the grilse are running in June and July and after a rise in water in September. The stand at 'the back of the boxes' has been known to give 120 fish in one six-hour period. The next best stretch is for 1 mile down from the Corroy River confluence. It is said that this fishery can produce up to 1,500 fish in a week when the grilse are running. It is heavily fished.

3 MOUNT FALCON SALMON FISHERIES

(Belass, Foxford, Co. Mayo, *telephone* 094 56690)

Permits

Mount Falcon Castle Hotel
Ballina
Co. Mayo
Telephone 096 21172

The Fishery Office
Mount Falcon Castle
Ballina, Co. Mayo
Telephone 096 71296

This company controls extensive fishing rights over approximately 7 miles of river, extending upstream from the Corroy River to near Foxford on the right bank and a substantial part of the left bank. It includes such well-known fisheries as Mount Falcon Castle Water, Scott's Fishery and Baker's Fishery.

The company has two private beats (six rods per beat) which are let with a gillie. It also lets day and weekly permits on its association water. A season ticket to the association water is also available.

REPORTED CATCH - MOUNT FALCON SALMON FISHERIES

	Private beats inc. gillies' catch	House rods	Assoc. water
1987	1049	134	2800
1988	952	140	2100
1989	879	120	1900
1990	670	106	2100
1991	568	77	1700
1992	861	92	2300

The fishery has several good pools with plenty of streams and nice fly water. Worm fishing and spinning are practised but shrimp and prawn are allowed only at certain times and never on the private beats.

4 ALPINE HOTEL FISHERY

Permits

The Alpine Hotel
Enniscrone, Co. Sligo
Telephone 096 36144

This fishery consists of about half a mile of single-bank fishing. It is a deep stretch and is good holding water.

5 ARMSTRONG'S FISHERY

Permits

Mr George Armstrong
Ballina Road
Foxford, Co. Mayo
Telephone 094 56580

Armstrong's Fishery is approximately one mile of single-bank fishing and has about 300 yards of nice fly water. The rest is deep holding water and very productive. A limited number of season tickets are issued and the remainder of the fishing is let by day tickets. All legal methods are allowed.

6 BEAL EASA FISHERY

LECKEE FISHERY

Permits

Mr P. Gannon
The Post Office
Foxford, Co. Mayo
Telephone 094 56101

The Beal Easa Fishery is 1½ miles of single-bank fishing downstream of Foxford. It is all good holding water with some nice fly fishing at Moran's

Rocks.

The Leckee Fishery is $\frac{1}{5}$ mile long and is situated on the right bank upstream of Foxford.

Limited season tickets are let and day tickets are available. A gillie service can be provided and Mrs Gannon provides Irish Tourist Board registered accommodation in the town of Foxford.

7 FOXFORD SALMON ANGLERS' ASSOCIATION

Permits

> Mr Jack Wallace
> Swinford Road
> Foxford, Co. Mayo
> *Telephone* 094 56238

This fishery consists of about one mile of double-bank fishing upstream of the town of Foxford. Part of it is suitable for fly fishing and the rest is more suited to worm fishing and spinning.

8 FOXFORD WATER

This is a short stretch in the town of Foxford where the proprietor has given local anglers permission to fish.

9 CLONGEE FISHERY

Permits

> Mr Michael Ruane
> Cloongee
> Foxford, Co. Mayo
> *Telephone* 094 56634

This is one of the most interesting fisheries on the river. It is located upstream of Foxford at the confluence of the outflowing river (the Cross River) from Lough Cullin and offers over 2 miles of fishing on the right bank as well as fishing on the left bank and on part of the Lake River. This fishery offers lots of variety for fly fishing, spinning and worm fishing and is said to produce enormous numbers of salmon every season. There is spring fishing from the end of March and high water in September always makes for a good finish to the season. Only day permits are issued and there is no limit on the number of rods on the fishery.

The Cross River can give excellent brown trout fishing in mayfly time, especially with a wind on the water. The trout can run to 3 lb.

10 EAST MAYO (SWINFORD) ANGLERS' ASSOCIATION

Permits

Mrs Florence Wills
Ballylahan Bridge
Foxford, Co. Mayo
Telephone 096 56221

Boland's Lounge
Bridge Street
Swinford, Co. Mayo
Telephone 094 51149

This is the most extensive fishery on the Moy. It stretches upstream on both banks from the Cloongee Fishery for about 8 miles. Permits are available on a daily or weekly basis at a modest charge. It fishes best in medium to high water and can give really excellent results for both spring salmon and grilse when water levels are right. The 'Gub' at the confluence of the Gweestion River offers some of the best fly fishing on all of the River Moy and there is some lovely fly fishing up at Oldcastle too. There is spring fishing here from early April and the grilse fishing can be brilliant in June. It is not an easy river to fish in places and wading is necessary but can be difficult.

11 THE UPPER MOY

The Upper Moy is largely uncharted and undeveloped. The fishing is free and there is a lot of lovely water up as far as Banada. It is badly overgrown in places but well worth exploring, especially in periods of high water.

12 PONTOON BRIDGE

Permission

Free.

This fishery is located in the short channel between Lough Conn and Lough Cullin. It is highly regarded as a lie for spring salmon and is estimated to produce 150 spring fish per season. Often, the first spring fish on the Moy system is taken here. The grilse fishing can be good here too, especially in May, but quickly slows up as the water drops. There are anglers who specialize in fishing this stretch. Fly fishing and spinning can take fish but a bunch of worms is especially effective. The fishing is adversely affected by a flood in the Moy backing up Lough Cullin and reversing the flow.

RIVER DEEL   G 13 17

The Deel forms part of the headwaters of the Moy to the west. It rises in north Mayo and flows east for 28 miles past Rake Street, through Crossmolina, and then describes a semicircle round the top of Lough Conn before entering the lough from the north-east.

Possibly because it is free fishing, the River Deel is very underrated, both as a salmon and brown trout river.

There is very good spring salmon fishing (spinning and worm) from Deel Castle to the river mouth. This fishing commences on 1 February and can last till June or when the lough starts to drop. From June the fishing improves up river for both grilse and salmon. The best stretch has some nice fly water and extends for at least 5 miles from Richmond Bridge (near Rake Street) upstream to Carrowgarve Bridge, on to Cammoge Bridge and for about 1 mile upstream of Cammoge Bridge. The good fishing in this stretch continues into July and improves again after a flood in late August or September. The top half of this stretch flows through moorland and the remainder through marginal farmland and the banks are undeveloped. A gillie service is available through Mr Barry Segrave, Cloonamoyne Fishery, Enniscoe House, Castlehill PO (near Crossmolina), Ballina, Co. Mayo (telephone 096 31112, fax 096 31773) and Tourist Board approved accommodation is available nearby at Kilmurry House, Castlehill PO (near Crossmolina), Ballina, Co. Mayo (telephone 096 31227).

There is about 2 miles of good trout fishing at Knockglass House, north-east of Crossmolina, 5 miles of trout fishing from Ballycarron House upstream past Richmond Bridge and Carrowgarve Bridge and a further mile of fishing immediately upstream of Deel Bridge.

The trout range in size from $\frac{1}{2}$ lb to $3\frac{1}{2}$ lb. In May and June, the best fishing is at Knockglass, but later, when the lough trout start running, all areas fish well. Try spider patterns early, such as a Greenwell's and in September try a Wickham's Fancy and Watson's Fancy.

CLYDAGH RIVER	M 23 97

CASTLEBAR RIVER	M 20 93

MANULLA (BALLYVARY) RIVER	M 23 95

Permission: The river is leased by the Round Tower Anglers' Association. Permits are available from Canning's Lounge, Ballyvary, Co. Mayo (*telephone* 094 31285)

These three rivers join west of the village of Ballyvary and flow into Lough Cullin. They offer some excellent spring salmon fishing and hold good stocks of brown trout. The spring salmon fishing starts at the confluence of the Castlebar River and Manulla River and extends downstream for about $3\frac{1}{2}$ miles to a point 1 mile below the confluence of the Clydagh River. There is another short stretch about 1 mile upstream of Lough Cullin. This fishery is estimated to produce at least 200 spring salmon every season – mainly in March, April and early May. In a very wet summer, with the Moy in flood, it can fish well in June for grilse. It has some lovely fly water.

The Manulla River holds a good stock of brown trout to 2 lb from Moyhenna Bridge downstream for about 3 miles to Ballyvary Bridge on the N5 Road.

The Castlebar River holds an excellent stock of brown trout to 3 lb with plenty of fish between $\frac{3}{4}$ lb and $1\frac{1}{2}$ lb. It is deep and rich near Turlough village.

The North-Western Regional Fisheries Board has opened up a lot of the fishing on these rivers by erecting stiles and footbridges.

GWEESTION RIVER	M 30 97

POLLAGH RIVER	M 33 92

GLORE RIVER	M 35 92

TRIMOGUE RIVER	M 33 97

Permission

Free.

The Gweestion River is a tributary of the Moy and the Pollagh, Glore and

Trimogue Rivers are tributaries of the Gweestion.

The Gweestion lies between Swinford and Bohola. It is a limestone river and holds grilse in June and an excellent stock of brown trout ranging from 10 oz to 1½ lb, with some fish to 3½ lb. Stiles and footbridges have been erected up to the confluence of the Glore River. The banks are quite overgrown with alder in places, but it has some nice pools and riffles and prolific fly hatches, including mayfly. It can be recommended and it doesn't weed up as many rivers do in summer.

The Pollagh river holds a great stock of trout averaging 10 oz – some to 2 lb – from Bushfield Bridge downstream to the confluence. It has some lovely pools, but, sadly, it is very overgrown.

The Glore River consists of mainly fast water with occasional pools. The trout average ½ lb – some to 2 lb – and the best stocks are in a short stretch upstream of the bridge on the R 320 Swinford–Kiltimagh Road.

The Trimogue River holds a good stock of trout up to ¾ lb upstream from the confluence to Kinaff Bridge. The average width of the channel is 12 feet and it has some lovely pools.

SONNAGH RIVER   G 42 03

The Sonnagh rises south west of Charlestown and joins the Moy downstream of Bellanacurra Bridge. It is no more than 15 feet wide and holds an excellent stock of trout to 1½ lb. It is rarely fished.

MULLAGHANOE RIVER   G 41 05

The Mullaghanoe rises near Charlestown and flows west to the Moy upstream of Bellanacurra Bridge. It, too, like the Sonnagh, holds excellent stocks of trout to 1½ lb. It is a narrow river – about 12 feet wide. It has recovered well from drainage works but is rarely fished.

OWENGARVE RIVER   G 44 07

The Owengarve flows through the village of Curry and joins the Moy downstream of Cooleen Ford. The 3 mile stretch downstream of Curry holds an excellent stock of trout up to 1½ lb. It has a nice mix of streams and pools. Unfortunately, there is very heavy bank cover along the entire stretch, which makes fishing very difficult.

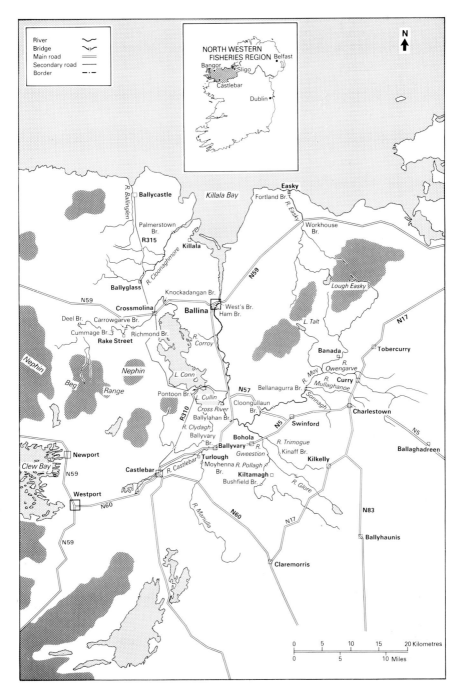

The rivers Ballinglen, Cloonaghmore, Easky, Moy and tributaries

CLOONAGHMORE (PALMERSTOWN) RIVER   G 17 31

Season

Salmon: 1 June to 30 September.
Sea-trout and Brown trout: 1 June to 12 October.

The lower reaches of this river are leased by Ballina and Cloghans Angling Club and the fishing on a stretch up at Owenmore, near Ballyglass, is reserved. The rest of it is regarded as free fishing. It was a great sea-trout river in the past, but now the stocks are barely surviving. The best chance of a fish now is late in the season. Fish a small spoon in the deep water up at Doobehy.

BALLINGLEN RIVER   G 10 38

The better pools on this small spate river are leased by Ballina and Cloghans Angling Club. Further upstream the river is badly overgrown and unfishable. Like the Palmerstown River above, its run of salmon and sea-trout has greatly declined over many years.

MUINGNABO RIVER   F 88 37

GLENAMOY RIVER   F 89 34

BELLANABOY RIVER   F 85 31

GLENCULLIN RIVER   F 85 27

Season

These are all end-of-season rivers and the statutory closing date for all species on each of them is 30 September.

Permits

Mr Seamus Henry
Bangor Erris
Co. Mayo
Telephone 097 83487/83461

These four small spate rivers are all located in north-west Mayo. Some hold salmon and sea-trout, but mainly sea-trout. You could expect a fish in any of them from June. All of them get a late but quite prolific run of both species. Since they are small spate systems, the fishing can be unpredictable, but if the month of September comes wet – and this is an area of particularly high average rainfall – they can provide terrific sport. The sport they provide for the angler is only part of their attraction. The remoteness and tranquillity of the lovely unspoiled countryside is good for the soul.

The Muingnabo River is just 9 miles long with a 16 square mile catchment. Being so remote, it is rarely fished, but is well worth fishing for sea-trout on a spate in September. There are some fine pools for about 1½ miles above Annie Brady's Bridge and it can be fished right to the estuary.

The Glenamoy River has a catchment of 33 square miles and is just 14 miles long. It has been developed with stiles and footbridges by the North-Western Regional Fisheries Board. This one is a real treasure. The tidal section fishes well for sea-trout from late July. In a spate, there is about 6 miles of fishing, from Glencalry Lodge down to the tide. It is basically a sea-trout river, fly-only, but I have known anglers to come away with half a dozen salmon for an evening's fishing. Some of the nicest pools are from the graveyard downstream past the new concrete bridge.

The Bellanaboy River flows into Carrowmore Lake from the north. It is a deep, narrow little river and can be very good for sea-trout or even a salmon, on a spate. Fish it from the bridge to the lake.

The Glencullin River flows westwards into Carrowmore Lake. It holds a good stock of sea-trout and salmon on a flood. They probably back down to the lake again as the flood drops. It can be fished from April but is best from June. There is only one bridge over it, with a few good pools upstream. Downstream, it can look a bit canal-like, especially near the lake, but this is all good water and well worth fishing when the wind breaks the surface.

Flies

A Black Pennell, Bibio, Watson's Fancy, Shrimp Fly, Garry Dog and Hairy Mary in various sizes will serve the angler well on these rivers.

OWENMORE RIVER   F 87 24

Season

Salmon and Sea-trout: 1 February to 30 September.

The Owenmore drains a large area of the bogs, moorland and mountains of north-west Mayo into Tullaghan Bay, north of Achill Island. It is every inch a brilliant salmon and sea-trout fishery. Much of the fishing is reserved and not let. One 4 mile stretch in the middle reaches is leased by the Bangor Sporting Club. This is lovely water, well endowed with good pools. A limited number of day tickets are available – but not at weekends – from:

> Mr Seamus Henry
> Bangor
> Co. Mayo
> *Telephone* 097 83487/83461

This is really a big spate river which produces a remarkable number of salmon every season. It holds spring fish to 20 lb from February and can be fished confidently from mid-March. The grilse come in early June and it gets another run of big autumn fish from August. The fishing is fly only – a by-law – and Curry's Red Shrimp, The Garry Dog, Silver Garry, Thunder and Lightning and Hairy Mary are all good flies.

It gets a good run of sea-trout from mid-June to the end of September. The average weight is about ³/₄ lb and, while most are caught as a by-product of the salmon fishing, they can provide good night fishing in some of the bigger pools.

OWENINY RIVER   F 98 21

The Oweniny River is a tributary of the Owenmore. It flows down for 14 miles from Maumakeogh and joins the main river at Bellacorick Bridge.

Permission

The ownership of the fishing rights is very fragmented. Glenalt Syndicate and the Office of Public Works have about a quarter of a mile upstream from the confluence which is not let. Upstream from here, permission to fish can be obtained from John Gillespie, Dominic McLoughlin, John Ruddy, Bord na Mona, Tony Cosgrave and Michael McGrath, while Pat Mullarkey gives permission on the Sheskin River, which comes in from the west. All the above have addresses at Srahnakilly, Bellacorick, Co. Mayo.

Access to the lower reaches is up a road at Bellacorrick along the right bank. However, the river stretches for several more miles into the mountains and these upper reaches are best reached via a forestry road off the Crossmolina–Ballycastle road at Garranard Post Office.

This is a wild moorland river and very remote and all twists and bends. The banks are clear for walking, but go prepared for biting midges. In summer they can be terribly troublesome. The lower reaches can get very stained and dark as treacle with peat from the bogs. This is also a problem on the Owenmore (see page 83).

This river holds a lot of spring salmon from April, grilse from June and sea-trout from July. The fishing extends up to Cluddaun.

From Cluddaun above the Srahmeen confluence, downstream for $1\frac{1}{2}$ miles to the footbridge (at the end of the forest road from Garanard PO) the river consists of streams and pools. Downstream of the footbridge, there is a mile of deep slow water and the rest is a mix of shallow water and pools. It is very much a spate river but the deep pools can fish well in a strong SSW or NNW wind.

Some anglers' approach to fishing the river is to have a car drop them off at the footbridge in the morning. They fish all the way downstream and arrange to be collected at Dominic McLoughlin's in the evening. This is a distance of 8 miles approximately and it can take up to 12 hours to fish it all. The fly-only by-law does not extend to this river.

For gillies, contact Mr Barry Segrave, Cloonamoyne Fishery, Enniscoe House, Castle Hill PO, near Crossmolina, Co. Mayo (*Telephone* 096-3112, *Fax* 096-31773) or Val and Martin Irwin or Jackie Conway, Srahmeen, Garanard PO, Co. Mayo.

OWENDUFF RIVER   F 81 15

Season

Salmon: 1 February to 30 September.
Sea-trout: 1 February to 12 October.

This is another of those exceptionally attractive and prolific salmon and sea-trout fisheries in north Mayo. Together with its tributary, the Tarsaghaunmore, it drains a 52 square mile catchment of wild moorland and mountain into Tullaghan Bay, a few miles north of Ballycroy. The river is all privately owned except for the estuary below the weir at Srahnamanragh Bridge. In this estuary, there is about a mile of free fishing. It can produce a salmon on occasions and the sea-trout fishing can be exceptionally good at the turn of the tide. Up river, there are five private fisheries and three fishing lodges – Shrahnamanragh Lodge, Lagduff Lodge and Shean Lodge, while a fourth fishery is served by Rock House near Ballycroy.

The water in the Owenduff is clear and both salmon and sea-trout are noted for their free-taking qualities when the water is right. The spring

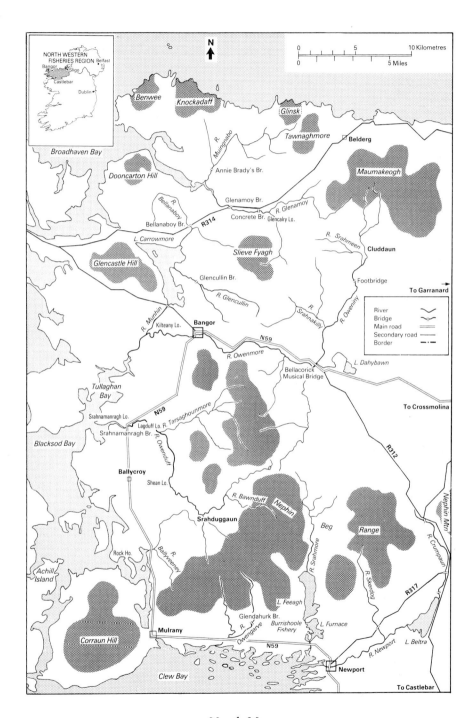

North Mayo

salmon run from 1 February and March is prime time for spring fish at Lagduff and on the bottom of the Shean Lodge water. The grilse come in May, the sea-trout run peaks in August and there is a late run of salmon. I would estimate that it produces about 350 fish annually to the rod. This is a fly-only river (by-law) and useful patterns are Lemon and Grey, Black Doctor, Thunder and Lightning, Shrimp Fly, Dunkeld, Connemara Black, Invicta, and Black Pennell.

Access

Occasionally, a week comes available in one of the lodges. Details are available from Mr Roy Craigie, Owenduff, Celbridge, Co. Kildare, for Shean Lodge; The Proprietor, Rock House, Ballycroy, Co. Mayo, and Mr Colum O'Briain, New Park, Bray Road, Foxrock, Dublin 18, for Shranamanragh Lodge.

BALLYVEENEY RIVER   F 82 04

Season

Salmon: 1 February to 30 September.
Sea-trout: 1 February to 12 October.

Permission

> The Proprietor
> Rock House
> Ballyveeney
> Ballycroy, Co. Mayo

This small deep river has about 2,000 yards of fishing. It used get a great run of sea-trout and the average size was above normal.

OWENGARVE RIVER   F 90 97

Season

Salmon: 1 May to 30 September.
Sea-trout: 1 May to 12 October.

Permits: Mr J.B.Healy, Rostork Castle, Mulrany, Co. Mayo

Newport Angling Club leases part of this small spate river from the proprietor of Rosturk Castle and lets day tickets.

Mr Peter McGee	Mr Ciaran Moran
Newport	Moynish Guesthouse
Co. Mayo	Mulrany, Co. Mayo

The Owengarve holds salmon and sea-trout in August and September and fishes best on a wild, stormy day with a good spate on it. It is fly fishing only and Black Pennell, Bibio, Dunkeld and Black and Orange all work well.

BURRISHOOLE FISHERY   L 96 96

Permits

> The Manager
> Burrishoole Fishery
> Newport, Co. Mayo
> *Telephone* 098 41107

This is really a lough fishery comprising Loughs Furnace and Feeagh. How can I omit it, since it was there I caught my first salmon and sea-trout?

Lough Furnace has three good bank stands for salmon which would earn it the right to be included in this work. They are at the Mill Race, the Salmon Leap and the Back Weir and have saved the day for many a fisherman who likes to play his fish with feet firmly on terra firma.

NEWPORT RIVER

Season

Salmon: 20 March to 30 September.
Sea-trout: 20 March to 30 September.

Permission

> Newport House Hotel
> Newport
> Co. Mayo
> *Telephone* 098 41222

The Newport River drains Lough Beltra and a 56 square mile catchment into Clew Bay. This river is something of an enigma, for, though it holds salmon right from opening day, its value, particularly as a salmon river, is not really appreciated and hence it is quite under-exploited. It gets a good run of spring salmon right from the start of the season and can produce three or four salmon on opening day. It holds good fish too, and has fish of 16 lb, 17 lb, 18 lb, 19 lb and 22½ lb to its credit in recent years. Somehow, it is overshadowed by Lough Beltra and it would appear that most of the patrons of Newport House Hotel prefer the luxury of lough fishing with a gillie to walking the river. Little do they know what excellent sport they may be missing.

The river is approximately 7 miles long and bends and twists its way through rough pasture, bog and woodland. The bottom alternates from gravel to silt and the banks are all negotiable, well maintained with stiles and bridges, and it is not necessary to wade. There are numerous access points with car parks strategically placed and nowhere is it necessary to walk more than 200 yards to the river bank.

It is a river that is very well endowed with pools and streams. There are at least 24 named pools and even though it is not divided into beats it could easily take eight or ten rods per day.

The present proprietor, Kieran Thompson, took off the draft net at the mouth in 1987, as a conservation measure, and this contributed, on average, an additional 600 spring salmon and grilse to the river and the lough.

The better pools for spring fishing are the Upper and Lower Cement Bridge, the Bush Pool, Sheridan's Pool, the Long Pool (below Sheridan's), The Brigadier's Pool, Welsh's Pool and Upper and Lower Flags. For the grilse, in addition to the above, add the Junction, Jack Mack's Pool and the Road Pools.

The spring fish run from before opening day right up to the end of May and sea-liced fish have been taken in early June.

The grilse begin running on the first flood after 10 June and continue through the summer. It also gets a good run of bigger autumn fish and this run starts with the first flood at the end of August.

Some would say that this is a river for the experienced salmon fisher.

You can fish a stream and a pool down – or back it up – rest it and fish it again and be successful on the second or even the third attempt. A 14-foot double-handed rod is comfortable to use on good water, but when the water runs low a single handed rod to take a No. 8 or 9 line is adequate. Floating lines are the norm, with a sink-tip being preferred in spring.

Flies

It is a fly-only fishery and the most favoured patterns are Garry Dog, Silver Doctor, Silver Wilkinson, Lemon and Grey, Thunder and Lightning, Beltra Badger and Dunkeld. Fly size depends on water height and rarely is anything larger than a size 8 treble or size 4 single required. Often the angler who dares to err on the small side is the one to take a fish.

The sea-trout begin running in early July and the best of the fishing is through July and August.

Trout can be taken anywhere in the fast water when they are running – even during the day – but the bigger trout are taken at night. The best of the night fishing is from 11.30 p.m. to 1.30 a.m. For daytime fishing, the favourite fly patterns are Green Peter, Silver Stoat's Tail, Delphi Silver (on the point), Bibio (on the bob), Thunder and Lightning, Teal, Blue and Silver (for fresh-running sea-trout) and a Dunkeld can work marvellously well. For night fishing, many locals consider a Silver Stoat's Tail in size 10 or 12 single or size 12 and 14 double to be the number one choice.

Srahnamanragh Lodge on the Owenduff River, Co. Mayo

·5· Western Fisheries Region

The Western Fisheries Region extends from Westport in Clew Bay south to Hags Head in Co. Clare. It covers south Mayo, most of Co. Galway and north Co. Clare. The headquarters of the Western Regional Fisheries Board is at The Weir Lodge, Earl's Island, Galway, (*telephone* 091 65548).

The region offers a varied and rich choice of game fishing. It is probably true to say that it has a greater number of well managed fisheries available to the visiting angler than anywhere else in the country. The rivers of south Mayo and Galway virtually all get runs of salmon and some of them get them in spectacular numbers.

The sea-trout fishing has been rightly famous for generations. The Connemara district of west Galway is especially suited to the production of sea-trout. Virtually all of its sea-trout fisheries are managed with a view to catering for visiting fishermen.

A sudden decline in sea-trout stocks first manifested itself in 1987 and has continued for four seasons. The Sea-trout Action Group (STAG) is a body made up of government, fishery and angling interests and is working to discover the cause of the decline.

The best of the brown trout fishing is confined to the limestone rivers of east Galway and Mayo.

CARROWBEG (WESTPORT) RIVER   M1 84

Season

Brown trout: 15 February to 12 October.

Permits: Not usually required.

The Carrowbeg River flows through the town of Westport. It is 10 miles long and drains a 22 square mile catchment. It holds a fair stock of wild brown trout. The best of the fishing is in the pools from Westport up to Cooloughra Bridge, where it runs close to the Ballinrobe road.

OWENWEE (BELCLARE) RIVER   L95 82

Season

Salmon: 1 February to 30 September.
Sea-trout: 1 February to 12 October.
Brown trout: 15 February to 12 October.

Permits

> Mr Vincent Bourke
> Bridge Street
> Westport, Co. Mayo

A small spate river, 2½ miles west of Westport, it is 11 miles long and drains a 19 square mile catchment into Westport Bay. It gets a fair run of grilse and sea-trout from July and the best of the fishing is in the last two miles.

BUNOWEN RIVER   L80 81

Season

1 April to 30 September.

Permits

> Charles Gaffney's Bar
> Louisburgh, Co. Mayo.
> *Telephone* 098 66150

The Bunowen River drains the Sheeffry Hills and a catchment of 29 square miles. It flows through the town of Louisburgh into Clew Bay. Part of it is owned, developed and managed by the Western Regional Fisheries Board and it is that part that is let. It gets an excellent run of grilse from mid-July and holds sea-trout from early July. It is deep and sluggish below the town and there are some nice pools upstream, the best known being Carr's Pool. It is fly-fishing only and useful patterns include Silver Doctor, Silver Rat, Hairy Mary, Blue Charm, Black Pennell, Watson's Fancy, Bibio and Bloody Butcher.

CARROWNISKEY RIVER   L75 77

Season

Salmon and Sea-trout: 1 April to 30 September.

Permits

> Mr Charles Gaffney's Bar
> Louisburgh, Co. Mayo.
> *Telephone* 098 66150

The Carrowniskey River flows west into the Atlantic 3 miles south of Louisburgh. It is very much a spate river with a catchment of about 14 square miles. That part of it that is let is owned, developed and managed by the Western Regional Fisheries Board. It flows into Roonagh Lough before entering the sea and the best of the fishing is on the flats from the lough up to Carrowniskey Bridge. It gets a good run of grilse from mid-June and fishes best on a falling spate. It holds sea-trout from July. Fly-fishing only.

BUNDORRAGHA (DELPHI) RIVER   L84 63

Season

Salmon: 1 February to 30 September.
Sea-trout: 1 February to 12 October.

Permits

> Mr Peter Mantle
> Delphi Lodge
> Leenane, Co. Galway.
> *Telephone* 095 42213/42246   *Fax* 095-42212

The Bundorragha River is $1\frac{1}{2}$ miles long and drains a catchment of 20 square miles, including the salmon and sea-trout loughs – Finlough and Doo Lough – which constitute the renowned Delphi Fishery. The fishery

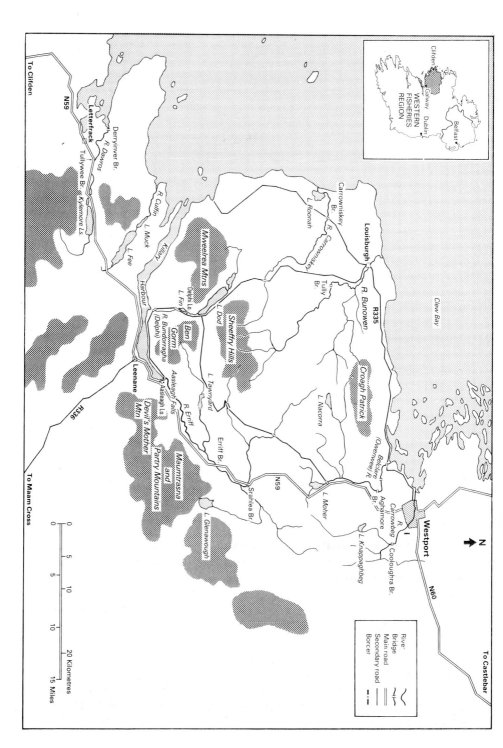

The Erriff, Delphi and S.W. Mayo

is run from Delphi Lodge, which was completely refurbished in 1989 to cater for anglers. The lodge offers anglers accommodation and has its own rod room and tackle shop, serving all the anglers' needs. Self-catering cottages are also available.

The Bundorragha River which flows down from Finlough into Killary Harbour, is a stunningly beautiful fishery, with a backdrop of wild, rugged mountain scenery. It drains a completely unspoiled valley that is totally isolated from the modern world. The river has nineteen named pools, some of which were created by the building of stone weirs in the 1860s. These have magnificently withstood the worst winter floods ever since.

This is a prolific little salmon and sea-trout fishery with an amazingly long season. A unique feature of the fishery is that you can fish for spring salmon using small flies and floating line right from opening day. The river usually produces the first salmon of the season in the west of Ireland and it is often taken on opening day.

Rod Catch, Delphi Fishery, 1987-92

Year	1987	1988	1989	1990	1991	1992
Salmon	93	143	88	61	39	156
Sea-trout	832	675	309	112	437	494

Fish don't run straight through to the loughs but rest in the pools. The most popular salmon pools on the river are the Turn Pool, Quarry Pool, Rock Pool, Whin Pool and Meadow Pool. Three rods are allowed and it is such a straightforward river that a gillie is not necessary.

The spring fish average 9 lb in weight and run in February, March, April and May. The grilse average 4 lb and run in June and July. A feature of the river is that it gets a small run of very big summer salmon, some of which weigh over 20 lb. The best fish in recent years was 19 lb and was a summer fish.

The fishing is fly-only, from 9 a.m. to 7 p.m., with evening permits for residents in the summer. The best salmon flies are Delphi Badger (a deadly 1-inch tube fly), Silver Wilkinson, Wilkinson Shrimp, Hairy Mary, Garry Dog and Silver Rat.

The sea-trout run begins in early July and the river is noted mainly for producing finnock rather than the larger sea-trout. This is a strange phenomenon because in the records of the Irish Specimen Fish Committee the Delphi Fishery rates second in Ireland to Lough Currane for producing large specimen sea-trout. It is fly only and there is a 10-

inch size limit. Expect to meet a sea-trout anywhere, but particularly good pools are the Hut Pool, Waterfall Pool, the pool above the school, Horse Shoe Pool and the Turn Pool where sunk-line tactics work well at night. Small flies work well including Delphi Silver, Teal, Blue and Silver, Silver Doctor, Watson's Fancy, Kingsmill, Black Pennell, Connemara Black and Silver Invicta.

RIVER ERRIFF   L90 64

Season

Salmon: 1 February to 30 September.
Sea-trout: 1 February to 12 October.

Permits

> Mr Jim Stafford, Manager
> Erriff Fishery
> Aasleagh Lodge
> Leenane, Co. Galway
> *Telephone* 095 42252

The River Erriff is a remarkable little spate salmon river draining into the top of Killary Harbour, near the village of Leenane in Co. Galway. It is just over 20 miles long and drains an area of 69 square miles. The last 8 miles flow through a spectacular and very beautiful glacier-formed valley and it is here that the rod fishery is situated. It is divided into nine beats with a total of forty-eight named pools and streams. Beats take two or three rods and the total rod capacity of the main fishery is twenty-two rods. After a high spate, there is salmon fishing further upstream (above Srahlea Bridge) but this is not regarded as part of the fishery proper in low water. The river is characterized by the spectacular Aasleagh Falls waterfall near the sea, and a series of long, deep pools, glides and streams. The bottom consists of stones, sand and glacial deposit, the result of centuries of erosion that appears to be getting worse with every passing season.

The fishery is owned and managed by the Central Fisheries Board. The property includes Aasleagh Lodge and Aasleagh Cottage, where anglers are accommodated during the fishing season.

The river is well developed and serviced by stiles and footbridges and access to the banks is easy, with the road running parallel to the bank of the river for its entire length. The banks are good and deep wading is not necessary.

The fishery opens on 1 April, by which time there are a small number of spring fish in the river. The peak of the spring run is around mid-May. This fishing can last into June and anglers who fish at this time have a chance of a good fish. The grilse begin running in early June and the river peaks in late June and early July. These fish provide the bulk of the fish for the angler for the rest of the season, but there is a fair run of summer fish averaging about 9 lb and these arrive early in August.

The heaviest fish weighed 45 lb and was taken on fly in the early 1960s by the late Mrs Alice Dodds-Marsh, a former lessee of the fishery. The best one in recent years weighed just over 20 lb and was taken by Mr Patrick Savage, of Dublin.

River Erriff, Catch Data, 1987-92

Year	1987	1988	1989	1990	1991	1992
Salmon	640	875	450	322	316	608
Sea-trout	450	308	127	*	*	*

* all sea-trout returned alive to the water

The Erriff is a productive summer salmon fishery. July is always the best month for catches and June, August and September are about equally productive. The effort per unit catch in 1984 was 5.4 rod days; in 1985 it was 4.6; in 1986, it was 4.2 and in 1987 it was 3.1 rod days.

Fly-fishing is the rule on the fishery, but spinning, worm and shrimp are allowed by the fishery rules for a short period each day.

Flies

Fly sizes vary from size 6 trebles down to size 12 doubles, with the smaller patterns fishing best on the higher beats. Popular fly patterns include Black Pennell, Hairy Mary, Shrimp Fly, Silver Rat, Silver Doctor, Garry Dog, Stoat's Tail and Thunder and Lightning.

Fishing down and across with a floating line is the usual method on the streams in summer and the bigger pools are best fished by backing up, using two flies (one being the Black Pennell on the dropper) and using a sink-tip line.

For fly-fishing, a $9\frac{1}{2}$ – 11-foot single-handed rod capable of casting an 8 or 9 line is adequate. For high water, a 12–15 foot double-handed rod with floating and sinking-tip lines will prove useful. For spinning, an $8\frac{1}{2}$-10 foot rod is generally used and Mepps spinners and Toby spoons are most popular. The river does not get a big run of sea-trout and they are generally caught as a by-product of the salmon fishing. I found the slow pools on Beats 1 and 2 as well as the Sea Pool and Coronation Pool and Gowlan to be the most productive areas for sea-trout at night. Small flies – sizes 10 and 12 – work best.

CULFIN RIVER   L74 76

Season

Salmon: 1 February to 30 September.
Sea-trout: 1 February to 12 October.

Permits (for the North Bank)

Mrs. R. Willoughby	Mr Owen King
Salruck	Lettergesh PO
Renvyle, Co. Galway	Co. Galway
Telephone 095 43498	*Telephone* 095 43414

The Culfin River is about a mile long and drains Loughs Muck and Fee and a 9 square mile catchment to the sea. It tumbles down from Lough Muck in a spate and can be well worth fishing, especially in June and July. It flows through a bog and the banks are high and difficult in places but there are some nice pools too. It is a lovely peaceful place for a quiet holiday and Mrs Willoughby has three holiday cottages to let and boats on the lake. This river also gets a good run of sea-trout in July and a few big ones come in May.

DAWROS RIVER   L70 59

Season

Salmon: 1 February to 30 September.
Sea-trout: 1 February to 12 October.

Permits

For the pools downstream of Derryinver (Dawros) Bridge

Renvyle House Hotel
Renvyle
Co. Galway
Telephone 095 43511

For the river upstream of Derryinver Bridge

    Mrs W. Aspell
    Kylemore, Co. Galway
    Telephone 095 41145

The Dawros River is about 4 miles long and drains a catchment of 20 square miles, including the Kylemore Loughs, into Ballynakill Harbour. It lies 1 mile north of the village of Letterfrack in Co. Galway and is noted for a small run of spring salmon and a really excellent run of sea-trout and a good run of grilse. The pools below Derryinver Bridge are especially good on the tide in late May and June. The banks have been cleared between Tullywee and Derryinver Bridges and there are some good deep pools in this stretch. The Rock Pool in the grounds of Kylemore Abbey can be especially good for grilse.

OWENGLIN (CLIFDEN) RIVER   L68 50

Season

Salmon: 1 February to 30 September.
Sea-trout : 1 February to 12 October.

Permission

The river is owned by members of the Clifden Anglers' Association and day tickets are available from: Mr Percy Stanley, Clifden or from Mr Declan Moran, also of Clifden.

    The Clifden River rises in the Twelve Bens mountains in the heart of Connemara and flows due west for $11\frac{1}{2}$ miles to the sea at the town of Clifden. It is an extreme spate river with a catchment of a mere 14 square miles. There are three waterfalls on the river, Salmon's Falls, Creggs Falls and the falls at Barnournaun village. The river is well endowed with good pools and when the water is right it can provide some exceptionally good grilse fishing. The first big run comes up on the first flood in June and it is estimated that the river can produce up to 300 grilse for the month of June alone if the water levels remain favourable. Grilse continue to run on the spate for the rest of the season and can be taken as far up as Barnornaun – 7 miles upstream. A feature of the grilse run is that the fish all tend to be small – averaging 3 lb. Traditionally, it used to be a sea-trout fishery and salmon were introduced – according to local information – about thirty years ago. The fishing methods are fly and worm. Spinning and shrimp are prohibited. Best flies are Badger, Silver

Badger, Garry Dog, Stoat's Tail, Silver Stoat's Tail, Hairy Mary and small Shrimp Fly.

The Ivy Pool and the Green Pool are best fished for sea-trout at night. A by-law prohibits fishing with rod and line between Ardbear New Bridge and Ardbear Old Bridge after 15 May each season.

DERRYHORRAUN RIVER   L68 49

Season

Salmon: 1 February to 30 September.
Sea-trout: 1 February to 12 October.

Permits

Mr Percy Stanley   Mr Declan Moran
Clifden, Co. Galway   Clifden, Co. Galway

This small stream drains half a dozen loughs into the Salt Lake, just south of Clifden. Occasional salmon run it in summer and it gets a good run of sea-trout in July. The sea-trout mainly run through to the loughs. A by-law prohibits fishing off the Weir Bridge across the Salt Lake or being in possession of a fishing rod and line on the same bridge.

BALLINABOY RIVER   L66 58

Season

Salmon: 1 February to 30 September.
Sea-trout: 1 February to 12 October.

Permits

Col. A. Morris
Ballinaboy House
Clifden
Co. Galway

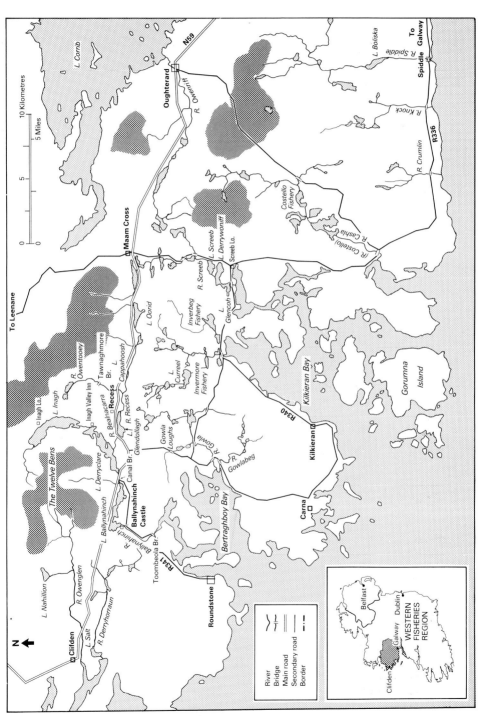

Connemara

The Ballinaboy River flows into the sea near the monument commemorating the landing of the first transatlantic flight by Alcock and Brown. Sea-trout run here from July. There are at least a dozen good loughs on the system and they hold most of the interest for anglers.

OWENMORE (BALLYNAHINCH) RIVER   L76 46

Season

Salmon: 1 February to 30 September.
Sea-trout: 1 February to 12 October.

Permission

There are eight separate fisheries on the Ballynahinch system. A number of them are private and I shall deal only with those that are available for letting to the general public.

The Ballynahinch system is strung like a necklace around The Twelve Bens in the heart of Connemara. Benlettery, Bengower and Bencorr patiently look down on the angler as he drifts the loughs and walks the river banks on this, one of the most beautiful and prolific fisheries in the west of Ireland.

The system is 15 miles long and from the top of the Inagh valley to the north and Lough Oorid near Maam Cross to the east it drains a catchment of 68 square miles. It once formed part of the sporting estate of the Martin family, one of whose best known members, 'Humanity Dick' Martin MP, is commemorated by a plaque at Ballynahinch Castle. In this century it was owned for a time by His Highness, The Maharaja Jorn Sahib of Nawanagar, better known on the cricket field as Ranjitsinhji. Ranji spared no expense in developing the fishery by building footbridges and weirs and a feature of the work was the construction of stone-built casting piers which still stand all along the fishery.

BALLYNAHINCH CASTLE FISHERY

Permits:

The Manager
Ballynahinch Castle Hotel
Ballinafad PO, Co. Galway
Telephone 095 31006
Fax 095 31085

The Ballynahinch Castle Hotel fishery consists of $2^1/_2$ miles of river, Ballynahinch Lake Lower and a narrow neck at the top of the lough known as Sna Beg, which is developed as a salmon throw. The fishery is at the bottom of the system, stretching upstream from Toombeola Bridge. This makes it a most prolific fishery since all the salmon and sea-trout coming in from the sea must pass through the fishery. It also has its own spawning beds right under the hotel.

The fishery is divided into eight salmon beats plus four sea-trout pools. It is let by the beat, which is rotated daily, and the tenant of the beat for the day may take one guest. Gillies are available on request from the fishery manager, Michael Conneely, himself one of the finest fishermen it has been my privilege to meet.

The first spring salmon run through in February and March and fish begin resting in the Ballynahinch pools in April. A number of spring fish are taken every year in April and May but the river is not heavily fished at this time. There is a belief among fishery staff in the area that the early-season run may be greater than is suspected. A lot of big fish, 10 lb – 12 lb and some well over 20 lb turn up on the redds every autumn and these have obviously been in the system from early spring.

It is the big grilse run that draws the anglers to Ballynahinch. It begins in late May or early June and peaks in late June and early July. It is these fish, with a small injection of September-run fish, that provide the best of the salmon fishing at Ballynahinch. The hours of fishing are from 10 a.m. to 7 p.m. and from 8.30 p.m. to dusk, a custom based on the belief that salmon pools should be well rested. Fly-fishing is the rule but a shrimp or worm may be used between 5 and 7 p.m. by persons who have not caught a fish on fly before 5 p.m. Spinning is allowed only in high water.

The Ballynahinch Fishery is characterized by short streams and big, deep pools. In character, it is far removed from the perceived image of a classic salmon river with its long streams and glides. However, for the angler who knows his fishing, it can be just as productive.

The streams are fished with the fly in the usual manner, casting across and allowing the fly to fish round in the current. In the slow water, movement must be imparted to the fly by retrieving line.

A small double-handed rod is useful on the river and a single-handed rod is essential. It can double up for the sea-trout fishing as well.

The popular fly patterns on the river are Ballynahinch Badger, Silver Badger, Silver Doctor, Blue Charm, Hairy Mary, Stoat's Tail, Silver Stoat, Silver Rat, Silver Grey and Shrimp Fly.

ROD CATCH, BALLYNAHINCH CASTLE FISHERY, 1985-92

Year	1985	1986	1987	1988	1989	1990	1991	1992
Salmon	120	171	168	359	325	23	43	100

Sea-trout

The sea-trout fishing at Ballynahinch has to be as good as an angler could hope to experience anywhere.

The first fish begin running in late June, and July and August see the best of the night fishing.

The season for daytime sea-trout fishing is from July to October. Sea-trout take well here, even in daylight conditions. Tactics are important and a single size 12 or 14 fly on floating line and fine leader gets best results. Favourite patterns are Duckfly, Connemara Black, Bibio or Watson's Fancy. A dry fly can also work by day – try a Grey Duster, a Black Gnat, a small Brown Sedge or a Daddy.

The hours for night fishing are from dusk to 12.30 a.m. A floating line and size 10 or 12 Silver Doctor, Bloody Butcher or Delphi Silver are the best choice. Fish only two flies on the leader. A good day or evening's fishing can produce up to a dozen trout to 5 lb – the average is about 1 lb – and with a good run of sea-trout on the river the annual catch must number nearly 3,000 trout. No one has ever counted or kept an accurate record of just how many are taken.

LOUGH INAGH FISHERY (BALLYNAHINCH SYSTEM)   L85 52

Permits

Della MacAuley
Inagh Valley Inn
Recess, Co. Galway
Telephone 095-34608

Lough Inagh Lodge Hotel
Recess
Co. Galway
Telephone 095-34706

The title of the Lough Inagh Fishery is somewhat misleading in that it conjures up images of a lough fishery. In fact, there are six bank beats at the fishery in addition to the lough fishing. The beats are rotated daily between the Inagh Valley Inn and Lough Inagh Lodge Hotel, two establishments where an angler will always find a welcome.

The spring salmon fishing begins in early March and peaks in May. The fish average 10 lb but with some to 25 lb. The best lie on the fishery is probably Derryclare Butts. (The point where a river enters a lough is known as a butt in Connemara and Derryclare is one of the most famous).

The grilse come in June and can be taken from the bank and from a boat on the lough up to the end of September.

The sea-trout fishing starts in late June. The large fish come early and the finnock arrive in July and August to give sport of an equal standard to that enjoyed farther downstream at Ballynahinch.

The Corloo Beat is located on the Inagh River at the outflow from Lough Inagh above the weir. It gives excellent sea-trout fishing and is a good throw for a salmon in high water when fished off the top two casting piers. A boat is provided to allow anglers to fish the lake here.

The Trout Pool on the Inagh River is located upstream of the forest road down to Derryclare Butts. As the name implies, it is an excellent sea-trout pool which takes one rod by day and three at night. There is a good high-water lie for salmon in the middle of this pool by the right bank.

Derryclare Butts is where the Inagh River enters Derryclare Lake. It is probably the most likely location on the whole system for taking a spring salmon and there is a tastefully constructed hut close by, where the angler can light a fire and keep warm on a cold March day while resting the beat. There is another pool above the footbridge – that can also hold a fish. In high water, this butt fishes high up – right underneath the footbridge and the fish lie farther down as the water drops. It is a good grilse lie too. A boat is provided for fishing the upper end of Derryclare Lake.

Glendalough Butts is located where the Bealnacarra River enters Derryclare Lake. It fishes best on high water but needs to be developed further.

Pine Island is one of the landmarks of Connemara. It is located at the bottom of Derryclare Lake just north of the Recess–Clifden road. Access is by boat. It is noted for its big sea-trout and grilse can be taken here too. It is a quite restricted location and best suited to night fishing.

The Green Point Beat lies between Derryclare Lake and the Canal Bridge. There are really only two good pools here. The first is for salmon and grilse and is immediately above the Canal Bridge and the fish lie close to the bottom of the island. The other pool is at the hut and is excellent for sea-trout and good for salmon on high water. The lie is by the right bank and a long cast across from the top casting pier. The best flies for spring fish are a Collie Dog variant, Wilkinson Shrimp, Silver Doctor, Curry's Red Shrimp and Ballynahinch Badger. A similar selection to that for Ballynahinch (above) tied on size 10 and 12 double hooks work for grilse. The sea-trout flies are as for Ballynahinch.

THE UPPER BALLYNAHINCH FISHERY   L 87 47

Permits

Mrs Iris Joyce	Mr Leslie Lyons
Tullaboy House	Tullaboy
Maam Cross	Maam Cross
Recess, Co. Galway	Recess, Co. Galway
Telephone 091 82305	*Telephone* 091 82462

This is a river and lough fishery, situated 2 miles west of Maam Cross at the village of Recess. It comprises the right bank of the Owentooey River from Tawnaghmore Bridge on the little road up to the Lehanagh Loughs down to the Chapel Pool and the left bank of the Recess River from the top of McCreedy's Pool up to the junction of the Owentooey River and both banks up to Cappahoosh Lough.

This is chiefly a sea-trout fishery but it also produces an unknown number of salmon – mainly caught by locals. The best of the fishing is after the first spate in July. The stretch towards the end of the beat at the run into McCreedy's Pool can nearly always be relied upon to produce a grilse in a spate.

Anglers will find delightful accommodation at Tullaboy House.

GOWLA RIVER   L 81 40

Season

Salmon: 1 February to 30 September.
Sea-trout: 1 February to 12 October.

Permits

The Zetland Hotel
Cashel PO
Co. Galway
Telephone 095 31111

The Gowla River is just over 3 miles long and drains a catchment of 20 square miles and a chain of sixteen loughs into Bertraghboy Bay. It is mainly a sea-trout fishery and gets a small run of grilse. It is divided into four beats and the three lower beats have some very good holding pools. Daytime fishing is best in wild, windy conditions and there is excellent night fishing when the sea-trout are running. The bigger fish run in

June, evening fishing is good in July and August and daytime fishing is best in September–October. Try a Bloody Butcher or Silver Doctor at night. The Camusunary Killer, Watson's Fancy, Peter Ross, Bibio and Black Pennell are recommended by day.

GOWLABEG RIVER   L 82 39

Season

Sea-trout: 1 February to 12 October.

Permits

> Cashel House Hotel
> Cashel
> Co. Galway
> *Telephone* 095 31001

This little river flows north-west into Bertraghboy Bay. It is small and there are those who would describe it as only a bog river, but it gets a run of sea-trout from July and there are a few holding pools where the sea-trout rest on their way to the loughs above. It is best fished on a falling spate but a good ripple on the pools can also provide the chance of a trout.

INVERMORE RIVER   L 90 38

Season

Salmon: 1 February to 30 September.
Sea-trout: 1 February to 12 October.

Permits

> Mrs Mary McDonagh
> Glenview
> Cashel
> Co. Galway
> *Telephone* 095 31054

This little river is not more than half a mile long and drains twenty or so loughs of the famous Invermore Fishery into the top of Kilkieran Bay. It holds salmon and sea-trout. The salmon fishing can be good from early June and the sea-trout run about mid-June. There are about six pools in all and there is a road of about 400 yards long to the sea pool. A feature of this river is that it fishes best under average to low water conditions because the fish tend to run through it in a flood. It is said to fish better by day – with a ripple on the pools – than at night. The usual sea-trout flies will do – Bibio, Connemara Black, Delphi Silver, Peter Ross, Green Peter, Daddy, Camusunary Killer, Kingsmill and Black Pennell.

THE SCREEBE FISHERY   L 95 40

Season

Salmon: 1 February to 30 September.
Sea-trout: 1 February to 12 October.

Permits

> The Fishery Manager
> Screebe House
> Camus PO, Co. Galway
> *Telephone* 091-74110

The Screebe Fishery is situated at the head of Camus Bay, a tortuous winding estuary six miles due south from Maam Cross. It consists of an interconnecting series of about sixteen loughs and, while one might be tempted to conclude it is a lough fishery, it is surprising to find that there are five productive bank beats too. Maybe it would be more correct to call them stands, because, with the exception of the river beat, the others there are short, but on their day can be just as productive as many a beat a mile long.

This is a salmon and sea-trout fishery but the salmon fishing predominates on the beats. The fishery is managed by the Burkhart family at Screebe House, with professional advice from Dr Martin O'Farrell, a young fishery scientist. It is one of the few fishery catchments in Connemara unaffected by modern development such as forestry, and the wild salmon run is enhanced every year by the release of 50,000 smolts reared in the Screebe hatchery. Even though the Screebe catchment is small – about 22 square miles – the river holds the water after a flood for five or six days as a result of the slow-release effect of all the upstream loughs.

The fishery gets a small run of spring fish – 11 lb and 12 lb – in April and these are usually taken at the Salmon Pool. The grilse run about 20 June and peak in July, and some fresh fish continue running for the rest of the season.

Starting at the top of the fishery, the first location where an angler might expect to catch a fish from the bank is at the butt at Aasleam, where the river flows under the road. This butt is worth knowing about by anyone boat fishing Aasleam Lough. It fishes best with a flood in June, July and August and is totally dependent on the wild fish stocks to provide a salmon for the angler.

The Lady Pool is between the road and Cornaree Lake and this pool and Cornaree Butt, some twenty yards below it, give best results in a flood. The same holds true of Cornageeragh Butt at the inflow to the next lough down the system.

Next we come to the first proper river beat, which extends from the bottom of the cascade at the hatchery to the top of the Salmon Pool. Again this beat fishes best in a spate in August and September. Fishing it is like fishing for salmon in a small trout stream because it is no more than 4–5 yards wide. There are a few small pools where fish rest and the best one by far is Wing's Pool.

Next we come to the Salmon Pool, also known as Screebe Butt - at the top of Screebe Lake - and one of the best salmon pools in the west of Ireland. The shape of the river mouth with its natural rock formation and the two drystone jetties means that the fishing extends over a distance of 300 yards on both banks and there is a footbridge to facilitate crossing over to suit casting in windy conditions. It is a remarkable pool to produce salmon and when I visited it in 1988 the figure was 58 fish in 73 rod days. My own experience there bore out what has been said about it. A single-handed rod is adequate to fish this place; in fact is essential, because the water is practically still at the bottom and stripping the line is essential to give the flies life. It is an ideal location for backing up with a good wind blowing over your left shoulder.

For decades Screebe was a private fishery and only now are some of its secrets being discovered by the present fishery manager, Philip Clesham. Like Derrywoniff Butt! At the inflow to Derrywoniff Lough this is another hot spot and produced fifteen fish in June 1990. It is a most out-of-the way place to reach. It must be approached by boat and the angler runs the gauntlet of all the submerged rocks in Derrywoniff Lough.

Glencoh Butt between Derrywoniff and Glencoh Loughs is a very nice place and is fished – using a taxi boat to get there – in conjunction with the Road Pool and the Sea Stand. It is tidal and probably fishes only on the high tide.

ROD CATCH, SCREEBE FISHERY, 1986-92

Year	1986	1987	1988	1989	1990	1991	1992
Salmon	180	37	114	140	40	10	75
Sea-trout	1200	600	412	37	-	-	-

For fly-fishing for salmon, the favourite fly has to be a local dressing called the Screebe Badger. After that, a Thunder and Lightning is said to be good – or any fly with orange in it! Hairy Mary, Blue Charm, Silver Doctor and Black Pennell work too.

The Salmon Pool is fly only and Derrywooniff will probably be made fly-only. All methods are allowed on the river, on the Road Pool and at Glencoh.

The bulk of the sea-trout are taken on the loughs at Screebe but there are stories of good night fishing for sea-trout at the bottom of the Salmon Pool.

Screebe House provides accommodation and has a nice restaurant.

THE CASHLA (COSTELLO) RIVER   L 98 26

Season

Salmon: 1 February to 30 September.
Sea-trout: 1 February to 12 October.

Permits

The Manager
Costello and Fermoyle Fisheries
Costello, Co. Galway
Telephone 091-72196 *Fax* 091-72366

The Costello Fishery and its famous Cashla River is located near the village of Costello, about 22 miles due west of Galway City. Looked at on a map, it appears only a few miles 'out the road' from Galway, but its remoteness, situated as it is in bare, boulder-strewn, desolate countryside, makes it the ideal base for piscatorial romantics and fanatical sea-trout fishers.

The Cashla River is 3½ miles long and drains a watershed of 32 square miles and a chain of twenty-two lakes, at least fifteen of which hold sea-trout. It was to Costello that the late T. C. Kingsmill Moore, the father of Irish sea-trout fishing, came for twenty years to sample the marvellous 'white trout' fishing.

The river links Glenicmurrin Lake with the sea and is perhaps less well known than the loughs above, but equally deserving of attention. It is a typical moorland river, with a character all of its own. There are huge pools, perhaps forty yards wide – little loughs, really – and short tantalizing streams. All the loughs upstream make for a gradual drop in water. The flow is really self-regulating but a series of sluices are operated on the outflow from the loughs to maintain the flow. It has some of the finest sea-trout pools any angler could wish to lay eyes on –The Cabbage Pool, the Rock Pool, the Round Reedy, Paddy's Stand and the Dinner Pool, to name but a few.

The river is divided into four beats with two rods allowed by day and more at night. The main salmon taking places are Beat 1, which probably produces 70 per cent of the salmon, Paddy's Stand, the Butt of Rusheen, the Butt of Formoyle, the Clogher Pools, located about 150 yards below Clogher Lough, and the Butt of Clogher.

Such is the reputation of the loughs above that the river is often forgotten. The fishery opens in May and the first grilse begin running about 20 May. They continue running in June and it gets a run of big summer salmon (12 – 16 lb) towards the end of July.

The peak of the sea-trout run is around 12 July, even though the big sea-trout come up in May.

Flies

The following is a selection of killing sizes and patterns on the river. For grilse, with a good wind on the pools, use a size 10 or 12 Connemara Black on the dropper and a Watson's Fancy on the point. Alternatively, try a Blue Zulu and a Black Pennell. A Jeannie works well on the streams, as does a Blue Charm, Hairy Mary and small Curry's Red Shrimp. For daytime sea-trout fishing, a size 14 or 12 Watson's Fancy has to be the number one choice when fished on a 4 lb leader. A small Connemara Black with an orange tag is also highly rated. For night fishing, the choice has to be made between a Blue Zulu, Bibio, Bloody Butcher, Donegal Blue, Dark Mackerel (all size 10) and a big Black Pennell.

ROD CATCH, COSTELLO FISHERY, 1986-92

Year	1986	1987	1988	1989	1990	1991	1992
Salmon	50	55	71	75	24	12	101
Sea-trout	2300	1960	2110	489	420	410	475

CRUMLIN RIVER   M 3 22

Season

Salmon: 1 February to 30 September.
Sea-trout: 1 February to 12 October.

Permits

The Manager
Crumlin Lodge
Inveran
Spiddal, Co. Galway
Telephone 091-93105

This small spate river drains a number of loughs. It gets a small run of grilse and sea-trout.

THE KNOCK RIVER   M 9 22

A tiny spate river that drains a number of loughs west of Spiddal. It may get a few sea-trout on a spate.

THE SPIDDAL RIVER (OWENBOLISKA)   M 9 22

Season

Salmon: 1 February to 30 September.
Sea-trout: 1 February to 12 October.

Permits

Part of this water is private and part is leased to an angling club and day tickets are not available. There is a dispute regarding the fishing rights on part of the system.

The Spiddal River is about a mile long up to Boliska Lough. There is a further mile of water above Boliska Lough to Derryherk Lough.

Boliska Lough is used as a water supply and a dam at the top of the river once impeded running fish. This problem has been put right in recent times.

The river gets a fair run of grilse in June-July and sea-trout as well. Its main problem is that it is a small river, located close to a big centre of population, and this creates all sorts of problems. The best of the fishing is downstream of the waterfall and there can be quite good fishing on the upper section – above Boliska. Here the banks are clear, unlike the lower river, which is quite overgrown but is being cleared by the club.

CORRIB RIVER (GALWAY FISHERY)   M 29 24

Season

Salmon and Sea-trout: 1 February to 30 September.
Brown trout: 1 March to 30 September.

Permits

> The Manager
> Galway Fishery
> Nun's Island, Galway
> *Telephone* 091 62388

The Corrib River drains Lough Corrib and its tributaries, including Loughs Mask and Carra – a catchment of 1,212 square miles – into Galway Bay. It is 5½ miles long and flows through Galway City. It is owned and managed by the Central Fisheries Board.

This is one of Ireland's top salmon fisheries. In practice, from an angling viewpoint, it is divided into four distinct sections.

The water level on Lough Corrib is controlled by a weir with sixteen hydraulic gates. This weir is located about three-quarters of a mile below the point where the river flows out of the lough. The first fishery reaches from the Friar's Cut at the lough to The Weir. This water is deep and slow. It holds salmon, coarse fish and brown trout. Anglers troll and spin here for salmon and trout and a lot of coarse fishing is done here too. No permits are issued to fish here and the board does not at present exercise its rights of control on this stretch except immediately above the weir.

The next fishery down is what anglers refer to variously as The Weir or The Galway Fishery. It stretches from the weir down to the Salmon Weir Bridge, a distance of about 250 yards, and this is the stretch of water that salmon anglers make application in their thousands to fish every season.

The fishing for spring salmon, which average 12 lb, can begin as early as 1 February, depending on the water levels. For good spring fishing conditions, it is necessary that at least six gates be closed in the weir. The peak of the spring run takes place during April and up to the end of the first week in May. Spinning, shrimp fishing and fly fishing, using tube flies or size 4 treble-hook flies, are the usual methods.

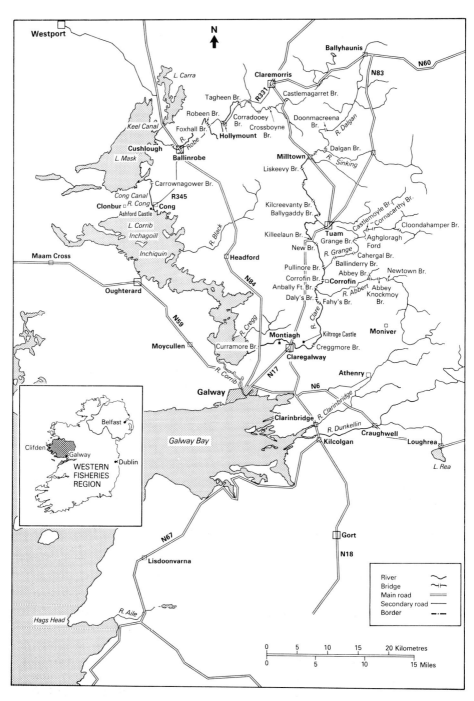

The Corrib system (east) and Galway

The grilse run from about 10 May, so there is no appreciable gap between the spring and grilse fishing. In a sense, they overlap in May. The grilse run in big numbers into early July and from mid-July there is a small but steady run of fresh fish for the rest of the season, with good fishing dependent on a good flow of water. In low water conditions, a fly-only rule applies for all but the last two hours of each session; when two or fewer gates are open, shrimp or spinner may be used, with a three-fish limit bag.

A maximum of six rods is allowed on the fishery. A fishing session lasts from morning up to 8.30 p.m. till mid-May. From mid-May until early July there are two angling sessions per day, from 6 a.m. till 1 p.m. and from 1.30 p.m. until 8.30 p.m. There is an evening (fly-only) session right through the season.

Fishing tactics and equipment are important even on a fishery as prolific as this if good results are to be obtained. It is essential that the angler be able to cast well with a double-handed rod and, furthermore, be able to cast a long line to slow down the speed of the fly. Body waders and a wading staff are essential. A sink-tip line should always be used for the grilse fishing; a floating line is rarely of any use. It is most important to mend the line well to prevent the fly from skating. The leader should be of at least 12 lb BS for grilse and from 15 to 20 lb for spring fish. Line of 25 lb BS is not too strong when spinning in spring.

In low water conditions the fishing is best in the early morning and late evening. The stream known as the Clonrickard Cut is a favourite in these conditions.

In high water, a Yellowbelly spun in front of the bridge or a shrimp fished in the pool at the Weir Lodge is recommended.

The favourite flies by day are Garry Dog, Munro Killer, Green Highlander, Willie Gunn, Tosh, and Black Goldfinch, while dark flies work best in the evening. Fly size is important. A size 10 treble is favoured in summer for grilse and a size 12 treble can be used in very warm weather.

The next stretch down is known as the New Beat. It extends downstream from the Salmon Weir Bridge to the traps and was first opened in 1989 by the then manager, Dr Paddy Gargan. It takes just two rods and is nearly as productive, pro rata, as the prime beat above. There is no bank fishing and it can only be fished by wading. It cannot be fished when more than two gates are open in the weir. All methods are allowed and it can be booked in advance but there is always the chance of being flooded out.

The final stretch is reserved for local anglers and reaches from McDonagh's turbine to the mouth of the river at Nimmo's Pier. It is bank fishing only. All fishing methods are allowed and it produced about 600 fish in 1989.

ROD CATCH, GALWAY WEIR, 1985-92

Year	1985	1986	1987	1988	1989	1990	1991	1992
Salmon	430	617	510	620	1905	1600	820	1100

Sea-trout

The fishery gets a big run of small sea-trout. They are usually fished for on the bottom two beats. They begin to run in June and the run peaks in July. The best of the fishing is in the evening and it is mainly availed of by local anglers.

OWENRIFF (OUGHTERARD) RIVER   M 12 43

Season

Salmon: 1 February to 30 September.
Brown trout: 1 March to 30 September.

Permits

The fishing is regarded as free for approximately one mile from Lough Corrib up as far as the hatchery opposite Oughterard House Hotel.

The rest of the river is privately owned or leased by, among others, Mr J. H. McCarroll, Clareville, Oughterard, Co. Galway and; Mrs I. Harben, Clonriff, Oughterard, Co. Galway.

The Oughterard River rises in Shannamona Mountain south of Maam Cross and flows east through Oughterard to Lough Corrib, draining on its way a chain of half a dozen loughs.

It is regarded primarily as a salmon fishery. The resident brown trout are small and it would be quite unsporting to fish the brown trout that run it in September to spawn from Lough Corrib.

The river gets a good run of salmon and grilse. Since it is very much a spate river, the runs are dependent on floods to take them up and the first good run coincides with the first good flood in late May or early June. Fish rarely run in July but will run again on a spate in August and September.

This is a river that is heavily fished by local anglers when the fish are running.

OWENWEE RIVER

JOYCE'S (MAAM) RIVER

BEALANABRACK RIVER

FARLMORE RIVER

CORNAMONA RIVER

All these rivers flow into the north-western end of Lough Corrib. They are spawning and nursery rivers for the lough and the fish that run them are quite often ripe with spawn. Angling is, therefore, not encouraged on any of these rivers, because it is quite unsporting to take such fish in rivers like these.

THE CONG RIVER   M 13 54

Season

Salmon: 1 February to 30 September.
Brown trout: 1 March to 30 September.

Permits

The fishing is free but a small fee is charged by Ashford Castle Hotel for admission to the grounds. The Cong River rises in the village of Cong. It is, in fact, the outflow from Lough Mask, further to the north, that escapes through huge fissures in the cavernous limestone of the district and rises again in the village of Cong. It is about one mile long. This is a big, wide river, perhaps 100 yards wide in places, and divided by an island at one point. It pushes down strongly past Ashford Castle. Some of it can be fished off the bank and it is possible to wade it, but more of it is better fished from a boat. To fish it well, the visitor would be well advised to employ one of the local gillies. They can be contacted through any hotel or guesthouse in the village of Cong.

The river gets an excellent run of spring salmon and fishing can start on opening day if the water is not too high. The peak of the spring run is in April and then the grilse come in May. June is particularly good, as is early July, and salmon are taken here in lesser numbers for the rest of the season.

The early-season fish are mostly taken by spinning but the fly can take fish from April onwards and shrimp and worm are also used.

The river also holds excellent stocks of good brown trout and some are very large. It has good hatches of olives, mayflies, sedges and midges and dry-fly fishing can be especially good. Body waders are very useful for the dry-fly fishing but care should be exercised while wading.

THE CONG CANAL   M 13 59

Season

Brown trout: 1 March to 30 September.

Permit

Free fishing.

The Cong Canal was intended to link Lough Mask with Lough Corrib and extends from Ballinchalla Bay towards the village of Cong. It is interesting both from an historical perspective and especially as a superb brown trout fishery.

The canal was proposed by the Board of Public Works in 1844 and work began in 1848. By 1850, 500 men were employed in its construction. Famine was widespread at the time and the scheme afforded much-needed relief for the men and their families. The engineer's report for 1848 refers to the greater portion of the men being so destitute and badly nourished that they were unable to realize a wage greater than 3d (1¼p) a day. By the end of 1833, the main channel was completed.

The suspension of the work in 1854 gave rise to much speculation over the years. The porous nature of the limestone through which the canal was cut created considerable difficulty and required much staunching. A report of a House of Lords committee in 1852 that the Board of Public Works at that time was having severe difficulties in financing schemes, and that the prospects of a sufficiency of traffic on the new canal were poor, would appear to be as good a reason why the navigation work was abandoned as the frequently expressed view that the canal was an engineering failure.

The canal was further deepened for drainage purposes in 1983.

Whatever the reason for its closure as a navigation route, we should remember the distressed and underfed workmen who gave us a very fine trout fishery.

The canal is about 3 miles long and the best of the fishing is from Lough Mask down to Carrownagower Bridge. It is approached by the Inishmaine road, which branches off the Ballinrobe–Clonbur road, and the permission of the riparian owners should be sought as necessary. The canal dries up in summer below Carrownagower Bridge and for some distance above it. In springtime, the water flows swiftly and the canal offers good wet-fly fishing and spinning produces several trout over 10 lb every year. The Cong Canal trout are beautifully conditioned fish. The average weight of trout caught on wet-fly and dry-fly is marginally under 2 lb, which makes it one of the fisheries with the highest average weight in the country. The canal has all the usual fly hatches associated with an Irish limestone river. Dry-fly fishing to the sedge is especially good on summer evenings at its outlet from Lough Mask and plenty of trout are hooked and landed here up to 5 lb. Many much bigger fish are hooked that are impossible to land. This is popular fishing and it can get crowded. In a wet summer, try further downstream, where the fishing can be just as good.

BLACK RIVER   M 20 48

Season

Brown trout: 1 March to 30 September.

Permit

Part is free and part can be fished with Regional Fisheries Board permit, obtainable from:

Weir Lodge
Earl's Island, Galway

The Black River flows into Lough Corrib north of Greenfields and Inchiquin Island after a journey of about 15 miles past Shrule and Headford. It is a rich limestone river but was drained in the late 1960s and runs low early in the season. It offers some prospects for wet-fly fishing in March and April.

THE CREGG RIVER   M 32 35

Much of this river is too deep to hold trout and its upper reaches mainly provide spawning and nursery waters.

CLARE RIVER   M 32 35

Season

Salmon: 1 February to 30 September.
Brown trout: 1 March to 30 September.

Permit

> The Buckley Fishery
> Spiddal House
> Spiddal
> Co. Galway
> *Telephone* 091 83393

Corofin Fishing Association permits are available from:

> Western Regional Fisheries Board
> Weir Lodge
> Earl's Island
> Galway
> *Telephone* 091 63118.

> Mr Matt Furey
> Anbally, Corofin
> Co. Galway
> *Telephone* 093-41565

> Mr Patrick Balfe
> Secretary
> St. Colman's Angling Club
> Corofin
> Cummer P O, Co. Galway

> Mr Sonny Martin
> Esso Station
> Galway Road, Tuam
> Co. Galway
> *Telephone* 093-24151

Riparian owners have the remainder of the fisheries and much of the fishing is as good as the controlled stretches and is available on request.

The Clare River rises north of Ballyhaunis in Co. Roscommon and flows south through Tuam before turning west through Claregalway to enter Lower Lough Corrib. It is over 58 miles long (it changes its name to the Dalgan River above Milltown) and together with its tributaries it drains a huge area of East Galway.

It is mainly a limestone river and holds excellent stocks of spring salmon, grilse and good-quality brown trout.

The spring salmon run the river from early in February and the best of the fishing is from 17 March to the end of May. Fish are taken all the way up to and above Tuam but some of the best of the fishing is in the

Claregalway–Corofin area.

The grilse begin running in late May, with the best fishing being in June and July. As the season progresses the fish move upstream with every rise in water and fish are sometimes taken on the Dalgan River up near Ballyhaunis.

No records are kept by any of the fisheries or clubs along the river, but all agree that both the summer and spring fishing is very good. The spring salmon average 10–12 lb and the grilse 5–6 lb. Worm fishing is the most popular angling method and the Yellowbelly and Toby are also popular. The Corofin Fishing Association has a fly-only stretch from Daly's Bridge to Anbally footbridge. The most popular salmon flies are Garry Dog, Green Highlander, Munroe Killer, Silver Doctor, Hairy Mary, Blue Charm and Stoat's tail.

The quality of the brown trout fishing is first rate and anglers travel a long way to fish some of the better water. The average weight is about $1\frac{1}{2}$ lb and there are reports of trout being taken on fly up to $8\frac{1}{2}$ lb. In addition, the river stock is augmented by a run of big trout up from Lough Corrib when water conditions are right in July and August. Photographs on anglers' mantlepieces from Claregalway to Tuam testify to the quality of the trout fishing. Where else could a recent catch of three trout – 5, 4 and 3 lb – taken in one evening on a Grey Midge be matched.

The trout fishing begins in April and this can be a good month. May brings the mayfly on several stretches and reed smut are very plentiful and give good fishing. The evening fishing in July and into August can be especially good to sedges, blue-winged olives and white moths. The Pheasant Tail, Orange Quill and Tup's Indispensable, all size 14, fish well for the blue-winged olive hatch. Various diptera get blown on to the water too – especially the hawthorn fly and the cowdung.

The Buckley Fishery covers 8 miles of the right bank from Lough Corrib up to Kiltroge Castle and about 3 miles of the left bank downstream from a point half a mile above Claregalway Bridge. The lower section is slow, wide and deep and bank access is difficult. Salmon can be taken near the lake and there is good salmon and trout fishing from Montiagh upstream to above Claregalway Bridge.

The Corofin Fishing Association Water is in four parts or beats. The first stretch up from Lough Corrib is on the left bank at Curramore Bridge on the Galway–Headford road. This section is slow and deep but is good salmon-holding water.

The next stretch is also on the left bank half a mile up from Claregalway Bridge and extends for nearly 2 miles.

The third stretch is on both banks below Creggmore Bridge for a mile and a mile on the right bank upstream.

The fourth stretch is quite extensive and consists of nearly 3 miles of both banks from just above Fahy's Bridge to above Anbally Castle. From Anbally footbridge down to Daly's Bridge is fly-fishing only.

The trout fishing on the latter three beats can be of quite exceptional quality – especially on summer evenings.

St. Colman's Angling Club has a couple of miles of excellent salmon and grilse fishing as well as trout fishing on the right bank from Pullinore Bridge to a point about half a mile below Corofin Bridge and the club has fishing on the left bank above and below Corofin Bridge.

Tuam and District Angling Association has extensive fishing rights on the river – either leased or the trespass rights from riparian owners. On sections of this water, there is good and even excellent spring-salmon fishing from mid-April, grilse fishing in June and July, and marvellous brown trout fishing.

The Tuam water begins above Corofin village on the left bank and extends for about 1,000 yards at the junction of the Grange River. This is prime spring salmon, grilse and brown trout fishing.

One mile above Pullinore Bridge, at Cloonkeen, the river holds excellent stocks of trout for about 400 yards.

The next worthwhile stretch for brown trout is from the New Bridge up to Killeelaun (Cloonmore) Bridge and the trout stocks are excellent at Gardenfield, 1 mile above Ballygaddy Bridge.

There is good clean salmon water half a mile above Kilcreevanty Bridge (at the back of the graveyard) and this stretch also fishes well with wet-fly for brown trout.

There is good wet-fly fishing below Lehid and dry-fly-fishing from Lehid up to Liskeevy Bridge. This same stretch below Liskeevy Bridge is also noted for spring salmon and grilse.

Finally, quite a few salmon are taken every year around the village of Milltown.

DALGAN RIVER   M 42 64

The Dalgan River is an extension of the River Clare. It fishes well for salmon above Dalgan Bridge and fish are taken up as far as Doonmacreena Bridge every season. The brown trout fishing is quite good in this area too.

ABBERT RIVER   M 50 42

The Abbert River is 25 miles long. It flows west from Monivea through Abbeyknockmoy to join the Clare River at Anbally. This was one of the favourite trout streams of J. R. Harris (of *An Angler's Entomology* fame) but it was ravaged by an arterial drainage scheme. Most of it is too shallow but there is still a bit of good trout fishing with fish to 3 lb above Abbey Bridge and at the old mill. There is some nice trout water at Newtown Bridge too. Inquiries to Mr Sonny Martin, *(see page 120)*

GRANGE RIVER   M 48 50

The Grange River flows west for 17 miles to join the Clare River about 3 miles south of Tuam. It flows through the bog from Cahergal Bridge down to the confluence and is of no interest to the game angler. It too was affected by an arterial drainage and there is not a sound to be heard from the famous Ahgloragh Ford (the roaring ford in Irish). Some rehabilitation work has been carried out and the river has recovered well from Grange Bridge upstream. It holds good stocks of brown trout to 3 lb and fishes especially well to wet-fly on high water in August and September. It also gets a small run of grilse. The best of the brown trout fishing is from Grange Bridge to Castlemoyle Bridge, the stretch downstream of Cornacartha Bridge holds some very large trout and the tributary coming in from the south is worth fishing from Cloondahamper Bridge downstream. Inquiries to Mr Sonny Martin, *(see page 120)*

SINKING RIVER   M 50 63

The Sinking river flows through Dunmore and joins the Clare River below Dalgan Bridge. It flows through bog from Dunmore downstream and it has fair to good trout fishing upstream of Dunmore.

ROBE RIVER   M 20 65

Season

Brown trout: 1 March to 30 September.

Permit

Free fishing.

The Robe River is nearly 40 miles long. It rises near Ballyhaunis and flows west past Claremorris through Hollymount and Ballinrobe and enters Lough Mask north of Cushlough. This rich limestone river was drained in the early 1980s but has now recovered well with the help of rehabilitation works carried out by the Western Regional Fisheries Board. It holds a fair stock of brown trout – some very good ones to over 6 lb – and is a firm favourite with many dry-fly anglers. It has good hatches of olives and mayflies and a prolific hatch of sedges. The banks are well developed and have had stiles erected by the Fisheries Board on all the good trout-fishing water from downstream of the town of Ballinrobe right up as far as Castlemagarret, near Claremorris.

Access is reasonably good, either from the bridges or at points where the river flows close to the public road. One stretch is virtually inaccessible, midway between Hollymount and Foxhill Bridge. Fortunately, this is mostly deep water and holds very few trout. Another short stretch with no access lies midway between Robeen Bridge and Ballinrobe.

Some parts of the river can suffer from an algal problem in summer.

THE KEEL CANAL   M 15 68

Season

Brown trout: 1 March to 30 September.

Permit

Free fishing.

The Keel Canal is a mile long and links Lough Carra and Lough Mask. Its water is gin-clear and it holds trout to over 6 lb. It flows fast and strong in spring and later has prolific fly hatches of all the usual limestone species, including mayfly. Access is good from Keel Bridge, with stiles and footbridges provided. The lovely silver Keel trout and their clear-water habitat can provide a good test for the very best dry-fly angler. It runs low and becomes weedy in summer.

CLARINBRIDGE RIVER   M 42 21

A small river that might just produce a few brown trout to the wet-fly in late March or April.

DUNKELLIN (KILCOLGAN) RIVER   M 42 18

Season

Salmon: 1 February to 30 September.
Sea-trout: 1 February to 12 October.
Brown trout: 17 March to 15 September.

Permits

The Western Regional Fisheries Board, Earl's Island, Galway, (*telephone* 091 63118) for a short stretch of less than half a mile on the right bank. The rest is free or with riparian owner's permission.

The Kilcolgan River is over 30 miles long and drains a catchment of over 140 square miles, including Lough Rea. It flows west through the village of Craughwell into Galway Bay. It is a rich limestone river and the porous nature of the district causes part of the river to dry up in summer.

It gets a run of salmon and sea-trout and holds fair stocks of brown trout.

The spring fish run in April and May and the grilse in June and July. The river offers good prospects for fly-fishing in the last mile above the tide.

The best of the sea-trout fishing is in July and early August, from the Old Bridge at Kilcolgan down to the top of the estuary. The river gets a larger average size of sea-trout than those found in Connemara. The best fishing is from about 10 p.m. to 11.30 and again from 1 a.m. to 4 a.m. Favourite flies are Bloody Butcher, Silver Doctor and Teal, Blue and Silver.

The Kilcolgan also holds some very big slob trout, but these are rarely taken by conventional fly-fishing methods.

The river holds a big stock of relatively small brown trout but also some good ones to $3\frac{1}{2}$ lb. It can fish well in April, when every half-dozen trout taken will include one or two of 1 lb or better. April and May see the peak of the brown trout fishing. The main brown trout fishing stretch is from the old bridge up to the waterfall, as far as Dunsandle House and it is very good at Craughwell. The fly hatches are a bit erratic though the river has everything except mayfly. Local anglers favour a Wickham's Fancy on the top dropper, a Greenwell's Spider on the middle dropper and an Orange and Green Grouse on the point for the wet-fly fishing in spring.

AILLE RIVER   M 10 97

Season

Sea-trout: 1 February to 12 October.
Brown trout: 15 February to 12 October.

This little river flows down off the Burren through Lisdoonvarna to enter the sea at Doolin Strand. It flows in places through deep gorges and is very overgrown. There are several deep holes along its course, both above and below Lisdoonvarna, which hold good brown trout. They are best fished with worm after a flood. Access to one of the better stretches is at the old Protestant church above the Spectacle Bridge. The river runs dry in summer from Roadford downstream but sea-trout and a few grilse are said to run it on a spate. It is mainly only suited to worm fishing and spinning.

Greenpoint Two on the Ballynahinch River

·6· Eastern Fisheries Region

The Eastern Fisheries Region extends from the boundary of the Republic of Ireland and Northern Ireland in Carlingford Lough to Kiln Bay, Co. Wexford. It includes part of Co. Monaghan and Counties Louth, Meath, Westmeath, Dublin, Wicklow, Kildare and Wexford. The Headquarters of the Eastern Regional Fisheries Board is at Mobhi Boreen, Mobhi Road, Glasnevin, Dublin 9, (*telephone* 01 379209).

The Fane, Dee, Boyne, Liffey and Slaney are some of its major rivers. With Dublin, the capital city, being located right in the middle of the region, one could be forgiven for concluding that the fisheries are all overcrowded and overfished. This is not the case. There may be some overcrowding in specific areas, but there are also miles of river holding quite good stocks, especially of good quality wild trout, that are only lightly fished. The reason perhaps, has been lack of information – and that is what this chapter aims to provide.

THE COOLEY RIVER   J 17 05

Season

Salmon and Sea-trout: 1 February to 30 September
brown trout: 1 March to 30 September

Permission

Riparian owners

It is also known as the Piedmond River or the Big River and the Little River. This is a small spate river which tumbles down the Cooley Peninsula along a 62 mile course and enters Dundalk Bay east of Giles Quay. It has a lovely gravel bed and is heavily overgrown on the lower reaches and is unfishable except with worm. It holds plenty of small brown trout further up but the last 2 miles bear signs of chronic pollution. It is just possible that it gets a small run of sea-trout after an August or September spate.

BALLYMASCANLAN RIVER   J 10 08

Season

Salmon and Sea-trout: 1 February to 30 September
Brown trout: 1 March to 30 September

Permission

The Dundalk and District Brown Trout Anglers Association claim fishing rights. Apply to:

> Mr John Clarke
> Hon. Secretary
> 31 Fatima Park
> Dundalk
> Co. Louth
> *Telephone* 042 36352

Also refer to riparian owners.

The Ballymascanlan River (also known as the Flurry River) rises on Camlough Mountain west of Newry and flows 132 miles in a southerly direction into Dundalk Bay. It drains an area of some 37 square miles of mainly mountainous countryside and the last four miles flow through old pastureland and woodland consisting of mature oak, ash and beech. This is a beautiful little spate river, about four yards wide, with some nice pools. It has a lovely gravel bed with clumps of ranunculus. The banks are reasonably clear. It gets a good run of sea-trout and grilse from mid July and unfortunately, it is reputed to have a poaching problem. The early run of sea-trout range from 1 lb to 3 lb. It fishes best after a flood and five or six sea-trout and even a grilse can be expected. In all, there is about four miles of fishing that starts at a good pool above Curralhir Bridge and continues downstream to Ballymascanlan Bridge.

   There is a size limit of 8 inches for the trout.

CASTLETOWN RIVER   J 03 09

Season

Salmon and Sea-trout: 1 February to 30 September
brown trout: 1 March to 30 September

Permission

The Dundalk and District Brown Trout Anglers Association claim the fishing rights. Apply to:

Mr John Clarke
Hon. Secretary
31 Fatima Park
Dundalk, Co. Louth
Telephone 042 36352

Refer also to riparian owners.

The Castletown River (also known as the Creggan or Courtbane River) flows into the head of Dundalk Bay and together with its tributaries, the Cully Water (Fallmor or Dungooley River) and the Kilcurry (Forkhill) River, it drains an area of 98 square miles.

The Dundalk and District Brown Trout Anglers Association claims extensive fishing rights. Membership is open and costs £6 per annum. Day tickets are also available. The Association is very active in developing the waters and co-operates with the Regional Fisheries Board staff in carrying out fishery protection.

The system holds brown trout and gets a run of salmon and an excellent run of sea-trout. It is also stocked with brown trout. This river has heavy angling pressure, particularly when the sea-trout are running.

The grilse run with the first flood in July and the sea-trout come in late July. This river fishes well through August and September when conditions are right.

ROD CATCH, CASTLETOWN RIVER, 1987-92

Year	1987	1988	1989	1990	1991	1992
Salmon	5	10	12	25	79	111
Sea-trout	3000	350	1000	270	295	351

The Kilcurry (Forkhill) River is usually fished for sea-trout from the Annagh Road Bridge down past Millbrook Bridge to the confluence, a distance of about 2 miles. This is a fast-flowing river, 5–7 yards wide and well overgrown with brambles. It is best fished with worm or a small spinner. Mee's Pool is the most productive spot.

Brown trout

The Castletown River flows in a southerly direction from Newtownhamilton and through Cullyhanna in Co. Armagh. It becomes a worthwhile trout stream from Ballybinaby Bridge downstream just south of the Armagh border. In all, there is about five miles of brown trout fishing, mainly to wet-fly in April and early May. There is a bag limit of six trout and a size limit of 8 inches.

Sea-trout

The sea-trout fishing can be very good from early July, through August and September. There is a bag limit of six trout. The best of the sea-trout fishing is from Bellew's Bridge (Coffin Bridge) downstream for a distance of about three miles to the estuary. The river is about 10 yards wide at Bellew's Bridge (with its 1674 inscription) and it has a nice sequence of pools and glides over a gravel bottom.

Water abstraction takes place above Tubberona Bridge and below the bridge is a big pool and a weir. This is a favourite area for sea-trout fishing. Most of the fishing is done at night and silver bodied flies are most popular - Teal, Blue and Silver, and Silver Doctor in small sizes. Maggots are also used either alone or attached to an artificial fly. Angling pressure is very heavy on the river when the sea-trout are running.

Salmon

The run of salmon has improved in recent years with the improved fishery protection and it is commonly believed that it can be increased. Some fish enter the river in July but the run doesn't peak till August, when the draft nets go off. It is, therefore, considered to get a late run.

The fishing is best after a flood and the main salmon angling areas are, working upstream, below Tubberona Weir, Tubberona Pool, then there are a few nice pools between Bellew's Bridge and the Court Bridge and, finally, Philipstown Pools. There is a nice long pool about $\frac{1}{4}$ mile above Philipstown Bridge and it is a good place to take a fish on fly from the right bank, especially in a September flood. The pool below the bridge is small and turbulent and best suited to a worm.

Shrimp patterns are the most favoured salmon flies on the river.

RIVER FANE

Season

Brown trout: 1 March to 30 September
Salmon and Sea-trout: 1 February to 12 October

Permission

The fishing rights on parts of the river are in dispute between Dundalk Salmon Anglers' Association; Dundalk and District Brown Trout Anglers' Association; the Village Anglers, Inniskeen; and riparian owners.

Dundalk Salmon Anglers claim continuous fishing rights on the right (south) bank from the sea to Knock Bridge, on Campbell's Fishery at Channonrock and Mulholland's and Monaghan's Fisheries at Ballintra, Inniskeen. Membership is limited to 250 senior members and costs £20 per season. Day tickets are available at £3 per day and £5 per day for out-of- state visitors. The Secretary is:

Patrick Wehrly
Jenkinstown
Dundalk, Co.Louth

Day tickets are available at:

Island Fishing Tackle
58 Park Street
Dundalk, Co.Louth
Telephone 042 35698

Dundalk Brown Trout Anglers' Association disputes all the fishing rights on the right bank upstream from Fane Valley Bridge, excluding Monaghan's Fishery at Ballintra, and from the top of the Fortescue Fishery above Fane Valley Bridge to the Armagh border, except Monaghan's Fishery. Membership is open and costs £6 per annum and day tickets are available. The Secretary is: Mr John Clarke, 31 Fatima Park, Dundalk, Co. Louth, (*telephone* 042 36352).

The Village Anglers at Inniskeen claim fishing rights on about 1 mile of water at the village of Inniskeen. Day tickets are available at Ruddy's Filling Station, Inniskeen, Co. Monaghan and cost £5 for salmon fishing and £3 for trout fishing. The Secretary is: Mr Arthur Campbell, Monvallet, Louth, Dundalk, Co. Louth, (*telephone* 042 74511).

It is also worth noting that riparian owners exercise their fishing rights on certain stretches.

The rivers Fane, Casletown, Ballymascanlan and Cooley

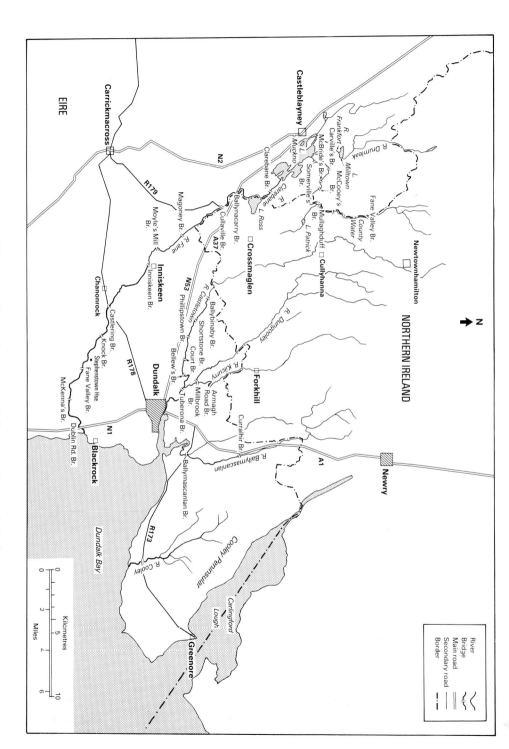

The River

The River Fane rises north west of Newtown Hamilton in Co. Armagh and flows for a distance of 38 miles to the sea at Blackrock in Co. Louth. It drains a catchment of 135 square miles. Its upper reaches before it enters Lough Muckno at Castleblayney are variously known as the County Water, the Mullaghduff River and the Little Fane. It flows along the Monaghan–Armagh border for 6 miles. Another tributary, known as the Drumleak River, flows into Milltown Lough and the river from Milltown Lough to Lough Muckno is known as the Frankfort River.

The Clarebane River joins Lough Muckno and Lough Ross in Co. Armagh. From Lough Ross, the river marks the border between Co. Monaghan and Co. Armagh for a distance of about 5 miles and meanders along through drumlin type countryside towards the stony grey fields of Inniskeen and the country of the poet, Patrick Kavanagh.

From Inniskeen, the gradient lessens and, ever so gradually, the flow slows down as it makes its way to meet the tide, which can often back up the water as far as Craig's Pool, below Fane Valley Bridge.

The river follows its natural course and has never been drained. In 1988 a new dam was constructed at the outflow from Lough Muckno and a reservoir is being built above Fane Valley Bridge. The intention is to abstract millions of gallons of water to service the needs of north Louth, though it is promised that this will not affect the fishing in any way. It is mainly a rain-fed river.

There is a net fishery in Dundalk Bay but no nets or traps on the river.

Jurisdiction

In those areas where the river flows along the border between Northern Ireland and the Republic, the matter of licences and opening and closing dates depends on which jurisdiction the angler is fishing in. The Northern Ireland season is much longer but it is illegal for an angler in the Republic to have a fish in his possession after 12 October, even though it might have been legally caught in Northern Ireland.

Salmon

The extent of the salmon fishing depends on water height. In low water, the majority of the fish are confined to the lower reaches and the best fishing is from Craig's Pool to the tide below McKenna's Bridge.

In high water, salmon fishing extends right up to Lough Ross, though some would contend that the best of it is from a point about a $\frac{1}{4}$ mile above Magoney Bridge. In high water there are at least three good lies from the old mill down to Magoney Bridge. Below Magoney Bridge, the

best of the fishing is at the Island Pool, the Flats and the Linnies Pool.
Access to this stretch is down along the old railway line halfway between
Blackstaff National School and Magoney Bridge. From Moyles Mill
Bridge downstream the best fishing is at the village of Inniskeen. The Hall
Pool above the village is a noted lie.

Passing down from Inniskeen, the first pool of note is the Splink Pool,
regarded by many as the most productive high water pool on the river.
The next pools of note are Pepper's Wall and Campbell's Mill Pool, where
a 54 lb fish was allegedly poached in 1938. The Hall Pool 100 yards above
Castlering Bridge, is the last pool of note on this stretch.

Between Castlering Bridge and Knock Bridge there are half a dozen
pools, any one of which could produce a fish. The last of them and
probably the best, is McArdle's Pool – a big triple pool. The flat above it is
also well worth some attention.

Below Knock Bridge, McGeeney's Pool and Kirk's Pool are favourite
throws and from the weir at Stephenstown House down to Fane Valley
Bridge there are five or six pools, all of which hold fish.

From Fane Valley Bridge downstream it is nearly all deep water except
for one shallow stretch and Craig's Pool is a noted lie. This is definitely
the most heavily fished stretch on the whole river.

The Season

The river got a nice run of spring fish till about 1970. After that, the
effects of UDN and overnetting decimated the spring run. The river gets
a small run of grilse in June, but it is not significant. The main run – and
it can be very substantial, with a lot of big fish in double figures – arrives
with the first floods in August and these are the fish that provide the best
fishing of the season all the way up to and above Magoney Bridge and it
can be very good indeed.

Access

Access to the rivers can be gained at all the bridges. Other well defined
access points are at the old railway track at Blackstaff, Monahan's
Bungalow, Coburn's, Campbell's Lane (but remember to park the car at
the main road), Craig's Lane and Lamb's Lane.

Fishing Methods

Worm and shrimp fishing are very popular, especially from Fane Valley
Bridge downstream. Fly fishing has gained greatly in popularity in recent
times and popular patterns are Goldfinch, Green Highlander and
Shrimp Flies. On good water, the river offers ample opportunities for the

fly all the way from Magoney Bridge downstream. Fly fishers should note that water temperatures can drop very fast on this river in autumn and large flies, sizes 2 and 4, may be called for. Of the spinning baits, the most popular are a No. 3 brass Mepps or a No. 4 copper Mepps.

ROD CATCH, DUNDALK SALMON ANGLERS ASSOCIATION WATER 1988-91

Year	1988	1989	1990	1991
Salmon	300	79	68	56
Sea-trout	553	501	279	225

Sea-trout

This river used get a really good run of sea-trout, but numbers have declined in recent years. The sea-trout fishing extends up as far as Knock Bridge and the best of it is from $\frac{1}{4}$ mile below Knock Bridge to Stephenstown House – good fly water – and from Craig's Pool to McKenna's Bridge and downstream about a mile to the Fiddler's Hole. From Craig's Pool downstream the river is heavily fished.

The peak of the season is from mid-July through August and daytime fly fishing can be quite good, as is the fly fishing at night, though a lot of anglers choose to fish maggot and worm.

Small flies – size 12 – seem to work best and the locals recommend anything with silver in it. Some of the recommended patterns are Butcher, Bloody Butcher, Teal, Blue and Silver, Dunkeld and Watson's Fancy.

Brown trout

The brown trout fishing on the Fane is generally considered to extend upstream from Knock Bridge to Cullaville Bridge and there is some nice wet-fly fishing in the Stephenstown area in spring. This is a relatively rich river and, while the average size is about $\frac{1}{2}$ lb, it holds trout to $2\frac{1}{2}$ lb and better. The average weight of the trout in the Castlering Bridge to Knock Bridge stretch is close to $\frac{3}{4}$ lb. There is a size limit of 9 inches. The river holds an excellent stock of trout from Cullaville Bridge down to Inniskeen and there is some nice dry fly water for $\frac{3}{4}$ mile above the Mill of Moyles.

The best daytime fishing is from late April, through May and into early June, with very good evening fishing through the summer.

The river is reported to have hatches of dark olives, iron blue duns, grey flags, black sedges and black gnats.

The river is not heavily fished for brown trout and a visiting angler is likely to find plenty of space, especially on weekdays.

CLAREBANE RIVER   H 87 17

Permission

Riparian owners.

The Clarebane River is about 12 miles long and joins Lough Muckno with Lough Ross. Two-thirds of it is in the Republic of Ireland and the lower part flows along the border with Northern Ireland. The access to it is good, with a road close to part of the right bank on the upper reaches and again at Clarebane Bridge roughly halfway along its course.

This is a substantial river, nearly 30 yards wide in places with firm banks, some nice riffles and glides and some very deep water. It holds an excellent stock of good brown trout with some to 6 lb. It is the kind of river that is always likely to produce a couple of nice trout early in the season and it gives really good dry fly fishing, mainly to sedge but also to small olives and their spinners on summer evenings.

This is a river where a nymph fished deep and slow is reputed to give very good results in late April and May.

MULLAGHDUFF RIVER (LITTLE FANE RIVER)   H 85 20

Permission

Riparian owners.

Season

1 March to 30 September.

Trout

The Mullaghduff River rises north west of Newtownhamilton in Northern Ireland and flows in a southerly direction for about 7 miles, forming the border between Northern Ireland and the Republic. It then swings sharply north west and meanders and glides through drumlin hills for a further 3½ miles to Lough Muckno.

This is a beautiful trout stream, comprising short riffles and glides and innumerable deep holes – ideal for holding brown trout. An angler who fished it all his life once described it as 'a river what you would never get tired looking at'. It ranges in width from 4 yards to 6 yards.

Unfortunately, it has suffered serious bouts of pollution in recent years, but it is a river that is quick to recover if given half a chance.

There is good fishing from Fane Valley Bridge (not to be confused with the other Fane Valley Bridge on the River Fane) on the Castleblayney – Newtownhamilton Road down to Mullaghduff Bridge and the fishing can be excellent from Mullaghduff Bridge past McCooey's Bridge, McBride's Bridge, Carville's Bridge to Somerville's Bridge. The stretch from this point to the lake is too deep to hold trout.

Access to the river is from the bridges and the banks are clear for the most part and very fishable.

The trout average 10 oz and a catch of 8 or 10 trout used be considered normal when the river was pollution free.

It fishes best from April onwards with the best fishing being from 11 a.m. to 4 p.m. The popular early season wet-fly patterns are March Brown, Hare's Ear and Greenwell's Glory. Later in the season dry- fly fishing comes into its own and olive spinners and small sedge patterns are especially useful.

FRANKFORT RIVER   H 83 21

Permission

Riparian owners.

This river flows from Milltown Lough for a distance of 2 miles to Muckno Lough It holds a fair stock of half pound trout and much better fish – 3 lb or more – are always a possibility. It is stocked by Castleblayney Anglers Association with 2 year old trout.

The best fishing is in May and June, when you might be lucky enough to get up to six trout in a day. The better trout are usually taken on dry sedge late in the evening in June and July.

The banks are good all along. There is access for the wet-fly fisher at Milltown Lough (fish it down) or from either of the bridges.

DRUMLEAK RIVER   H 85 23

Permission

Riparian owners.

This small river flows into Milltown Lake and holds a nice stock of trout from $\frac{1}{2}$ to $1\frac{1}{2}$ lb. Access to it is good with a road running parallel to the bank for its full length – about 1 mile. A recent drainage scheme has had adverse effects on the fishing but it may recover in a few years.

MONAGHAN BLACKWATER   H 68 35

Permission

>   Mr G. Hughes
>   Hon. Secretary
>   Monaghan Angling Club
>   Killygoan
>   Monaghan

Riparian owners

Season

1 March to 30 September.

The Monaghan Blackwater rises on Slieve Beagh on the Tyrone–Monaghan border and flows in a south-easterly direction through Scotstown towards Monaghan town. From there, it turns north-east towards the border at Ardgonnell Bridge and Middletown and on to Lough Neagh. From its source to the border is approximately 25 miles.

It underwent an arterial drainage scheme in 1987 and there were problems with agricultural and urban pollution. These are now well under control.

Before its pollution and drainage problems, it was regarded as one of the most productive trout rivers in the northern part of the country and catches of more than twenty trout per angler per day were not unheard of. The average size of the trout was about 12 oz, with plenty to 1 lb and some to 4 lb.

Now that the drainage scheme is completed this is a river that will recover quickly, and already anglers are reporting good catches. It is clear that rehabilitation work to restore the character of the river would be more beneficial than a restocking programme. It has good hatches of dark olives, and iron blue duns and a prolific hatches of sedges.

Wet-fly fishing after a flood is now probably the most productive course to take and popular fly patterns are Hare's Ear, Greenwell's Glory, Olive Quill, Iron Blue and various small sedges.

The banks have all been cleared of bushes on one side and this makes for easier access but the drainage works have also left the banks

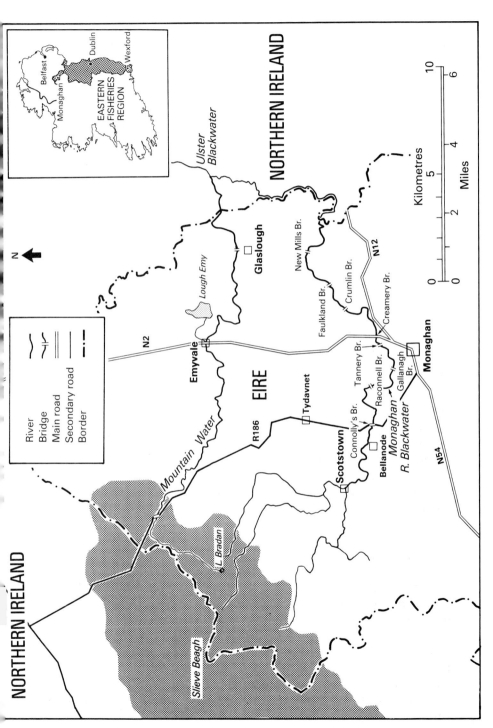

Mountain Water and the Monaghan Blackwater

impossibly high in some places. In most instances it is better to wade than to try and fish from the bank.

Access to the river is good, with numerous bridges along its course, none of them more than a mile apart.

The Fishing

In the river's present condition, the size of the trout and the stock density varies greatly. There is a bit of fishing at Cadden's midway between Scotstown and Ballanode. From Ballanode to Connolly's Bridge and from Connolly's Bridge to Raconnell Bridge the river is too shallow to hold trout. From Raconnell Bridge to Gallanagh Bridge, there are a few pools that hold trout but the banks are very high.

The Tannery Bridge is next downstream and there is a nice pool about 200 yards above it that holds trout. From the Tannery Bridge to the Creamery Bridge – on the N2 Monaghan–Emyvale road – is quite shallow but holds some trout up to $\frac{1}{2}$ lb.

There is a lot of shallow water from the Creamery Bridge to Crumlin Bridge and on to Faulkland Bridge, but there are occasional pools which are well worth fishing in springtime. The banks are high here and wading is essential.

The stretch from Faulkland Bridge to New Mills Bridge now provides the best fishing on the river since drainage took place. It can hold a lot of trout and to fish it properly, it is necessary to wade all the way.

From New Mills Bridge to the border the water is mainly deep and heavy. It holds a small stock of big trout.

Rehabilitation

A rehabilitation programme is planned for this river and when it is completed, the river should revert to being a really worthwhile trout stream.

THE MOUNTAIN WATER   H 68 43

The Mountain Water rises in Lough Bradan and flows through Emyvale to join the Blackwater 2 miles north of Glaslough. An arterial drainage scheme was carried out there in the late 1980s and the river has now little or no trout angling potential. It functions as a spawning and nursery stream for Emy Lough.

Before drainage, it was surveyed by the Central Fisheries Board in the early 1980s and was found to hold a good stock of moderately fast-growing trout from Glaslough up to Emyvale and to above the weir that diverts water to Emy Lough. Trout up to 3 lb were encountered in the Glaslough area. It was very overgrown and hard to fish.

RIVER DEE   0 8 93

Permission

Permission is discussed in detail at the end of the entry.

The Dee rises at 1,119 feet above sea level on Loughanlea Mountain near Bailieborough in Co. Cavan. It flows in an easterly direction for 38 miles, draining a 151 square mile catchment, and enters Dundalk Bay at Annagassan where it shares a common estuary with the Glyde.

The tributaries above Whitewood Lake are fast flowing over clean gravel bottoms and have all the appearance and qualities of excellent salmon spawning and nursery streams. The character of the river varies. From Whitewood Lake downstream it is slow flowing, silted and overgrown, with some fast, streamy water. From the village of Nobber to Garvey Bridge, it is mainly fast flowing. From Garvey Bridge to Ardee, there is a lot of deep, slow water, and from Ardee to the sea it varies with a lot of nice streams interspersed with deep, slow flats, ideal holding pools for salmon and occasional big brown trout.

A feature of the river is its high banks, which make the river almost inaccessible in places.

These are the result of an arterial drainage scheme that took place between 1950 and 1956. It was one of the first – if indeed not the first – arterial drainage schemes in the country, financed by the Marshall Aid Programme. In those days, drainage schemes were engineers' solutions to flooding and no consideration was given to a river as a fishery. Only now, forty years on, is a rehabilitation programme being considered.

By 1966, the river was showing good signs of recovery and in the following years, the trout and salmon stocks increased dramatically. At the present time, it is highly regarded as a brown trout, sea-trout and salmon fishery.

Fish Stocks

The river gets a fair to good run of spring salmon. It has the distinction of still getting a small run of three-sea-winter salmon ranging from 25 to 35 lb. It is one of the few remaining rivers in the country still getting a run of such fish. This is a stock that should really be preserved because of this unique factor. The gene may well be peculiar to the River Dee salmon. There is no fish counter on the system and consequently no means of accurately estimating the size of the runs of fish. The rod

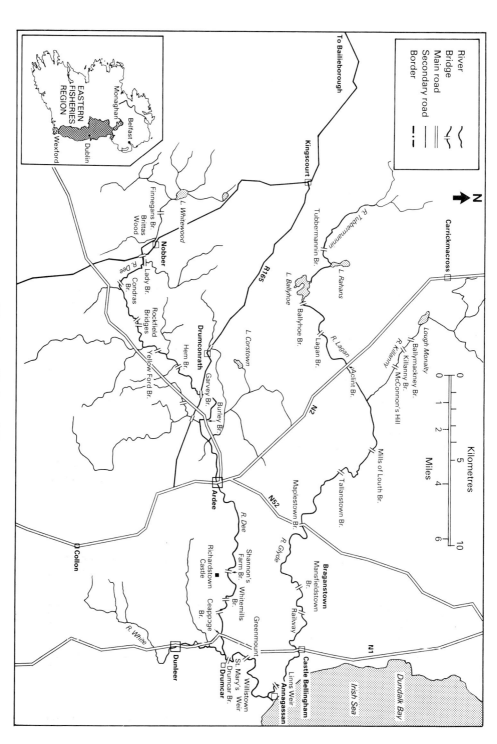

The rivers Glyde and Dee

fisheries don't keep accurate records but estimate that about 200 spring salmon and 300 grilse are taken annually. The only other means left of evaluating the fishing are reports – apparently well founded - that local anglers who fish the good fisheries regularly can take up to forty fish per rod from opening day up to early May. The consensus among anglers is that it is a good spring salmon fishery and the average weight is 12-14 lb.

The summer grilse fishing is patchy. It does not really pick up till August after the nets go off. The first grilse usually show in the river on the first flood after 22 June. They weigh from $3\frac{1}{2}$ to 7 lb. There is alleged to be a heavy run of fish in October after the season has closed and some of these fish will come up early if there is a flood in September.

It is generally agreed that the Dee gets an excellent run of sea-trout from mid July, through August and September. The first sea-trout appear in May. This is usually a small run of good fish from 2 to 5 lb. This run of good trout continues through June and early July. The river gets a big run of sea-trout averaging $1\frac{1}{2}$ lb around mid July and enormous numbers of $\frac{3}{4}$ lb trout usually arrive around the end of August. Finally, there is a big run of small 7–10 oz. trout in September. In some seasons, the majority of these trout are very small.

The Dee is a river with a lot of potential as a brown trout fishery. It holds big stocks of small trout and there are a lot of trout there averaging $\frac{3}{4}$ lb, some fish to $1\frac{1}{2}$ lb and occasionally much bigger trout. Some of the better brown trout fishing areas in the Nobber region have deteriorated greatly in recent times due to silting and banks becoming overgrown and impassable. This is one of the areas where a rehabilitation programme is urgently needed. If this takes place, the river will quickly recover and become once more the excellent brown trout fishery that it was ten or fifteen years ago. Overall, it is still a very impressive brown trout fishery, with a lot of potential and the capacity to take an awful lot more anglers than fish it at the present time.

Salmon

The spring salmon fishing is considered to extend upstream from Greenmount Pumping Station on the left bank and the bottom of the St John of God's Fishery on the right bank to Ardee, a distance of approximately 10 miles. The spring fishing lasts from February to May and, while all the fisheries are productive, the section from Parker's Weir, above Drumcar Bridge, down to Greenmount is jokingly referred to as the Golden Mile. However, there is also good fishing from Parker's Weir up to Whitemills Bridge, at Shannon's farm 2 miles above Whitemills Bridge (off the left bank) and on the stretch along the farmyard of St. Brigid's Hospital, Ardee, Co. Louth.

This is a mix of streamy water and deep, slow flats and pools. In low water, fish can be taken on fly from early February – otherwise it is spinning, with a blue Devon or a Yellowbelly being the popular choice.

The grilse fishing is more extensive and is generally considered to extend from Willistown Weir – and even a bit below it – upstream to Rockfield. Grilse are sometimes taken by trout fishers as far up as Nobber. The tide comes up to Willistown Weir but the river nets no longer operate since the weir was breached and all fish that escape the estuary nets at Annagassan now have a free run into the river.

Shrimp fishing is very popular over the summer months. A bunch of worms is said to be particularly good in May, and from June onwards it is believed that a single worm works best.

For the fly fisher, Stoat's Tail, Green Highlander, Shrimp Fly, Garry Dog and Collie Dog are recommended.

Sea-trout

The best of the sea-trout fishing is from Willistown Weir upstream to a point about 1 mile above Whitemills Bridge. Occasional sea-trout are caught up as far as Ardee. The choice fishing is from Willistown up to Drumcar Bridge and there are anglers who claim that the sea-trout fishing at Farraher's Fishery, above the weir, is as good as is to be found anywhere in Ireland.

All legitimate fishing methods are allowed on the river – worms, spinning, maggots, fly and maggot-and-fly. Night fishing can be excellent and daytime fly fishing in the streams or when a wind ripples to pools can also be very good. Silver-bodied flies are favoured and the Butcher, Priest, Teal Blue and Silver and Silver Doctor, all size 12, are especially effective by day. For night fishing, a Bloody Butcher, Connemara Black and Watson's Fancy are also used.

Such are the numbers of sea-trout taken on this water that many consider that a daily bag limit should be imposed. Certainly, it is worth considering a ban on the use of maggots.

Because of the quality of the sea-trout fishing, the better pools become very overcrowded at the peak of the season. It is necessary to find a method of spreading anglers more evenly along all of the productive water.

Brown trout

The brown trout fishing stretches from Drumcar up to Whitewood Lake and, while some of it may have diminished in quality, quantity and accessibility in recent years, there is a consensus among the fishery owners that the supply still far outstrips the demand.

From Whitewood Lake down to Finnegan's farm bridge the river is deep and sluggish and holds few trout. From Finnegan's Bridge to Summerhill (Brittas) Wood, the banks are very overgrown and the channel badly silted. This was fabulous trout water up to 1980. Brittas Marsh is again deep and silted but used to hold a lot of good trout. There is still good fishing for about 400 yards upstream from Casey's Forge just south of the village of Nobber. The next good stretch is from Lady's Bridge to a point 300 yards below Condras Bridge and there is some lovely fishing all the way to Rockfield Bridge. The opinion of the local club is that if the stretch from Whitewood Lake to Rockfield Bridge were developed, it could take up to sixty anglers. This may be true of evening fishing, but hardly holds for daytime fishing.

The next good stocks are to be found downstream of Rockfield Bridge (lower) between Yellow Ford Bridge and Hem Bridge and from Burley Bridge all the way to Ardee. There is very good fishing starting $\frac{1}{4}$ mile below Ardee, and from Ardee to Whitemills Bridge there are five or six good brown trout stretches. There is particularly nice trout water for a mile above and for some considerable distance below Whitemills Bridge. In July, there is good evening fishing to spent olives and sedges on the stretch below Drumcar Bridge.

Wet flies are favoured for early-season fishing. The river is said to have hatches of march browns, dark olives, iron blues, blue-winged olives, alders, black gnats, mayflies and various sedges. The mayfly fishing can be especially good with a rise in water in June from Hem Bridge upstream and upstream of Ardee. The evening fishing with spent olives and sedges can be very impressive in July.

Permission

Getting permission to fish the river is relatively simple. There are numerous owners of fishing rights and some of these rights are let and even sublet.

The following is a guide to where the fishery is located, from whom permission can be obtained, a brief description of the fishing on offer and the access route.

1 The right bank from the Bridge of Annagassan upstream to the confluence of the rivers Dee and Glyde and on to the corner of the field above Willistown Weir.

This is a good summer salmon and sea-trout stretch. One part of it is a private net fishery and the other part is a private rod fishery.

Inquiries about all the fishing should be made to Mr Peter Harmon, Strand Road, Annagassan, Co. Louth, *Telephone* 042-72249 or to Mr Peter McGuinness, Woodenstown, Castlebellingham, Co. Louth.

Access: As above.

2   From the field at Willistown Weir for a mile upstream is known as Farraher's Fishery.
A good summer salmon and sea-trout (good daytime fishing) stretch. Permits (£7 per season, £2 per day) may be had from:

Padge Reilly
Dee and Glyde Development Association
Cappack's Green
Ardee, Co. Louth

Thomas Durigan
Stickillen
Ardee, Co. Louth

Access: Via the lane 1 mile east of entrance to St. Mary's, Drumcar.

3   St John of God's Fishery, 2 miles of the right bank downstream from Drumcar Bridge. An application for permission to fish must be made in writing or in person to:

St Mary's
Drumcar
Dunleer, Co. Louth
Telephone 041 51211

Permits cost £10 per annum.
This is a spring salmon, summer salmon and sea-trout fishery and it has some brown trout fishing.

4   From Willistown Weir on the left bank upstream to Greenmount Pumping Station is a private fishery let by Mr P. O'Neill, Annagassan, Co. Louth. It is occasionally leased by the Dee and Glyde Development Association *(see 2 above)*. This is good summer salmon and sea-trout fishing with some spring salmon fishing.
Access: via Greenmount Lane

5   From Greenmount Pumping Station on the left bank upstream, for a distance of about 4 miles to near Whitemills Bridge, is mostly private fishing – some not let and some privately leased. Permission to fish can occasionally be obtained from riparian owners on the stretch downstream of Drumcar Bridge.

6 Cappoge Fishery, 1 mile of the right bank downstream from Cappoge Bridge. Permission from:

Mr Enda O'Callaghan
Victualler
Main Street
Ardee, Co. Louth

Very good sea-trout and good spring and summer salmon fishing. Most of it is deep and slow flowing.
Access: Via O'Callaghan's Residence, which is below Cappoge Bridge. Dee and Glyde Development Association members have permission to fish.

7 From Cappoge Bridge upstream on the right bank is private fishing for about 1 mile.

8 Permission to fish both banks from a point about $\frac{1}{2}$ mile below Whitemills Bridge to Hem Bridge, the left bank from Hem Bridge to Yellow Ford Bridge and both banks from Yellow Ford Bridge to the lower Rockfield Bridge can be obtained from the Dee and Glyde Development Association (above).
Access: to the good spring fishing above and below the farm bridge at Shannon's is gained via an old lane opposite Richardstown Castle. The lane is 1.9 miles west of Kaig's Cross.
   There is good salmon, sea-trout and brown trout fishing below Whitemills Bridge. The left bank can be reached at Charleville.

9 The fishing rights on the right bank between Yellow Ford Bridge and Hem Bridge are reserved by the riparian owners.

10 The stretch between the two bridges at Rockfield is private fishing.

11 Both banks from the upper Rockfield Bridge to Whitewood Lake, except for one stretch belonging to Mr J. Mulligan, is leased or controlled by Nobber Trout Angling Club. Permission should be sought from:

Michael O'Reilly   Bert Onions
6 O'Carolan Park   Main Street
Nobber, Co. Meath   Nobber, Co. Meath

The Club encourages fly fishing and spinning. Fishing with natural minnow is not allowed. This is a brown trout fishery.

RIVER GLYDE   0 6 95

Season

Salmon and sea-trout: 12 February to 20 August.
Brown trout: 14 February to 20 August.

Permission

Permits to fish the Dee and Glyde Development Association water can be had from the Chairman:

    Padge Reilly
    Cappock's Green
    Ardee, Co. Louth

The Association has a 2 mile stretch on the left bank from Castlebellingham downstream. It is mainly spring salmon and sea-trout fishing.

Bellingham Castle Hotel, (*telephone* 042 72176), has 1/2 mile of double-bank fishing in the hotel grounds. The fishing is free to hotel residents, otherwise the rule is that half the catch goes to the hotel.

The fishing on the rest of the river is part strictly private and part with the permission of the riparian owners.

The Glyde rises among the drumlin hills of Co. Cavan and Co. Monaghan in an area between Loughanlea Mountain and Carrickmacross and flows east for 35 miles before joining the River Dee a mile above Annagassan, where it flows into Dundalk Bay. It drains a catchment of approximately 135 square miles.

It was the subject of an arterial drainage scheme in the 1950s which has resulted in high banks in places and a general disruption of the fishery. It was a noted spring salmon river before drainage and is still a river with a lot of potential if it had a rehabilitation programme carried out and its pollution problems remedied.

Salmon

The river still gets a small run of spring salmon. The average size of the fish is remarkably big and they are in the river from opening day on 15 February.

The first fish of the season are usually taken from the stretch between Maplestown Bridge and Bragganstown Bridge where fishing is available from riparian owners on the left bank. It is best approached upstream from Bragganstown Bridge. The best of the fishing is considered to be above the railway bridge.

The Dee and Glyde Association water below Castlebellingham always holds spring fish and fish are taken every year on the Bellingham Castle Hotel water. There are a couple of very good holding pools for early salmon between Castlebellingham and Bragganstown Bridge.

Most of the fishing on the left bank from Maplestown Bridge to Tallantsown Bridge is strictly private but there is a bit of good salmon fishing off the right bank – with riparian owners' permission.

A couple of pools above the weir at Tallantsown hold spring fish and then there is a long barren stretch up to Tully, where there is good holding water for spring fish below the confluence of the Killanny River at a place called Tully Meadows.

Much of the Glyde is deep and slow and most spring fish are taken by spinning. Favourite baits are the Yellowbelly and brown and gold Devons and a Swinford spoon.

Sea Trout

The River Glyde was once noted for its magnificent sea-trout run but no longer gets a worthwhile run.

Brown Trout

The Glyde still holds good stocks of brown trout. They have a good growth rate and this isattributed by some anglers to the fact that there are a lot of minnows in the river. The average trout weight is 1 lb.

The best of the fishing is early in the season for the river tends to weed up badly in summer. The fishing becomes quite difficult after mid June and the best fishing is in a season with lots of rain and high water levels.

The river still has a terrific mayfly hatch at the end of May and for the first couple of weeks in June. There is also a good hatch of sedge and the grey flag hatch is especially prolific in the shallower areas with a stony bottom.

The main brown trout fishing stretches are downstream from Bragganstown Bridge, where there is some excellent fishing. The banks are difficult and, in places, very overgrown.

There are good trout stocks too in stretches downstream of Maplestown Bridge on the N52 Ardee–Dundalk road and there is a lot of good trout water up to Tallanstown. Access is difficult – really only from bridge to bridge – and deep to the right bank below Tallanstown.

The last good trout stretch on the Glyde is from McGuinness' Pool which is about 500 yards above the Mills of Louth, right down to Tallanstown where there is about $2^{1}/_{2}$ miles of trout fishing.

RIVER LAGAN   N 90 98

Season

Salmon and Sea-trout: 12 February to 20 August
Brown trout: 14 February to 20 August

Permission

Not usually required.

The River Lagan is a tributary of the Glyde and flows down from Ballyhoe Lake to join the Glyde at Tully. It is about 6 miles long and flows under the N2 Carrickmacross road at Aclint Bridge. It is deep and sluggish and was never any good for trout fishing.

THE KILLANNY RIVER   N 90 01

Season

Salmon and Sea-trout: 12 February to 20 August
Brown trout: 14 February to 20 August

Permission

Not usually required.
The Killanny River flows south east from Monalty Lake for 4 miles to join the River Glyde at Tully. In the past, this was really an excellent trout stream with plenty of 1 lb trout and many to 2 lb and 3 lb. It is still well worth fishing and dry sedge tactics always take the better trout. It has a prolific sedge hatch that includes the murrough or large red sedge. It is a bit overgrown above Ballymackney Bridge but is reasonably easy to fish from Ballymackney Bridge to a point ½ mile below McConnon's Mill.

TUBBERMANNIN RIVER   N 82 96

Season

Salmon and sea-trout: 12 February to 20 August
Brown trout: 14 February to 20 August

Permission

Not usually required.

The Tubbermannin River flows south from Northlands past Cabra Castle and into Rahan's Lake. Before drainage, it was reputed to be an excellent trout stream with trout averaging 1 lb and plenty to 2 lb or more. Today, it still holds trout but they rarely grow more than 8 ounces. The banks are reasonably easy to fish and there are small trout from the bridge on the R 179 Kingscourt–Carrickmacross road downstream to Rahan's Lake.

RIVER BOYNE (AND TRIBUTARIES)   O 07 75

Season

Salmon and sea-trout: 1 February to 15 September.
Brown trout: 15 February to 15 September.

In certain years, an extension of the trout and salmon season to September 30 has been granted.

Permission

The fishing on the main channel and on the tributaries is controlled either by private fishery owners or by angling associations and there is virtually no free fishing. Contacts for the various fisheries are given from page 156.

The Boyne rises near Edenderry on the borders of Counties Offaly and Kildare and flows in a north-easterly direction for 70 miles before entering the Irish Sea at Drogheda. Together with its tributaries, it drains a catchment of approximately 1,040 square miles.

This magnificent river drains the fertile plains of Royal Meath. Its valley is rich in archaeological remains and the prehistoric burial chambers at Newgrange, and the numerous ruins of medieval castles and abbeys bear testament to a colourful history.

It is one of the country's premier game fisheries and both the Boyne and its tributaries offer a wide range of angling from fishing for spring salmon and grilse to sea-trout fishing and extensive brown trout fishing.

The years 1965 and 1969 were significant dates for angling on the river. UDN appeared in 1965 and decimated salmon stocks. In 1969 an arterial drainage scheme was started on the system and disrupted angling for about eighteen years. As can be imagined, both of these events had disastrous effects on all fish stocks and on the character of the river.

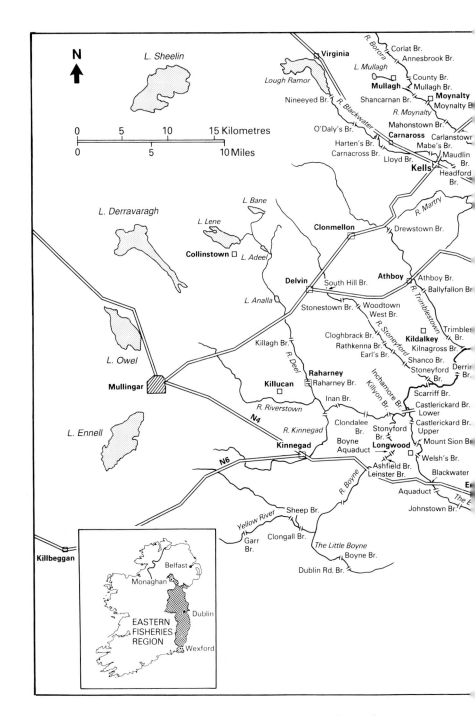

The rivers Boyne, Nanny, Delvin and Broad Meadow

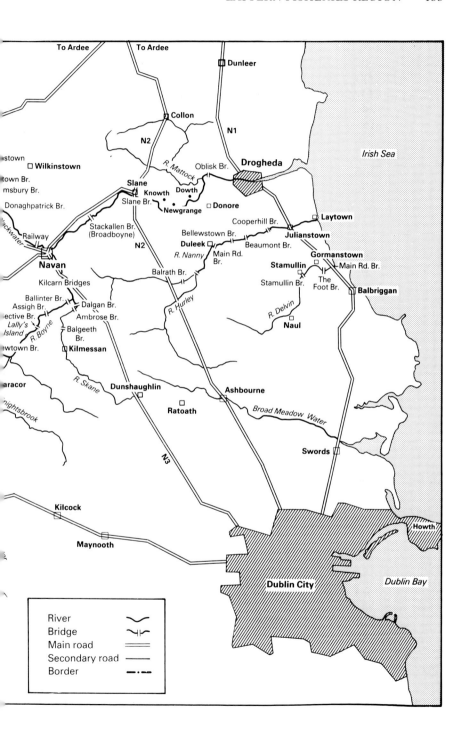

Fortunately, the stocks – particularly the brown trout – have recovered quite well and in some locations are as good, if not better, than before.

The dredging altered the character of the river completely and resulted in many cases in leaving very high banks. The main channel from Drogheda upstream to Navan was left untouched, as were a few stretches on the Kells Blackwater.

Salmon

The prime salmon angling water is now to be found on the fisheries between Navan and Drogheda and on a stretch of the Kells Blackwater immediately upstream of Navan. Occasional salmon are taken upstream of Navan, at Bective, Trim, Board's Mill below Scarriff Bridge, above and below Inchamore Bridge, on the River Deel at Riverdale and on the Kells Blackwater.

The river gets a run of big three-sea-winter fish from 20 to 30 lb. These fish generally arrive early in February and March. Smaller spring fish, averaging about 10 lb, arrive in April and early May and the grilse come in July. The river gets a further run of fish in late August and September and this run would appear to last long after the season closes.

The early fish run through and the first fish is usually caught between Slane and Navan and indeed, most of the spring fish come from this stretch of river, though some are taken below Slane.

The grilse fishing from July onwards is mostly confined to the fisheries between Slane and Drogheda.

In low water conditions, there can be a very big build-up of fish in the fisheries downstream of Slane in late August and September. If a flood comes down in September, there can be excellent salmon fishing all the way up from Drogheda to Navan and good fishing up to Trim and beyond. The distance up river that the good fishing extends in September appears to be directly related to water levels.

All legitimate fishing methods are allowed for salmon. Spinning is the most popular method for spring fish – followed by worm and shrimp. Occasional fish are taken on the fly from mid April, but only a minority of anglers fish fly. The salmon fisheries from Navan to Drogheda are made up of streams, glides, pools and stretches of deep water above the various weirs. There is ample water on all of the fisheries for fishing and since it is a big wide river, a 15-foot rod or longer is recommended. The river has a compacted gravel bottom and wading is possible in places.

The most commonly used baits are Yellowbelly, blue and silver, and brown and gold Devons and useful flies include Black Goldfinch, Garry Dog, Hairy Mary, Blue Charm and Thunder and Lightning – down to size 10 doubles for summer and autumn fishing.

Sea-trout

The river gets an excellent run of sea-trout and the fishing extends up as far as Slane Bridge. Sea-trout have been found as far as Navan and even Trim, but not in sufficient quantities to warrant fishing specifically for them. The biggest stocks are found downstream of the Oblisk Bridge at Drogheda.

The first sea-trout are usually taken in April, the run begins to peak in early July and there is good fishing through August and into September.

The various fisheries have different regulations but some or all of the following fishing methods are allowed – fly, worm, maggot or spinning. The fly produces best results at night and any of the recognised sea-trout flies will do.

An interesting fact about the Boyne sea-trout is that they feed on the natural insects of the river on summer evenings, in particular on blue winged olives and sedges.

brown trout

The River Boyne and its tributaries hold superb stocks of wild brown trout. Stock density surveys were carried out by Dr. Martin O'Grady of the Central Fisheries Board up to 1989 and his findings revealed stocks of trout that were as good as, if not better than, anything he encountered on the River Suir, one of Ireland's premier trout rivers. This is significant, for the Suir has not been drained. There is probably more trout fishing now on the main river than before drainage, but sections of good fishing were lost on the tributaries. More and more trout water is being regained as the rehabilitation work progresses.

At the present time, there is something in the region of 100 miles of trout angling water spread over the main river and the various tributaries. I will give more details of these later when I deal with the various fisheries. There are, of course, barren stretches that are unproductive and to be avoided. The best advice for the trout fisher is to fish the fast, streamy water and the glides and avoid the deep flats which hold only occasional large trout. The best time to fish the flats is at dusk. During the day, the best fly hatches are found in the glides and riffles.

Fly Hatches

The river has all the various fly hatches associated with a limestone river and fly fishing can begin about 15 April. On some stretches, certain species are missing and Sedges are especially prolific on the Kells Blackwater. Otherwise, expect to find dark olives, medium olives, iron blues, big hatches of stone fly in May, yellow May dun, alder, simulium and black gnats, mayfly, various sedges, midges, August dun, caenis and blue-winged olives.

A sedge, known as the grey flag *(Hydropsyche* spp) is by far the most important angling insect on the entire catchment at the peak of the daytime and evening trout fishing in May–June. It emerges on open water during the day and at dusk and flutters on the surface. It overlaps with the mayfly – last 2 weeks of May and first 2 weeks of June – and is taken by the trout in preference to the mayfly in those locations where the two insects hatch together. The mayfly tends to hatch in pockets and is found on the main channel and some of the tributaries including the Yellow River and the Upper Boyne. The August dun is a very important insect for both trout and angler in August. There is a secondary hatch of iron blues in September which are very small - size 16 hook - and you also find large dark olives, medium olives, blue-winged olives, big numbers of small red sedges and some big sedges on the deep flats, all hatching during the day.

Wading

Trout anglers would be well advised to use chest waders, especially in the tributaries, where banks are high. They contribute enormously to the angler's comfort. The bottom is firm and quite safe to wade, with a few important exceptions.

Weed Growth

Weed growth can be a problem from mid June but this is something that the angler has to learn to accept.

THE BOYNE FISHERIES (STARTING AT THE TIDE)

DROGHEDA AND DISTRICT ANGLING ASSOCIATION WATER

Permission

Mr Martin Carolan
Fair Green
Drogheda
Co. Louth
Telephone 041 34482

Sean Keenan
Military Connection
Laurence Street
Drogheda
Co. Louth

Drogheda and District Angling Association have three stretches of water between Drogheda and Newgrange. Most of it is on the right (south) bank. The bottom stretch at Drogheda is tidal and gives excellent sport with sea-trout from late June. The middle stretch (Fulham's and Glenmore) is the best of the salmon fishing (from June and very good in August and September) There is good sea-trout fishing there too and some brown trout. The upper stretch, below Newgrange wall, offers excellent brown trout to 2 lb and better, with some salmon and sea-trout. There is a good mayfly hatch here. Club membership is open and day tickets are available at a reasonable price.

THE OLDBRIDGE FISHERY

The Oldbridge Fishery is at Dowth and Oldbridge, east of Drogheda. At this point on the river the famous Battle of the Boyne was fought in 1600. The fishery consists of three miles of salmon and sea-trout fishing on both banks. The fishing is in two parts. The upper portion consists of about half a mile of prime summer salmon fishing. It is let on a yearly basis and the maximum number of rods is eight. It fishes best in low water and produced 94 salmon in 1991 and 80 fish in 1992. Inquiries about rods to Mr Jock Marry , Dowth, Drogheda, Co. Louth. *Telephone* 041-38745.

ROSSIN-SLANE ANGLING CLUB

Permission: Mr Barry Flood, Waterunder, Drogheda, Co. Louth
        Telephone 041-38514.

Rossin-Slane Angling Club has fishing at three locations between Slane and Drogheda. This is excellent fishing and is estimated to have yielded 600 salmon and 3,000 sea-trout in 1989 as well as lot of good brown trout. The Oldbridge Fishery at Oblisk Bridge, including the famous Curley Hole is mainly salmon and sea-trout fishing. The two upper fisheries (Law's and Johnston's) offer occasional salmon, very good sea-trout and excellent brown trout fishing with the trout averaging nearly $1\frac{1}{2}$ lb. Prolific hatches of mayfly, grey flag and blue winged olives.
   The trout fishing is fly-only from 1 June.
   Both club membership and day tickets are available.

SLANE CASTLE FISHERY

Lord Henry Mountcharles has extensive salmon and trout fishing at Slane, extending for approximately $3\frac{1}{2}$ miles on both banks from below Slane Bridge up to Beauparc. The fishing is not let at the present time.

O'CONNOR'S FISHERY

Enquiries to Mr Eugene O'Connor, Ardmulcan, Navan, Co. Meath.

This fishery is approximately half a mile long. It is situated on the right bank, midway between Navan and Broadboyne Bridge. This is good salmon-holding water from early spring. High water in autumn brings up a good late run. The brown trout fishing is excellent and it holds some very big ones.

THE BALLINACRAD FISHERY

This is a spring salmon, grilse and autumn salmon fishery. It also has good brown trout fishing. Inquiries about the fishing to: Mrs Ita McDonnell, Dowth, Drogheda, Co. Louth.

NAVAN ANGLING CLUB

Permission

> Mr Michael J. Connor
> Cill Ard
> Abbey Road
> Navan, Co. Meath
> *Telephone* 046 29007
>
> The Sports Den
> Trimgate Street
> Navan, Co. Meath

Navan Angling Club have access to extensive stretches of the Boyne above and below the town of Navan, totalling about 6 miles. It also has access to several fisheries on the Kells Blackwater between Bloomsbury's Bridge and Navan. Some are leased and others are fished by reciprocal arrangement with Kilbride Angling Club giving the club a further 6 miles of water.

The fishing on the Boyne above Navan extends for over a mile on the right bank and for 2½ miles on the left bank. There is a further stretch on the left bank above Ballinter Bridge. This is all excellent brown trout water and has a few noted salmon lies too.

The club has a further 2 miles below Navan on both banks including all but a short stretch of the famous Blackcastle Fishery. Further downstream it has over a mile of the fishing rights on the Dunmoe Fishery. Blackcastle and Dunmoe are prime spring salmon fisheries and have produced salmon to 26 lb in recent years. The season peaks here mid-April to mid-May. These fisheries can also provide good fishing in late August and September if the water is right to bring up the fish.

The trout fishing on this stretch can be superb but most of the angling effort tends to concentrate on the salmon.

Club membership and/or day tickets are available.

DALGAN ANGLING CLUB

Permission

Mr Joe Lenehan	Mr Joe Kinsella
Clonardon,	Kilcarn Bridge
Garlow Cross	Navan, Co. Meath
Navan, Co. Meath	*Telephone* 046 28009
Telephone 046 23530	

Dalgan Angling Club is the next club up river with good trout fishing and occasional salmon on the Boyne from Ballinter down towards Kilcarn, and good trout fishing on the River Skane (N 90 72).

The Skane rises near Dunshaughlin and flows northwards through Kilmessan and past the Hill of Tara before entering the Boyne at Dalgan Park. It is a lovely trout stream from the village of Kilmessan to the confluence and is at its best in spring as a wet-fly stream. After the drainage, it did not have adequate pool areas, but that situation has now been remedied by the erection of a series of small weirs. It holds big stocks of trout of 9-10 oz – but don't expect many over 1lb.

BECTIVE ANGLING CLUB

Permission

Mr Charles Woods
Tribley Road
Bective
Navan, Co. Meath
Telephone 046 22936

Bective Angling Club has the fishing at various points from Lally's Island, down past Bective Bridge and Assigh Bridge and almost to Ballinter Bridge. The club has a rule which states that the season opens on the Saturday before 17 March. A lot of rehabilitation work has been carried out in this area and trout stocks are excellent with fish from ¾ lb to 4 lb and even 5 lb. There are salmon here too – above and below Bective Bridge and at Brady's. They are mainly taken in March–April and late August–September. Try fly or a copper spoon. Club membership is limited but visiting anglers can be accommodated.

TRIM, ATHBOY AND DISTRICT ANGLING CLUB

Permission

Mr Gerard Lee	Mr Liam Henry
Loman Street	Dunlever
Trim	Trim
Co. Meath	Co Meath

This club has access to extensive fishing on the Boyne and Trimblestown River (N 77 56) The fishing on the Boyne extends from Scarriff Bridge downstream past the town of Trim to Lally's Island, with some stretches of private water in between. The club's rights on the Trimblestown River extends from the village of Athboy to the confluence with the Boyne.

The river here holds occasional salmon and they are taken on worm or spinner in April and May and in September if there is a flood to take them up.

The brown trout fishing can be excellent and as good as or better than any on the river. The average weight is 10 oz. but there are plenty of trout to 2 and 3 lb and better.

The best trout holding stretches are for $\frac{1}{2}$ a mile below Scarriff Bridge, from $\frac{1}{4}$ mile above Board's Mill to a point 400 yards downstream of Derrindaly Bridge, a $\frac{1}{2}$ mile stretch by the road at Higgins Brook and all the way from Newhaggard to Trim, to Newtown Bridge and downstream to Lally's Island.

The main salmon angling stretches are a short stretch below Scarriff Bridge, a short stretch above Board's Mill, a short stretch at the confluence of the Knightsbrook River and a stretch at Lally's Island.

Club membership is open and visiting anglers can be accommodated.

Note that there is a soft marl bottom upstream of the Trimblestown confluence and wading is very dangerous.

LONGWOOD ANGLING CLUB

Permission

Mr Michael Bird
Castlerickard
Longwood
Co. Meath
Telephone 044 74301

Longwood Angling Club has fishing rights on the Boyne between Scarriff Bridge and Leinster Bridge (6 miles) and on the Enfield Blackwater (N 71 50) from Johnstown Bridge down to the confluence with the Boyne.

There are trout to 2 lb in a 1 mile stretch upstream from Scarriff Bridge and in a short stretch of $\frac{1}{4}$ mile below Inchamore Bridge. Immediately above and below Stoneyford Bridge, there are trout to 1 lb and trout of the same size in a $\frac{1}{4}$ mile stretch at Ballinabarney. There is lovely trout fishing in the stretch from the Boyne Aqueduct to a point $\frac{1}{4}$ mile above Ashfield.

There is nearly 6 miles of fishing on the Enfield Blackwater (N 78 45). The lower reaches from Longwood down to the confluence with the Boyne are basically fast flowing with streams, pools and riffles. It holds substantial stocks of trout to $\frac{3}{4}$ lb. A rehabilitation programme is planned for this stretch. This should increase the population but the average size will probably remain the same. The best fishing is in the early season – from 15 April onwards.

Upstream of Longwood, the banks are very high and the river holds a moderate stock of trout to 5 lb. This is difficult fishing – only for the fit and agile, with steep, high banks. The reward will be, possibly, one trout per day, but it could weigh as much as 5 lb. This stretch is not very attractive. It is slow flowing, deep and difficult to fish.

RIVER BLACKWATER (KELLS)   N 74 76

Permission

Mr Thomas Murray
Kells Angling Club
Farrell Street
Kells, Co. Meath
Telephone 046 40205
Mr Michael Connor

Mr Thomas Byrne
Kilbride Angling Club
41 Walkinstown Drive
Dublin 14
Telephone 01 502289

Mr Michael Connor
Cillard, Abbey Road, Navan, Co. Meath.
Telephone 046-29007

These three clubs have access to extensive stretches on the river:

The Kells Blackwater drains Lough Ramor near Virginia in Co. Cavan and flows south east for 18 miles before joining the Boyne at Navan. It is a medium sized limestone river and is now recovering from the effects of the arterial drainage scheme. It was noted for its spring-salmon fishing and enormous stocks of fat trout. The salmon fishing is poor at present except on the Mollies Fishery at Navan, where some fish are still taken. The trout fishing varies from good to very good, with fair numbers of trout up to 2 lb and better.

There is virtually no trout fishing from Lough Ramor down to O'Daly's Bridge. The best of the fishing is from O'Daly's Bridge to Navan. The section from Lugawooly, below Carnaross Bridge, to Headford Bridge was not drained and can be especially good, with trout to over 2 lb. The river changes in character downstream of Headford Bridge and is less productive. A rehabilitation programme is proposed and it will extend from below Headford Bridge to 1 mile below Donaghpatrick Bridge. Fisheries staff are confident that it will greatly improve the trout stocks.

High banks are a problem for anglers at present, but it is proposed to dig secondary banks. There is also a lack of stiles and footbridges.

The Kells Blackwater has all the usual fly hatches found on a limestone river. Sedge patterns (both pupae and adult) are very important, especially the grey flag. Trout take the yellow May dun here and a dressing for the female blue winged olive is important for daytime fishing in September.

The salmon fishing in the Kells area has deteriorated from an average of 88 in the early 1980s to 2 in 1989. The fishing at The Mollies in Navan appears to have improved and has produced salmon to 22 lb in recent times.

BORORA RIVER   N 70 86

MOYNALTY RIVER   N 71 83

Permission

> Mr Gerard Farrell
> Borora Angling Club
> Moynalty
> Kells, Co. Meath
> *Telephone* 046 44317

The Borora River and the Moynalty River flow south from Bailieborough and Mullagh Lough to join the Kells Blackwater at Bloomsbury Bridge. This river was drained but has now recovered and there is about 7 miles of trout fishing in springtime from Corlat down to the village of Carlanstown. It is a lovely fast stream with a predominantly gravel bed. It is an especially nice stream in which to fish wet-fly in spring. The trout are small but plentiful and probably average 9 –10 oz. The best of the fishing is from March to June as the river runs too low after June.

Unfortunately, there are extensive stretches where the banks are very high and you must wade in order to fish. Thigh waders are adequate. Access is mainly at the bridges and at a couple of points off the Bellair road. Try a Greenwell's Spider, a Silver Spider or a Hare's Ear.

MARTRY RIVER   N 80 72

Permission

Inquire locally.

The Martry River joins the Kells Blackwater midway between Bloomsbury Bridge and Donaghpatrick Bridge. It is a small stream. The last half mile has some nice pools and holds trout up to 1 lb.

TRIMBLESTOWN RIVER   N 73 62

Permission

> Trim, Athboy and District Angling Club
> Mr Gerard Lee
> Loman Street
> Trim, Co. Meath

> Mr Liam Henry
> Dunlever
> Trim
> Co. Meath

The Trimblestown River rises west of Ballinlough in Co. Meath and flows south for about 23 miles, through Athboy to join the Boyne above Trim.

It is a fast flowing river with a continuous sequence of riffle, pool, and glide. It holds enormous stocks of trout to ¾ lb from Drewstown House for about 6 miles to a point 2 miles downstream of the village of Athboy, below Ballyfallon Bridge and from Trimblestown Bridge down to the Boyne. Early in the season, you can expect some bigger trout as a lot of fish migrate from the Boyne into the Trimblestown to spawn. This is a spring fed river and consequently has a continuous high volume of water and in that respect, it is like a chalk stream.

The banks are high and wading is necessary but quite safe as the river bed is stony and compacted.

It has an abundance of fly life and has all the ephemeropteran species as described for the Boyne, except mayfly.

STONEYFORD RIVER

Permission

> Mr Tom Conlon
> Stoneyford Angling Club
> 5 Killallon Road
> Clonmellon, Co.Westmeath

The Stoneyford River rises to the east of the village of Fane in Co. Westmeath and flows south past Delvin and Ballivor to enter the Boyne below Scarriff Bridge. This is an excellent trout stream with about 10 miles of fishing starting at South Hill Bridge near Delvin and continuing down to the confluence. It has a marvellous diversity of insect life and a big population of ephemeropterans. Sedge fishing is especially good from Stoneystown Bridge to Woodstown Bridge and from Shanco Bridge to the Boyne. This is a spring fed river with chalkstream characteristics. It is relatively small and easy to wade. Some sections are a little overgrown and the rest is quite good. It is all excellent trout water but some consider the best of it to be from Rathkenna Bridge, past Earl's Bridge and as far as Shanco Bridge.

RIVER DEEL   N 60 53

Permission

> Mr Jack Shaw
> Deel and Boyne Angling Club
> Riverdale
> Raharney, Co. Westmeath.
> *Telephone* 044 74301

The River Deel rises in Lough Lene and flows south through Raharney to join the Boyne above Inchamore Bridge. Deel and Boyne Angling Club has extensive fishing on it excluding the waters of Killyon Manor. This is another spring-fed river with chalkstream characteristics. It suffered greatly as a result of the arterial drainage scheme and some of it may never recover. A rehabilitation scheme has been carried out and there is a lot of good fishing now for trout to 1 lb, but mostly during high water in March and April and up to mid May. The best stretches are for 500 yards downstream of the bridge on the Delvin–Mullingar road; a 500 yards stretch immediately above Killagh Bridge; from Killagh Bridge down to the confluence of the Riverstown River; and from Clondalee Bridge to the Boyne. The stretch from Killagh Bridge to Raharney was rehabilitated in 1989 and should hold good stocks of trout to 1 lb by 1991. The banks of the lower Deel are not too difficult to fish and a secondary bank has formed. There are, however, many stretches where body waders are necessary to fish it properly. It has all the fly hatches one expects to find on a limestone river, including a small hatch of mayfly.

The Deel used to be a noted spring salmon fishery but that is now all in the past. However, there are reports that a few fish are still taken early in the season at Riverdale.

YELLOW RIVER   N 60 37

There are trout to 2 lb in a 1 mile stretch of this river immediately below Clongall Bridge.

> Mr Sidney Hopkins
> Edenderry Anglers' Association
> 66 J.K.L. Street
> Edenderry, Co. Offaly
> *Telephone* 0405 31425

The Little Boyne is strictly a spring fishery for trout. The best of the fishing is from the Boyne Bridge downstream to the confluence – a distance of about 3 miles. It holds trout up to 1 lb. It is not very attractive fishing and really is best suited to someone who wants to fish the worm. The river here is small and narrow and relatively slow flowing. Long sections have enormous high banks and it is an area that is not highly recommended.

KNIGHTSBROOK RIVER   N 81 54

The Knightsbrook River flows down from Summerhill and joins the Boyne 2 miles below Trim. It is difficult to get permission to fish from the riparian owners. This river holds a good stock of brown trout up to $^3/_4$ lb. The fish are mainly concentrated in a $2^1/_4$ mile stretch from Laracor to the confluence with the Boyne.

RIVER NANNY   O 10 70

Season

Sea-trout: 12 February to 15 September.
Brown trout: 15 February to 15 September.

Permission

There are three Angling Clubs on the river – Duleek, Drogheda and District Angling Club and Julianstown. Membership of Julianstown Angling Club is reserved. Tickets for Duleek Angling Club waters can be had from:

> Nicola's, Newsagent
> Main Street
> Duleek, Co. Meath

For the Drogheda water from:

> Mr Sean Keenan
> Military Connection
> Laurence Street
> Drogheda, Co. Louth

The River Nanny rises near Kentstown and flows east through Duleek and Julianstown to enter the sea at Laytown. It gets a small run of sea-trout up to Julianstown and the rest of the fishing is for brown trout. The river is stocked and more than half the trout taken every year are stocked trout. The trout fishing extends up to Balrath Bridge on the Nanny and to Dean's Bridge on its tributary, the Hurley River. The peak of the trout fishing is to the sedge in May–June. There is a fly-only stretch above Bellewstown Bridge. Trout average.³/₄ lb and the best fishing is to fly in the evening.

DELVIN RIVER   O 18 86

Season

Sea-trout: 12 February to 15 September.
Brown trout: 5 February to 15 September.

Permission

Gormanstown and District Anglers' Association. Day tickets are available from:

The Sail In Garage	Donnelly Electric
North Road	The Shopping Centre
Balbriggan	Balbriggan
Co. Dublin	Co. Dublin

This little river is just 10 miles long and drains a catchment of 27 square miles. It enters the sea less than 2 miles north of Balbriggan and is stocked annually by the local Angling Club with brown trout to augment the small stock of native trout. This is a small narrow river, very overgrown and difficult to fish with fly. It is best suited to bait fishing and can be fished all the way up as far as the Naul. Access is reasonably good and some stiles are provided.

It used get an excellent run of big sea-trout (1¼ - 4½ lb) but these have declined in recent years. Small numbers of sea-trout are still taken there from August onwards and the pool at the main road bridge is regarded as a prime location. The best fishing is at night. Occasional sea-trout are also taken in the stretch at the footbridge and at the back of Gormanstown College.

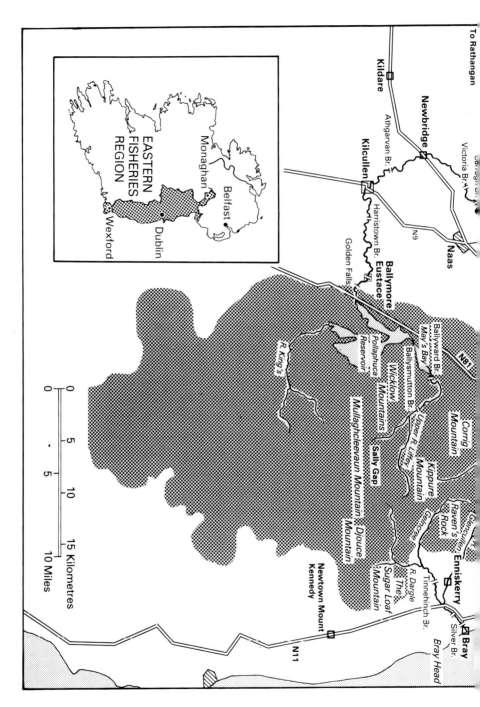

The rivers Tolka, Liffey, Dodder and Dargle

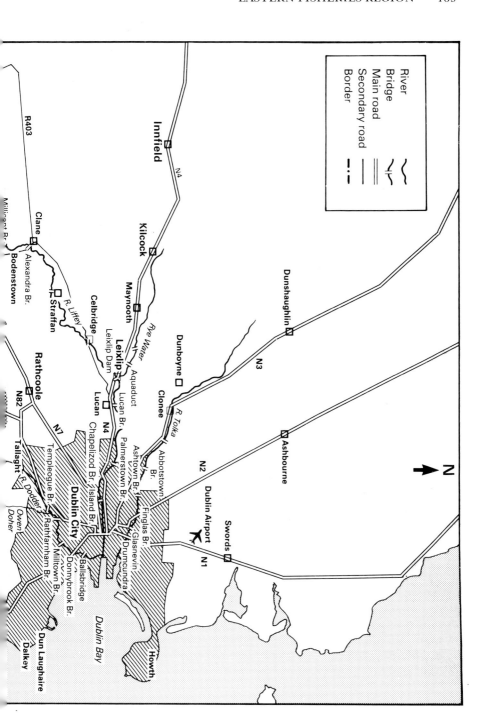

BROAD MEADOW WATER   O 18 47

Season

Sea-trout: 1 February to 12 October
Brown trout: 1 March to 30 September

The Broad Meadow Water, once famous for its magnificent double figure sea-trout is now but a shadow of its former self. The water runs off very fast, as the result of a drainage scheme and the river holds only occasional sea-trout in its lower reaches. It is proposed to carry out some rehabilitation work and create new pools. The Secretary of the Broad Meadow Angling Club is

> Mr Kenneth Rundle
> 119 Orlynn Park
> Lusk, Co. Dublin
> *Telephone* 01 438178

RIVER TOLKA   O 12 37

Season

Sea trout: 1 February to 12 October
Brown trout: 1 March to 30 September

The River Tolka rises near Dunshaughlin in Co. Meath and flows east via Dunboyne, Clonee, Blanchardstown and Finglas before entering the sea at Clontarf on the north side of Dublin city. For nearly half its length, it flows through urban sprawl and ironically, the only trout fishing left is within the urban area. It flows through some of the most fertile land in Ireland and is an extremely rich river. In the 1950s, it regularly produced trout up to 6 lb and trout of 4 lb were regularly taken at Ashtown. Today, it still holds some wild trout but it is drained, polluted and eutrophic and is really a put and take fishery, stocked by Tolka Anglers' Club. The best of the fishing is from Finglas Bridge to Abbotstown Bridge – a distance of about 3 miles. It still gets hatches of spring olives, midges, black gnats and a big hatch of blue-winged olives. It has no iron blue duns and the sedge hatch is patchy.

The Chairman of Tolka Anglers' Club is:
Mr Christopher Emmett
93 Tolka Estate, Finglas, Dublin 11

RIVER LIFFEY   0 10 34

Season

Salmon and Sea-trout: 1 January to 30 September
Brown trout: 1 March to 30 September

The Liffey rises only 12 miles south of Dublin and flows in a huge
crescent for over 82 miles before entering the sea at Dublin Bay. Along its
course, it drains a catchment of nearly 530 square miles. This is a big
river and a very interesting river with a great diversity of character. It
starts as a poor acid mountain river and is transformed into an
extraordinarily rich trout stream as it glides and meanders through the
plains of Co. Kildare. It flows over a range of differing geologies – from
granite, to sandstone, to sandstone-limestone and finally to pure
limestone. Dr Michael Kennedy, formerly of the Inland Fisheries Trust,
observed some of the fastest-growing brown trout ever recorded in
Ireland in the river near Lucan.

It goes without saying that a river which flows through a capital city the
size of Dublin cannot avoid the undesirable effects and demands of such a
thickly populated and heavily industrialized area. It has been dammed at
Pollaphuca to form one of the largest reservoirs in Europe and there is a
second reservoir at Leixlip (Leixlip means Salmon Leap, from the Norse
lax, salmon) Water abstraction is a huge problem. There are three
hydro-electric power stations along its course. Consequently, the flow is
controlled artificially and the river is subject to artificial spates which bear
no relation or have no connection whatsoever with natural rainfall.

The lower stretches from the city out to beyond Leixlip tend to be slow
and deep with a series of old mill weirs. Out in the country beyond
Celbridge, the river takes on a more natural character. Access to the river
downstream of Leixlip can be difficult in places and the banks are
undeveloped. Upstream of Straffan to Ballymore Eustace, a lot of good
work has been done by the Eastern Regional Fisheries Board which
organized a social employment scheme and there has been a lot of bank
clearance and stiles and footbridges have been constructed.

Most of the fishing is controlled by clubs or private interests. There is
free fishing at the Memorial Park at Islandbridge and on the left bank
immediately above Leixlip Bridge to the River Rye confluence. The latter
can provide useful summer grilse fishing and the access to it is via the car

park of the Ryevale Hotel.

Salmon

The salmon run has improved dramatically in recent times and the numbers recorded on the fish counter at Islandbridge have increased from a low of less than 220 fish in the early 1970s to over 4,000 in 1989. Spring salmon can be taken from early January and grilse run from June, with July providing the peak of the run. It is very difficult to quantify catches but it is estimated that well over 100 spring fish were taken in 1990. Most Liffey salmon are taken either by spinning or on worms. Most of the spring fish are taken at Islandbridge, while the grilse tend to run through and most are taken on the fisheries up to Leixlip and the rest upstream of the Leixlip dam in late August and September – water permitting. It takes a natural flood rather than an artificial spate to get the salmon to run up river and, of course, they cannot pass the dam at Golden Falls above Ballymore Eustace.

Sea-trout

The river gets a small run of sea-trout. The best of the fishing is in July on the Dublin and District Salmon and Trout Anglers' Association water immediately above and below the bridge at Islandbridge. Fly fishing at night is said to be most productive. Useful flies are Peter Ross, Butcher, Bloody Butcher and Teal, Blue and Silver.

Brown trout

The Liffey brown trout are not terribly big but they are there in good numbers and the water is extremely clean. Trout are found from Islandbridge upstream but the best of the trout fishing is above Leixlip and all the way to Ballymore Eustace. The average weight at Clane is 9–11 oz and one in six would weigh 1 lb. A 3 lb trout would be considered an exception. It is thought that the average size is declining on the river. It is noticeable that the weight of the trout increases the further downstream you fish.

The Liffey has all the usual fly hatches associated with a rich river. There are plenty of dark olives in spring but the iron blue hatch is patchy and mayflies are scarce. The best fishing of the season is in May and after that September can be very good. There are excellent hatches of sedges - including grey flags. You don't have to be too particular with your sedge pattern - the trout will usually take any small brown sedge pattern. The river has a heavy hatch of yellow evening duns around Clane. The trout take the hatching insect freely but are incredibly difficult to catch on summer evenings. The blue-winged olive is present and the trout take it spasmodically. It is important to note that the Liffey blue-winged olive has a very dark wing and if you are to imitate it successfully you must dress a very dark blue dun hackle on the Orange Quill.

SOME LIFFEY ANGLING CLUBS

Dublin and District Salmon and Trout Anglers' Association

Membership of this club is open and memberships may be purchased at Rory's Fishing Tackle, Temple Bar, Dublin 2.

The club has extensive water at Islandbridge, opposite the Wren's Nest Bar, at C.P.I., a stretch between Lucan and Leixlip and a stretch at Castletown near Celbridge.

Chapelizod Anglers' Association

Hon. Secretary
Mr Paul Devereux
23 St. Laurence's Road
Chapelizod, Dublin 20

Lucan Anglers' Association

Mr Alan Byrne
46 Newtown
Leixlip, Co. Kildare
Telephone 01 243010

Kilbride Angling Club

Mr Desmond Johnston (Hon Sec)
43, Avondale Park
Raheny, Dublin 5
Telephone 01-318786

The Kilbride Angling Club water is on the upper Liffey from The Sally Gap down to a point about 1 mile below Ballysmutton bridge.

Ballymore Eustace Angling Association

Mr Thomas Deegan
928 Breincan
Ballymore Eustace, Co. Kildare   *Telephone* 01-780222

This club has about 4½ miles of river. It is subject to sudden artificial floods up to 3 feet. The wild trout are small and stocking with 1 lb trout takes place.

Kilcullen Angling Association

Mr E. Delahunt
Bishop Rogan Park
Kilcullen, Co. Kildare

This club has about 4 miles of trout fishing and gets occasional salmon in September. River conditions and stocking policy as for Ballymore Eustace, above.

North Kildare Trout and Salmon Angling Assoociation

Mr Patrick Byrne
21 College Park
Newbridge, Co. Kildare

This is the biggest club on the river with nearly 30 miles of water from Kilcullen down to Millicent Bridge near Badentown. The average size of the wild trout improves at this point on the river and some stocking is carried out.

Clane Angling Club

Mr Anthony Doherty
Raheen, Rathcoffey
Naas, Co. Kildare

Good trout fishing extending from Millicent Bridge almost to Straffan.

Dublin Trout Anglers' Association

Mr J.R. Miley
4 Dodder Park Road
Dublin 14

About 3 miles of good trout fishing downstream of Straffan House. Open membership and day tickets available from:

Mr Dan O'Brien
New Road
Blackhall
Clane
Co. Kildare

Mr Sylvester Gallagher
Reeves
Straffan
Co. Kildare

UPPER RIVER LIFFEY   O 17 05

The upper Liffey flows down from the Sally Gap past Kilbride and enters
May's Bay on Pollaphuca Reservoir. The trout here average less than ¹/₂ lb
and the river tends to drop quickly. It is really spate river, suitable for
wet-fly fishing and occasional larger trout are taken early in the season.
These would be trout that came up from the Reservoir. Kilbride Angling
Club (Hon. Sec. Desmond Johnston - *see page 173*) have a lease
upstream from a point about 2 miles below Ballysmutton Bridge.

RYE WATER   N 99 37

Season

Salmon: 1 January to 30 September
Brown trout: 1 March to 30 September

The Rye water rises near Kilcock in Co. Kildare and flows east past
Maynooth to join the Liffey at Leixlip. It holds occasional salmon but has
the propensity to grow brown trout at a phenomenal rate. Trout to 8 lb
have been reported.
    The fishing on the Carton Estate is private. Inquiries about the rest of
the fishing should be directed to:
    Mr Aidan Crean, Westmanton Lodge
    Lucan, Co Dublin
    Telephone 01-6280496
    The upper Rye has hatches of dark olives and the iron blue hatch is
more dependable than on the Liffey. It has a very early hatch of blue-
winged olives in May and very consistent hatches in July and August.
The angler should note that the blue-winged olive found on the Rye has
an extraordinary delicate pale blue wing unlike its cousin on the Liffey. A
dressing of the female blue-winged olive is a great fly on the river in
September. There are good hatches of sedges and lots of alders on the
Rye.

RIVER DODDER   0 10 30

Season

Brown trout: 17 March to 30 September.

The River Dodder is another quite remarkable river in that it flows right through the city of Dublin and yet is well worth fishing for brown trout and sea-trout. It is a great tribute to those who care for it that its fish stocks still survive.

The Dodder Anglers' Club has a special interest in the river and there is a policy of making visitors welcome for a day's fishing. Membership of the club is open to all and membership cards are available at The Kiosk on Orwell Bridge; Rory's Tackle Shop, Temple Bar, Dublin 2; Watts Bros. Ltd, 18 Upper Ormond Quay, Dublin 7, and most fishing tackle shops on the south side of the city and in Tallaght.

The Dodder starts as three streams in the Dublin Mountains above Bohernabreena Reservoir. In that area, it is your typical mountain stream, flowing over granite and sandstone and has very good stocks of trout up to about $\frac{1}{2}$ lb. It changes dramatically between Oldbawn and Tallaght where it flows over limestone and from Firhouse to the sea the trout become relatively fast growing and average 9–10 oz with plenty to $1\frac{1}{4}$ lb.

The Dodder has now put most of its pollution problems behind it and the water is quite clean. In all, there are about 7 or 8 miles of good fishing from Firhouse down to Ballsbridge. It still holds trout to 3 lb and these are usually found in the weir pools. Because of the severe pollution in the past, a lot of the standard fly hatches have been killed off. It still has good hatches of olives and various midges – green, black, brown and all shades. It has very few sedges or other large flies. The fly angler has to fish very small for the brown trout – size 18 and 20. It is a very difficult river on which to learn to fly fish and the angler who masters it can really pride himself as a master fisherman.

The sea-trout seem to migrate in and out and can give quite good fishing in July, August and September. From the estuary up to the bus garage at Beaver Row, Donnybrook, fishing can be very good and sea-trout can be taken too at Clonskea, Milltown and Templeogue. It is difficult to fish during the day with so many people about but at dusk and into the night it can be good.

Access is reasonably good with public parkland stretching for miles on both banks.

OWENDOHER RIVER   O 13 24

This is an extraordinary little river flowing down from the mountain through Marley Grange to join the Dodder at Templeogue. It holds lots of small trout and has good hatches of olives and some sedges.

RIVER DARGLE   O 26 19

Season

Salmon: 1 February to 30 September
Sea-trout: 1 February to 12 October
Brown trout: 1 March to 30 September

Permission

Mr Alyn Turne
Secretary
47 Ardmore Park
Bray, Co.Wicklow

The Dargle Anglers Club has extensive fishing on the river. Membership is open and club members can avail themselves of day tickets on the Powerscourt Fishery. Membership application forms are available from:

The Jet Filling Station   Rory's Fishing Tackle
Dublin Road   Temple Bar
Bray   Dublin 2
Co. Wicklow

A private fishery offers season tickets and day tickets. Contact:

Mr Hugh Duff
Tinnehinch House
Enniskerry
Co. Wicklow
Telephone 01 868652

The River Dargle is 12 miles long and with its tributaries, the Glencree River and Glencullen River, drains a catchment of 47 square miles. It rises in the Wicklow Mountains and flows east through Enniskerry and enters the Irish Sea at Bray. It is a rather small river, coming off bare mountain and weathered granite cliffs, and is subject to violent spates. It flows through a deep valley from the confluence of the Glencree River down to Enniskerry and is well endowed with deep holding pools, some of which are very inaccessible.

This is one of Ireland's prime sea-trout rivers and comes closest to the famous Welsh rivers in its capacity to produce big sea-trout. I don't know of any other river in Ireland that can match it for producing double figure sea-trout and it is not insignificant that the biggest sea-trout ever recorded from fresh water in the Republic of Ireland, came from the Dargle. It weighed 12 lb.

The big sea-trout come in May and the run increases through June, July and August with plenty of 2-4 lb sea-trout. The best of the sea-trout fishing is above the confluence of the Glencullen river. This is a deep valley with fantastic big holding pools. There is beautiful water in Powerscourt Demesne and this is a beautiful place to fish. The upper limit of the good sea-trout fishing is at the top end of Powerscourt at the confluence of the Glencree River.

A single worm spinner and fly are all used for sea-trout. Some anglers have a preference for dark flies, such as Connemara Black, Zulu and Black Pennell but a Teal, Blue and Silver is also favoured.

The Dargle that can get a good run of salmon, though some seasons can be disappointing. The spring fishing can be excellent (some anglers take up to thirty fish) and the peak of the run is at the end of April and early in May. The grilse fishing can be good in a wet season, with the best of the fishing in August. The best of the salmon fishing is in the valley from the bottom of the Tinnehinch Fishery to the Silver Bridge.

The Tinnehinch Fishery (Hugh Duff) provides brown trout fishing and good night sea-trout fishing. It is fly fishing only and is limited to a maximum of eight rods at a time.

This is a most productive river in a beautiful setting. Unfortunately, being situated so close to a densely populated area, it is much abused and heavily poached.

VARTRY RIVER   T 30 96

Season

Sea-trout: 1 February to 12 October
Salmon: 1 February to 30 September

The Vartry River rises in Vartry Reservoir and flows down the Devil's Glen, through the village of Ashford and Mount Usher Gardens before meeting the tide at Broad Lough. It is a small, narrow river, 20 miles long, with a catchment of about 60 square miles.

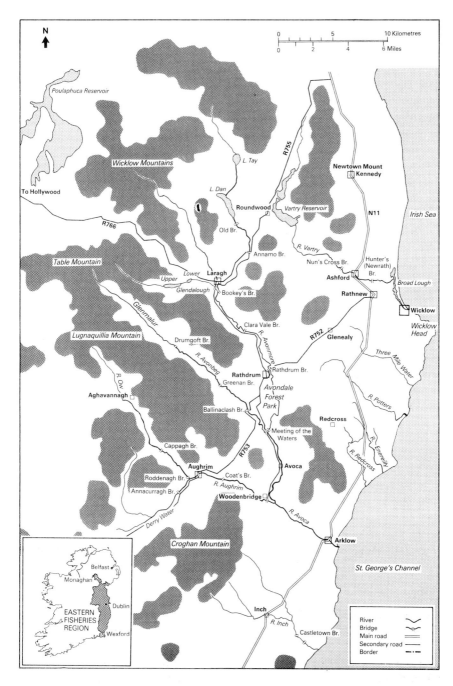

The rivers Vartry, Three Mile Water, Potters, Enereilly,
Redcross, Avoca and Inch

The upper reaches are overgrown and unfishable. From Nun's Cross Bridge to Ashford, the river flows through a densely populated area with private gardens, including Mount Usher Gardens. The only fishing available is the Vartry Angling Club water which is downstream of Ashford. The club has developed a couple of miles of fishing. Club membership is limited but there is a proposal to introduce day tickets and details are available from:

Mr Ray Dineen
Tara House
Redcross
Co. Wicklow
Telephone 0404 41645

The Vartry is primarily a sea-trout river and the trout run late. It is usually August before the run begins and it continues through to the end of the season. The sea-trout average about 1 lb but it is a river that produces a lot of nice trout up to about 4 lb.

Night fishing is by far the best and while all legal methods are allowed, fly fishing is regarded as being most effective. Useful patterns include Wicklow Killer, Teal, Blue and Silver, Peter Ross, Zulu, Bibio, Black Pennell and Green Peter. Size 10 is considered best.

THREE MILE WATER   T 32 87

POTTERS RIVER   T 30 84

ENEREILLY RIVER   T 29 80

REDCROSS RIVER   T 28 79

These four small rivers enter the sea between Wicklow Head and Arklow. They are mostly narrow and overgrown. None of them are recognized as great angling fisheries. Poaching is a problem. They get a run of sea-trout after a flood and an angler fortunate enough to be there at the right time might get a few sea-trout and possibly a grilse.

AVOCA RIVER AND TRIBUTARIES   T 20 76

Season

Salmon, Sea-trout and Brown trout: 15 March to 30 September.

The Avoca River and its tributaries drain a catchment of 252 square miles from the Sally Gap down to Arklow. This is a magnificent and very beautiful river system, world famous for its lovely setting among the Wicklow Mountains.

The Avoca River itself has been ruined by the run-off from disused copper mines and to a large extent is a dead river.

THE AVONMORE RIVER   T 19 89

The Avonmore flows down from Lough Tay and Lough Dan, through the villages of Laragh and Rathdrum, to join the Avoca River – a distance of 22 miles.

This is a lovely wide river with deep pools. It is very clean, with little industry or agriculture to pollute it. Wading can be dangerous and it is no place for children.

There is an active angling club – Rathdrum Angling Club. The secretary is Mr Christopher Bolton, 5 Ballinderry Road, Rathdrum, Co. Wicklow. New members are always welcome and the club spends a lot of money on the river, clearing banks and providing stiles and bridges.

The river holds big stocks of small brown trout. Some would say it has too many trout. A $\frac{1}{2}$ lb trout is considered good and a 1 lb trout is something of an exception but it can produce trout to over 3 lb. Some of the best fishing is in Avondale Forest Park, downstream of Rathdrum. One angler took five trout for $7\frac{1}{2}$ lb there recently. The best of the fishing is usually after a flood in May, June and July.

There are good hatches of olives – including blue-winged olives – sedges and black gnats. Popular fly patterns include Cowdung Fly, Wickham's Fancy, Small Brown Sedge, Greenwell's Glory, various olive patterns and a dry Red Spinner.

Access is good and mostly at the bridges. There is a car park at Avondale House, but you must pay a fee.

Be warned! Biting midges can be incredibly troublesome here in summer.

AVONBEG RIVER   T 17 85

The Avonbeg River is 17 miles long and flows down through Glenmalur, Greenan, and Ballinaclash to join the Avonmore above Avoca. It holds big stocks of small trout all the way from the top of the glen to below Ballinaclash. It is very overgrown at Ballynaclash and virtually unfishable, while farther up at Grennan there is no cover and it is easy to spook the trout in the clear water. It is a river with a lot of potential set in beautiful countryside. It is proposed to form an Angling Club in Ballynaclash.

For fly fishing, try a small Wickham's Fancy.

OW RIVER   T 10 81

The Ow River, 12 miles long, flows down from Lugnaquillia Mountain through a heavily wooded valley. Access is very difficult and the trout are small, with an occasional good trout in the deeper pools.

DERRY WATER   T 10 76

AUGHRIM RIVER   T 14 79

The Derry Water becomes the Aughrim River at Aughrim and joins the Avoca River below Woodenbridge. It is a superb little trout stream, the reason being that it flows over probably the only little bit of limestone in Co. Wicklow. It holds good stocks of trout at Annacurragh and is not heavily fished. The fishing extends for a mile up and down from the village. Access is at the GAA football pitch; park your car at the village hall. The trout average about ½ lb and you will meet trout to 1 lb or even 1½ lb more often than you might expect. The best fishing is in May, June, July and September, with night fishing being good in September with a big White Moth.

The Aughrim River is a big river by Wicklow standards, wide, with some deep, dangerous pools. Care should be taken when wading because the sand slides away from underfoot which can be dangerous.

The average size of the trout is ½ lb to ¾ lb, with the possibility of bigger fish to 4 lb – usually caught at night. There are three fish farms on the river and there is always the possibility of catching a few escapee rainbow trout.

The best of the fishing is from Roddenagh Bridge on the Ow River, down through the village of Aughrim to Coat's Bridge and down as far as

Woodenbridge.

Access is by the football field on the left bank at Roddenagh Bridge. There is a short stretch below the village of Aughrim where the landowner doesn't allow fishing, followed by a fishable stretch, then problems with heavy bank cover from the Woodfab Factory for about 1 mile to Coat's Bridge. There is no fishing allowed along by the fish farm at Coat's Bridge but below this there is a stretch known locally as 'the Slaney' with good access and good fishing down as far as the big fish farm at Woodenbridge.

The Aughrim River has probably the most prolific fly hatches of all the Wicklow rivers, especially olives and sedges. Some of the best fishing is to sedges on summer evenings. A Greenwell's Spider is a favourite early season pattern. A Coachman works well fished wet at night, or try fishing a dry White Moth.

This river holds occasional salmon and sea-trout above Woodenbridge.

INCH RIVER   T 64 23

Season

All species: 15 March to 30 September.

Permission

Riparian owners.

The Inch River and its tributaries drain a catchment of approximately 27 square miles in North Wexford into Courtown Harbour at Clone. It held an excellent stock of very fine east coast type sea-trout in the 1960s up to February. It has deteriorated greatly in more recent times but still gets a run of smaller sea-trout in July. The main fishing area is downstream of Castletown Bridge. The water is deep and slow and good fishing depends on a flood or an upstream wind.

OWENVORRAGH RIVER   T 20 56

Season

All species: 15 March to 30 September.

Permission

There is an active Owenavarragh Angling Club which leases part of the stretch from the tide up to a point about 1 mile above Boleany Bridge, a distance of about 3 miles. The rest of the fishing is with the permission of the riparian owners. Day tickets are available on the Angling Club water from:

> Whitmore's Jewellers Shop
> Main Street
> Gorey, Co.Wexford

This river is 18 miles long and drains a catchment of 63 square miles, south of Gorey, into Courtown Harbour. It was drained in 1975 and is relatively featureless and slow flowing and very overgrown, except where the anglers have cleared the banks.

It holds some salmon after the first flood in August and gets a good run of sea-trout up to 4 lb from July. The Angling Club stocks brown trout each season and some of these are known to run to sea and return as sea-trout. The best of the sea-trout fishing is from mid June through to August and the river is usually heavily fished at this time. All legitimate methods are allowed including maggot and spinner. The best of the fishing is at night and, for the fly fisher, dark flies get best results – Zulu, Butcher, Black Pennell and Connemara Black, sizes 12 and 14. The sea-trout here are thick and short and take best after a spate.

RIVER SLANEY   S 97 40

Season

Salmon and sea-trout: 26 February to 15 September for the River Slaney and tributaries downstream of its junction with the River Bann; 26 February to 31 August for the remainder of the River Slaney and its tributaries, including the River Bann.

Brown trout: 26 February to 16 September, for the River Slaney and tributaries downstream of Enniscorthy Bridge; 26 February to 30 September for the River Slaney and tributaries upstream of Enniscorthy Bridge.

Statutory Regulations

A by-law states that fishing shall be with artificial fly only from 1 April between Ballycarney Bridge and Aghada Bridge. From 1 May, it is artificial fly only on the river upstream of Enniscorthy Bridge and on the tributaries except on the River Bann above the Railway Bridge.

Permission

The Slaney Rod Fisher's Association represents the private fisheries which let rods mainly on a seasonal basis. Day rods occasionally come available. Information from the Hon. Secretary:

Mr John O'Gorman
Knochnagan House
Tullow, Co. Carlow
Telephone 0503-51335

Mr Chris Strong, Mill House, Kilcarrig Bridge, Clonegal, Co. Wexford, (*telephone* 054 77339), has fishing and fishing lodges to let at Kilcarrig Bridge – Kingsmill Moore's old home. Mr Strong can sometimes arrange rods on private beats.

The following Angling Clubs have fisheries on the river.

Tullow Salmon and Trout Angling Club

Mr Joe O'Neill
Carlow Road
Tullow
Co. Carlow
Telephone 0503-51288

Enniscorthy and District Angling Club

Mr Joe Cash
Tomnalossett
Enniscorthy, Co. Wexford,
Telephone 054 33490

Salsboro Angling Club

Mr Patrick Lacey
Mile House Road
Enniscorthy, Co. Wexford

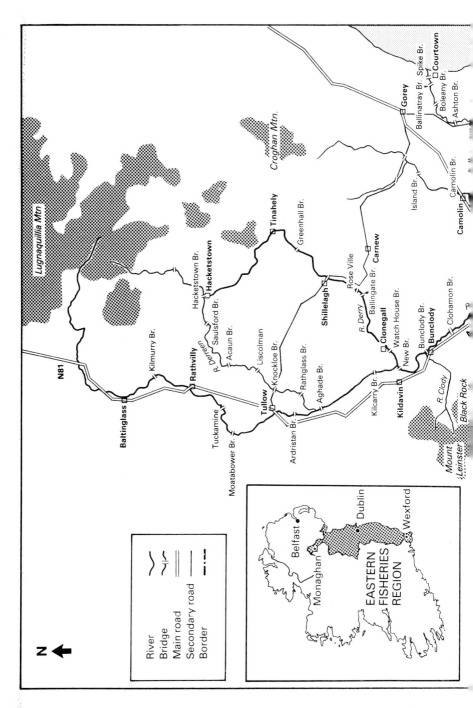

The rivers Slaney, Sow, Owenvorragh and the Bridgetown Canal

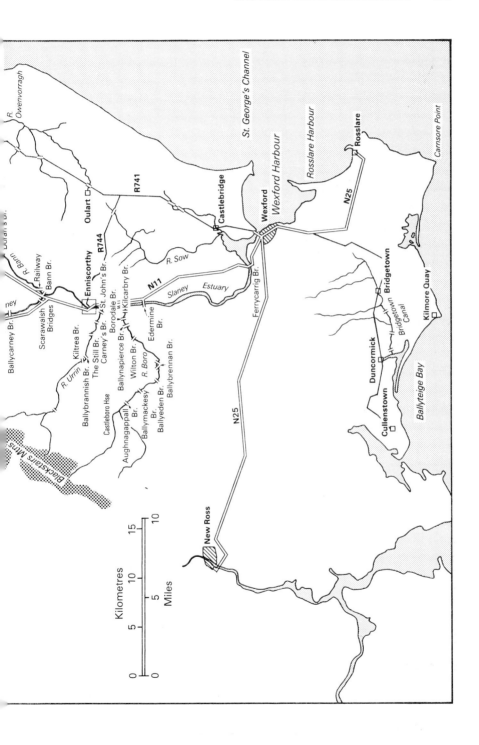

Island Angling Club

Mr William Cash
6 Bellefield Terrace
Enniscorthy, Co. Wexford, *Telephone* 054-35213

Free Fishing

The salmon and sea-trout fishing is free on the downstream side of the old bridge in Enniscorthy.

The River Slaney rises in the Glen of Imaal in Co. Wicklow and flows south through Baltinglass, Co. Wicklow, Rathvilly and Tullow, Co. Carlow and Bunlcody and Enniscorthy, Co. Wexford, where it meets the tide. It is 73 miles long and drains a catchment of approximately 680 square miles. In spring, it is a beautiful big fast flowing river, ideally suited for salmon fishing. Later in the season the water tends to run off rather quickly due to the extensive land drainage works carried out by farmers. The Slaney holds salmon, sea-trout and brown trout.

The Slaney is primarily a spring salmon fishery and is regarded as one of the top rivers in Ireland for early spring salmon fishing. It is probably for this reason that it has been called 'The Queen of Irish Rivers'.

The peak of the spring salmon fishing is from opening day (26 February) to the end of March. The fishing can be fair to good in April and even into May. In fact, the biggest run of fish comes in May but the majority of these are taken by the nets.

Water temperatures determine how far upstream the spring salmon fishing extends. With snow water the fish tend to lie below Bunclody, but in mild weather they can be caught up to Tullow in Co. Carlow. Very few grilse are taken on the rod.

The average weight of the salmon is 10 lb and they range from 7 lb to over 20 lb.

Spinning is the most popular early season fishing method. The most popular baits are yellow belly, brown and gold and blue and silver Devons – in that order. Sizes range from 3 inches maximum down to $1\frac{1}{4}$ inches. The majority of the fisheries don't allow worm or shrimp.

It is fly fishing only upstream of Ballycarney Bridge from 1 April. Yellow flies are popular, including yellow tube flies, the Garry Dog, and Black Goldfinch. In April, when the water is low and warm, the Blue Charm and Hairy Mary work well by day and a Thunder and Lightning is a favourite at dusk. Fly size depends on water temperature and height and can range from size 4 double to size 10. A Black Goldfinch variant with a broad silver rib and the Jock Scott were firm favourites in the old days – up to size 4/0.

Fishery Owners' Count of Rod-Caught Fish, 1981-92

Year	Total	Above Clohamon Weir	Below Clohamon Weir
1981	814	558	256
1982	361	212	149
1983	858	532	326
1984	1122	311	811
1985	1069	239	830
1986	712	102	610
1987	644	134	510
1988	287	81	206
1989	731	63	668
1990	415	83	332
1991	580	n/k	n/k
1992	344	136	208

Most of the fishing is done from the bank. Wading is not usually allowed, except where a fishery owner owns both banks.

The Slaney is a river with a very long, narrow estuary. It is over 12 miles from Enniscorthy Bridge to Ferrycarrig Bridge and a total of 75 nets operate from 1 April along the estuary. It is believed by many anglers that the 48-hour weekly closed period for the nets is too short to allow fish to run in low water conditions. The river, too, is not without its problems. Water abstraction takes place above Rathvilly and Clohamon Weir, where a new fish pass, installed by ministerial order in 1989, is a constant cause of concern to anglers.

Sea-trout

The river gets a very good run of sea-trout. They begin to run around 20 June and the peak of the run occurs in the first 2 weeks of July. The fishing remains good through July and into August when river fog often puts the trout off.

Certain stretches are especially good and include the free fishing from Enniscorthy Bridge down to the mouth of the River Urrin; from Scarawalsh Old Bridge down to the mouth of the River Bann; from Clohamon Weir down to Moyeady; the stretch opposite the cemetery at Bunclody; the stretch at Ballina Park downstream of Bunclody; the right bank opposite the mouth of the River Derry down to the confluence of the Kildavin Stream. Some of these stretches are private and some do not let permits.

The fishing methods can vary from fishery to fishery and may include fly, worm and maggots. The most popular flies are Killdevil Spider, Greenwell's Spider, Bibio, Butcher, Priest, Sooty Olive and Peter Ross in sizes 10 and 12.

For fly fishing, a floating, sink-tip or fast-sink line may be used, according to conditions. A slow retrieve is said to work best.

Brown trout

The river holds plenty of small brown trout averaging 6 oz. Anglers rarely bother fishing for them, except upstream of Tullow. Among the fly hatches observed in early spring are what appears to be the true March Brown.

RIVER DERREEN   S 86 70

Season and Regulations

As for the River Slaney.

Permission

The Tullow Salmon and Trout Anglers' Association (Mr Joe O'Neill, Carlow Road, Tullow, Co. Carlow, *Telephone* 0503-51288) has a short stretch on the right bank at the confluence with the Slaney. Upstream of that there is private fishing, and above Rathglass Bridge, it is possible to get fishing with the permission of the riparian owners.

Hacketstown and Rathvilly Trout Anglers' Association has 10 miles of trout fishing from Tobinstown Bridge to a point 2 miles south of Rathangan, Co. Wicklow. The Hon. Secretary is Mr Dermot Doyle, 26 Mountain View, Hacketstown, Co. Carlow, (telephone 0508 71334).

The River Derreen is 25 miles long. It holds salmon in spring and is considered by some anglers to be a better salmon fishery than the Slaney itself above the confluence of the 2 rivers upstream of Aghada Bridge. It fishes best in high water when the water temperature rises. It flows through rich agricultural land and holds good quality brown trout. There are good stocks of ¾ lb trout here and some even reach 3 lb. The best fishing is in March, April, May and June and there are good hatches of the various olives. It is a small river, easy to wade and a short fly rod is recommended.

RIVER DERRY   S 90 60

The River Derry rises north of Tinahely in Co. Wicklow and flows south west for 21 miles through Shillelagh to join the Slaney at Kildavin. It holds occasional salmon and small brown trout and is fished mainly by local farmers. It is a nice little river, but very overgrown and is, perhaps, best left that way because it is very important as a spawning and nursery river for Slaney salmon.

RIVER BANN   S 98 45

Permission   Mr Anthony Breen
The Angling Club
Milltown, Ferns
Co. Wexford

Season and Regulations

As for the River Slaney.

The River Bann rises in north Co. Wexford and flows south west for 28 miles past the town of Gorey, Camolin and Ferns to join the Slaney below Scarawalsh Bridge. It is regarded mainly as a sea-trout fishery and it has lots of small brown trout. The banks are overgrown and the river gets very weedy in summer. The best of the sea-trout fishing is on the stretch from the confluence with the Slaney up as far as the village of Camolin. There are some good pools here and the fishing can be great from mid July to the end of August. Access is difficult and the banks are very overgrown.

URRIN RIVER   S 96 39

Permission

There is one angling club operating on a two-mile stretch of the river and all inquiries should go to:

Mr John Horgan, Chairman
Kiltrea Angling Club
Ballybrannish
Enniscorthy, Co. Wexford
Telephone 054 34678

The River Urrin is 14 miles long and flows from the west into the Slaney estuary 1 mile south of Enniscorthy. It is primarily regarded as a sea-trout river. The fishing can be very good with lots of trout from $3/4$ to $1\frac{1}{2}$ lb.

The peak of the fishing is from around the first week in July to the end of the season. The fishing extends from the mouth up to the weir at Kiltrea, a distance of about 4 miles. This is a nice river – averaging about 10 yards wide – with good banks, relatively easy access and nice, deep pools. The fishing methods are worm, maggot and some fly fishing.

BORO RIVER   S 97 35

Permission

Free.

The Boro River is an impressive fast-flowing productive sea-trout fishery, 18 miles long, with some lovely streams and pools. The main sea-trout angling water reaches from the mouth up as far as Castleboro, a distance of 9 miles approximately. The river retains its natural character, with open banks, farmland and some forestry but no drainage works. The sea-trout fishing can be excellent with lots of fish up to $1\frac{1}{2}$ lb. They begin running around the last week of June, the peak of the season is around the third week in July, and the good fishing lasts till about mid-August. The best of the early-season fishing is from the mouth to Victoria Bridge and up to Wilton Bridge. From mid-August the better fishing is farther upstream and good local knowledge of the pools is necessary. This river is heavily fished with maggots. The season ends for sea-trout on 15 September.

RIVER SOW   T 5 26

Permission

Free.

Season

Salmon, sea-trout and brown trout: 15 March to 30 September.

The River Sow drains a 34 square mile catchment into Wexford Harbour at Castlebridge. It is regarded primarily as a sea-trout fishery with about 1 mile of tidal fishing located below the waterworks dam at Castlebridge. The fishing is above and below the main road bridge, and access is difficult, with high reeds. Nonetheless, this stretch produces 200–300 sea-trout every year from mid-July. It is tidal and fishing methods include worms and maggots.

THE BRIDGETOWN CANAL   S 93 8

Permission

Free.

Season

Sea-trout: 15 March to 30 September.

The Bridgetown Canal flows into the estuary about 4 miles north-west of Kilmore Quay in south Wexford. A recent survey by the Eastern Regional Fisheries Board found that it held good numbers of sea-trout up to 15 inches long. Further west, the estuary discharges into the sea at Cullenstown. The tide rushes through a narrow neck at Cullenstown and this location is known to produce good sea-trout to 5 lb in April and May. They are fished with spinners as the tide floods through.

A big one from 'The Mollies', Kells Blackwater

·7· The Shannon Fisheries Region

The Shannon Fisheries Region comprises all the rivers that flow into the sea between Hags Head in Co. Clare and Kerry Head. The Headquarters of the Shannon Regional Fisheries Board is at Thomond Weir, Limerick, (*telephone* 061 55171)

This is a huge region, extending from north Kerry in the south virtually to the border of Northern Ireland. The Shannon River is the biggest in these islands and drains the entire central plain. Most of it is on limestone and it has the characteristics required to produce and nurture huge numbers of fish of all species.

The fisheries are described below in detail, but a brief word is necessary on the Shannon, the greatest river of them all.

Traditionally, it is reputed to have produced large numbers of big salmon. In 1929, a hydro electric power station was commissioned at Ardnacrusha, near Limerick. A fish pass was incorporated in the regulating weir at Parteen. There are many who claim that the salmon did not all run the fish pass. In 1935, the Shannon Fisheries Act gave over the entire fishing rights of the Shannon to the Electricity Supply Board and in 1959 a Boreland lift was built at Ardnacrusha power station to get the salmon up the river.

At the present time, all of the salmon fishing on the river is controlled by the Electricity Supply Board. The company actively manages the fisheries on the lower river at Limerick – that is Castleconnell and the Mulcair River – and extensive stocking takes place. However, an Electricity Supply Board permit is required to fish for salmon anywhere on the Shannon or its tributaries. The trout fishing on a number of its tributaries – including the Suck, Inny, Brosna, Little Brosna and Camlin, etc. – is leased to the Central Fisheries Board and managed by the Shannon Regional Fisheries Board. Strictly speaking, a trout fishing permit is required on these rivers – issued by the Regional Board.

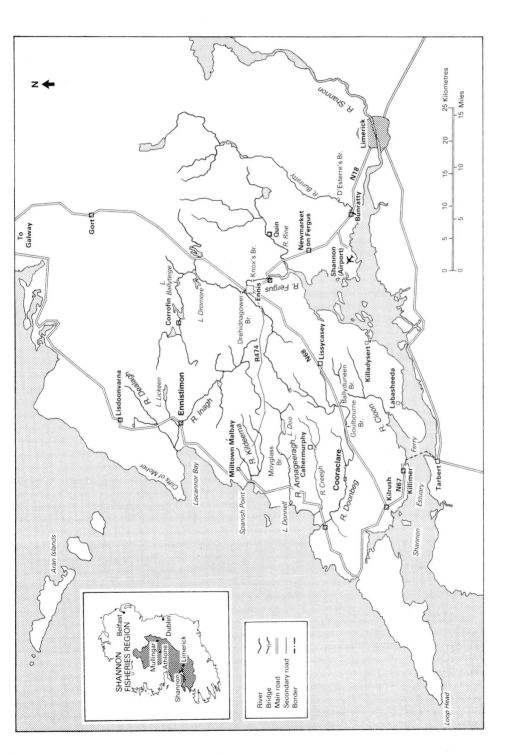

The rivers of County Clare

DEALAGH (KILSHANNY) RIVER   R 10 90

Season

Salmon, Sea-trout and Brown trout: 1 March to 30 September.

Permission

Free.

The Kilshanny River rises in The Burren and flows south west for 10 miles into Liscannor Bay where it shares a common estuary with the Inagh River. It flows through farmland and the banks are mostly clear. It is a spate river and has some nice deep holes for holding fish. It holds brown trout up to 10 oz and gets a fair run of grilse and sea-trout in June and July. Traditionally, the estuary of the Kilshanny and the Inagh River supported seven draft nets and the falls at Ennistimon were impassable, so the majority of the fish were possibly of Kilshanny River origin. It can be fished up as far as the bridge on the N67 Ennistimon–Lisdoonvarna road. Try a small Garry Dog or a worm for the grilse. If the water is coloured after a spate, the sea-trout can be fished during the day, otherwise the best fishing is at night. It can hold sea-trout to 3 lb.

INAGH RIVER (CULLENAGH RIVER)   R 12 88

This river is overrun with rudd and pike since the 1960s and it has little to offer the game angler. There is a fair stock of small brown trout in a 2 mile stretch above the town of Ennistimon and for a similar distance upstream of the village of Inagh.

KILDEEMA (BEALACLUGGA) RIVER   R 04 75

Season

Salmon, Sea-trout, Brown trout: 1 March to 30 September.

Permission

Free.

This little spate river enters the sea south of Spanish Point. It gets a fair run of grilse and an excellent run of sea-trout to over 3 lb on a spate in the months of June and July. The fishing is on the south bank in a half mile stretch from Bealaclugga Bridge up to the waterfall. Fish a fly or spinner by day, but the best sea-trout fishing is from dusk till dawn. Try a size 12 Silver Doctor, Bibio or Peter Ross.

ANNAGEERAGH RIVER   R 02 71

Season

Salmon, Sea-trout and Brown trout: 1 March to 30 September.

Permission

Free.

The Annageeragh River drains a 25 square mile catchment. It used to be a great little grilse river in the early 1970s and it also got a good run of big sea-trout to 4 lb in May and June. It can still give fair to good sea-trout fishing with the chance of a grilse on a spate from late June through to August. The best of the fishing is in the deep water for about 1 mile upstream of Lough Donnell and in the pools up as far as Moyglass Bridge.

CREEGH RIVER   Q 99 66

Season

Salmon, Sea-trout and Brown trout: 1 March to 30 September.

Permission

Free.

This little spate river enters the sea 2 miles north of Doonbeg. It gets a fair to good run of grilse on a flood from mid June and a marvellous run of sea-trout in July and August. It is a small stream – 15-25 feet wide. Access by road is good, the banks are relatively clear and on a spate it can be fished all the way to the bridge at Cahermurphy with either fly or worm.

DOONBEG RIVER   Q 98 65

Permission

Free.

This is one of the most underestimated salmon and sea-trout fisheries in the country. It has a lot of potential but requires a lot of work to help it fulfil itself. It rises near Lissycasey and flows west for 26 miles and drains a 52 square mile catchment into the sea at Doonbeg. The locals reckon it is worth fishing for spring salmon from 10 April, if there is plenty of water, and the spring run peaks in the first 2 weeks of May. The grilse are in the river from early July and September is always a good month for both salmon and sea-trout.

It has the potential to be as good a sea-trout river as any in the country with a run of spring sea trout in the 2-4 lb range arriving in April and early May. The smaller summer sea-trout come in late June and the river peaks in mid July, with finnock to follow later.

A Hairy Mary and shrimp flies are popular for salmon. The Dunkeld is a favourite sea-trout fly and Teal, Blue and Silver, Watson's Fancy, Peter Ross and Black Pennell are also popular in sizes 10 and 12. Bait fishing is widely practised. The best of the salmon fishing is from a point approximately 3 miles below Cooraclare up to a point one mile above Goulbourne Bridge and sea-trout are taken up to Ballyduneen Bridge. The early sea-trout run straight through to the upper reaches. The fishing is not easy, with the banks being high, difficult to walk and overgrown in many places.

CLOON RIVER   R 12 55

Season

Salmon, Sea-trout, Brown trout: 1 February to 30 September.

Permission

Regarded as being free.

The Cloon River enters the Shannon Estuary 2 miles north-west of Labasheeda. It gets a run of sea-trout in June and July and can be fished in places for about 2 miles upstream to the New Bridge. It is overgrown and inaccessible.

RIVER FERGUS

Season

Salmon, and Sea-trout: 1 February to 30 September.
Brown trout: 15 February to 30 September.

Permission

Generally regarded as free.

The River Fergus in Co. Clare is 37 miles long and drains a rich limestone catchment of 402 square miles which includes many interconnected loughs. It rises north-west of Corofin and enters the tide at Ennis. It is a noted brown trout dry-fly river and a worthwhile spring salmon fishery in its lower reaches. There is an 8-inch size limit for trout.

The brown trout average ³/₄ lb with some to 4 lb. The water is gin clear and it has good hatches of early olives, iron blues, blue-winged olives and sedges, but no mayfly. It is a noted dry-fly river. The banks are high and difficult in the middle reaches. It is tidal up as far as Knox's Bridge at Ennis.

The best trout fishing stretches are at Knox's Bridge; the stream opposite the Vocational School in Ennis; above and below Drehidnagower Bridge; the Cut, 1¹/₂ miles upstream of Ennis; the Upper Cut, below Templemaley Bridge; Addroon Bridge upstream to Ballyteigue Lough; Ballyteige Lough upstream to Ballyogan Bridge; Atedaun Lough upstream to Inchiquin Lough; Inchiquin Lough to Kilnaboy Bridge; and Kilnaboy Bridge, upstream to Elmvale. The banks are overgrown in places and the river runs low and becomes weeded in summer.

The Fergus is said to produce about 200 salmon and grilse every year. The best spring fishing is from opening day through February and March and anglers stand shoulder to shoulder at such well-known taking places as the Post Office Field, the Sandy Hole and The Meadow, all near the town of Ennis. The grilse come in mid June and there is always the possibility of taking one right through to September. The Fergus pools are deep and sluggish and worm fishing and spinning are the favourite fishing methods.

RIVER RINE (QUIN RIVER)

Season

Salmon and Sea-trout: 1 February to 30 September
Brown trout: 15 February to 30 September.

Permission

Part is free. For those parts that flow through the grounds of Dromoland Castle, contact:

> The Recreation Manager
> Dromoland Castle
> Newmarket-on-Fergus, Co. Clare
> *Telephone* 061 71144

The Quin River rises in the East Clare Lakes and flows south west through the village of Quin to the Fergus estuary. It is a nice clean little river, partly overgrown and part flowing through open pasture and parkland. It gets a small run of grilse and some sea-trout in July and there are six recognized pools and a number of flats from Drumoland to above Quin village. It is fished mostly by locals after a flood using worms or spinner.

It has a good stock of brown trout averaging ½ lb. It is a limestone river, and the hatches of fly are good. Useful wet-fly patterns are Partridge and Orange, Grouse and Green, William's Favourite and Waterhen Bloa. Drumoland Castle provides a gillie. Otherwise contact: (Dennis Exton, Keevagh Quinn, Co. Clare, *telephone* 065 25879), who has an excellent knowledge of the rivers and loughs in these parts, from the Shannon at Castleconnell west to the River Fergus.

BUNRATTY RIVER   R 46 72

Season

Salmon and Sea-trout: 1 February to 30 September
Brown trout: 15 February to 30 September.

Permission

Free.

The Bunratty River enters the Shannon estuary near the well known medieval Bunratty Castle. It is a fair sized river and drains several lakes in east Co. Clare. Access is either at the castle or on a few miles upstream at D'Esterre's Bridge, off the Cratloe–Sixmilebridge road. The banks are reasonably clear and were maintained recently. It holds small brown trout to 2 lb and gets a small run of grilse and a fair run of sea-trout. The best fishing is from mid June through July. There is some slob trout fishing at the tide. The best of the fishing extends upstream for about 3 miles to D'Esterre's Bridge. Try small sea-trout patterns.

THE RIVER SHANNON

Season

Salmon and Sea-trout: 1 February to 30 September
Brown trout: 15 February to 30 September.

The Shannon is the largest river in these islands. It rises in the mountains of West Cavan and flows south for 160 miles to the tide at Limerick. The total catchment of the main river and its tributaries is approximately 6,060 square miles. For the most part, this is a big, sluggish river which connects the three great loughs – Lough Allen, Lough Ree and Lough Derg.

The Shannon is a great mixed fishery and holds a wide range of coarse fish and pike as well as trout and salmon. Indeed, the fishing for the latter species is quite limited on the main channel and much better stocks are found in the tributaries.

There are three main areas where game anglers might concentrate their efforts on the main channel: the upper Shannon, Meelick, and the Shannon at Limerick.

UPPER SHANNON

The first stretch extends for a distance of about 6 miles from Bellantra Bridge (the Baily Bridge) at Lough Allen to just below Battle Bridge near Leitrim village and the fishing is free. This stretch holds fair stocks of brown trout to 2 lb and occasionally much bigger trout – to 9 lb – are taken on spinners. Fly hatches include olives, sedges, blackgnats and some mayfly above Battle Bridge. It is a stretch that is not heavily fished for trout. Roach have spread to this part of the river in recent years and quite a bit of coarse fishing takes place. The trout fishing water is: for a mile below Galley Bridge where access is fair; a short stretch above

Wooden Bridge where access is very difficult; midway between Wooden Bridge and Battle Bridge where access is very difficult, above and below Battle Bridge, where the access is fair; this being a developed coarse fishing stretch.

THE MEELICK FISHERY   M 94 13

Permits (for Salmon fishing)

Electricity Supply Board Office
Birr
Co. Offaly
Telephone 0509 20500

Electricity Supply Board Office
Ballinasloe
Co. Galway
Telephone 0905 42340

Mr Jim Robinson
Fishing Tackle Shop
Thomond Shopping Centre
Limerick
Telephone 061 44900

The salmon fishery at Meelick on the Shannon is situated approximately 5 miles downstream of the bridge at Banagher. The river here is very wide, with several islands. In the channel between the islands the water is relatively shallow and streamy with some nice salmon fishing stretches. The water level above the fishery is controlled by weirs and this can determine the quality of the fishing – in low water with all the sluice gates closed, the extent of the fishing water is greatly reduced. With a good flow of water, this is a handsome river, and when the salmon are running the fishing can be exceptionally good. There are no records kept but local opinion puts the annual catch somewhere between 300 and 400 fish, and some would say at least twice that number.

It is a fishery that is heavily fished at the peak of the season. For the first time visitor it presents an awesome prospect, such is the huge scale of things. It is one place where a gillie is really necessary but none is available. The next best thing is to observe the locals.

The fishery is really in two parts: the right bank, or Eyrecourt side, and the left bank or Offaly side.

Access to the right bank is off the Banagher–Eyrecourt road at Kilnaborris and thence to the pumphouse at the riverside. The water here is streamy and wading (with a staff!) is possible in places, but some locals use a boat to fish the runs and eel gaps. Two prime locations are above the pumphouse where the electric wires cross the river and immediately above the weir when fish are running.

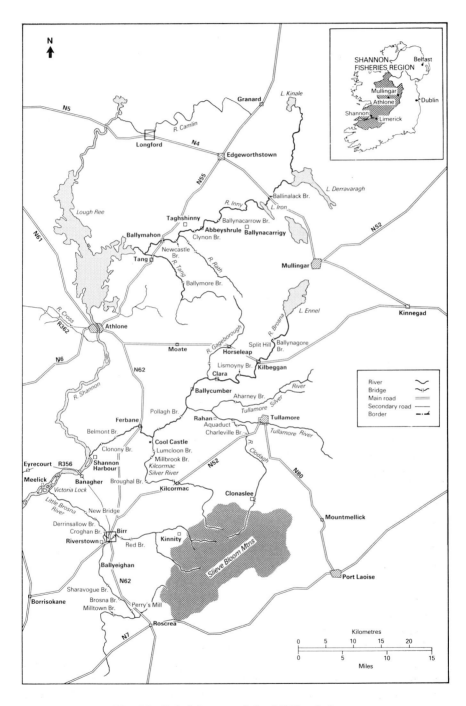

The Meelick fishery and the Midland rivers

Access to the left bank is from the town of Banagher, via Lusmagh village to Victoria Lock. A boat is virtually a necessity to fish this side. With a few gates open in Shaughnessy's Weir, fishing can be excellent in the pool under the weir and at the mouth of the Little Brosna River.

The salmon begin running at Meelick about the third week in May and the run tends to peak around the last week in June and early July. The fishing tends be quiet in late July and August but can get good in September with a rise in the water.

All fishing methods are allowed – spinning, worm and shrimp. For fly fishing, try a size 8 single or size 10 double Silver Doctor, Blue Charm or Thunder and Lightning – size 6 in high water.

THE CASTLECONNELL FISHERY   R 66 62

Permission

There are eight beats on the fishery. Five of these are let by tender every season and the remaining three are let on day tickets. For details, contact:

The Generation Manager	Mr Michael Murtagh
Electricity Supply Board	Castleconnell
Hydro Group	Co. Limerick
Ardnacrusha, Nr Limerick	*Telephone* 061 377289
Telephone 061 345588	
Mr Jim Robinson	The Angling Centre
Fishing Tackle Shop	Castle Oaks House Hotel
Thomond Shopping Centre	Castleconnell
Limerick	Limerick
Telephone 061 44900	*Telephone* 061 377666

This famous and prestigious salmon fishery lies close by the ancient village of Castleconnell, 7 miles north west of Limerick City and is owned and managed by the Electricity Supply Board.

The erection of a hydroelectric dam up river at Parteen greatly reduced the volume of the flow of the old river. The present fishery has been reconstructed to take account of the reduced volume of water. Some new streams and pools have been imaginatively created and many of the old pools retained with their lovely evocative names derived from the Irish – Fall na Hassa (Cliff of the Waterfall), Thraw-na-Knock (Strand of the Horses), Balchraheen (Place of the rapids), to name but a few. The pools are varied and interesting and most can be fished from the bank. Boats are provided to access difficult lies. A controlled flow is maintained from the dam to ensure that the water never runs too low.

The fishery is divided into eight beats, each about ½ a mile long. Four of them carry 3 rods and the other four 2 rods each. The beats are rotated daily. All legitimate fishing methods are allowed, except shrimp fishing. A small double-handed rod (14 feet) is advised but a single handed rod will suffice for grilse on some beats. A wading staff is necessary.

The season opens on 1 February and the fishery gets a few big spring fish in February and March. In the past, the Shannon was famous for its big fish – up to 45 lb, with some beats averaging an unbelievable 21 lb (*The Salmon Rivers of Ireland*, Augustus Grimble, 1913). The spring average is now about 10 lb and occasionally fish over 20 lb are taken. The month of April sees a good run of fish averaging 10 lb and known locally as 'April fliers'. These fish provide good sport through April and May.

The peak of the season is reckoned to fall between mid May and the end of June and coincides with the grilse run. Fish continue to rest in some of the bigger pools right through the season and fresh fish move up from the estuary with a rise in the water. In suitable conditions, good sport can be had till closing date on 30 September.

Accurate records are impossible to obtain but the annual catch is estimated to average 600 fish with 1,000 fish a possibility in a good season.

Fishing Methods

Spinning is the most productive method till 17 March. After that date, some anglers prefer to fish a fly or a worm. The most popular early season baits are 3-inch blue and silver Devons and 17-gram copper or silver Orklas. In March, local anglers prefer 3-inch Lane Minnows and drop down to 2-inch minnows as temperatures rise. Wooden Minnows and Mepps baits are not considered useful.

There is a short list of well tried fly patterns used at the fishery: Black Goldfinch, Silver Doctor, Hairy Mary, Garry Dog and Mephisto (Curry's Red Shrimp). Sizes range from 4 to 10. In spring, the big flies are very heavily dressed.

For gillies, contact:

Mr Jim Robinson
Fishing Tackle Shop
Thomond Shopping Centre
Limerick
Telephone 061 44900

The Angling Centre
Castle Oaks House Hotel
Castleconnell
Limerick
Telephone 061 77666

Mr Denis Exton
Keevagh
Quin
Co. Clare
Telephone 065 25879

Mr Michael Doherty
56 Pineview Gadens
Moyross
Limerick
Telephone 061 327770

THE LIMERICK FISHERIES PLASSEY

THE LONG SHORE

Permission

Electricity Supply Board Shop
Bishop's Quay
Limerick
Telephone 061 45599

An unlimited number of annual permits (bank and boat) are issued at reasonable prices. They are widely availed of by local anglers and the fishing can get crowded at peak runs.

Both of these fisheries offer excellent spring and summer salmon fishing. The Plassey stretch is located on both banks near the University of Limerick and the Long Shore is on the right bank downstream of the tailrace from Ardnacrusha power station.

Plassey is a lovely fishery with fast streamy water. The antics of fly fishers playing fish on the Black Bridge when the grilse are running, are worth seeing.

The Long Shore is very highly regarded as a spring fishery. Anglers here are fishing the undiminished width of the mighty Shannon. The river is deep and expansive – nearly ¼ mile wide - and many anglers fish from a boat.

The spring salmon fishing peaks in late March and April and a lot of fishing effort is concentrated on the Long Shore. No records are available but probably something in the region of 500 fish, averaging about 10 lb, are taken.

The grilse begin running in May and the Plassey stretch becomes very popular for it holds not only the Shannon fish but also the big runs of grilse for the Mulcair River. Again, no records are available for the summer fishing but estimates put the rod catch at 1,000 fish and possibly many more.

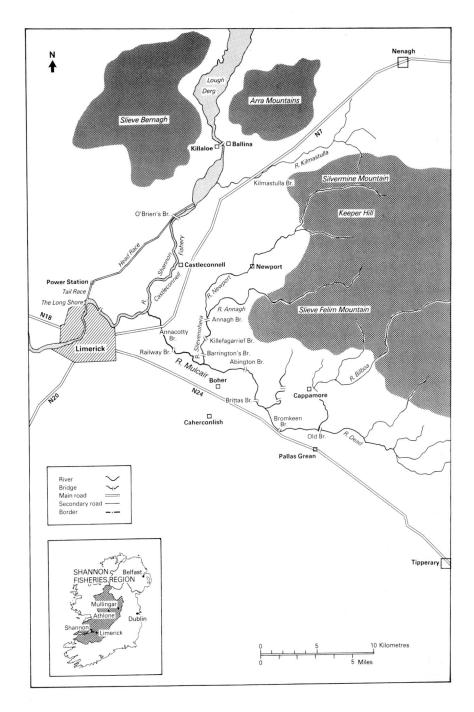

The Limerick fisheries

MULCAIR RIVER   R 65 55

DEAD RIVER   R 81 47

BILBOA RIVER   R 80 51

Permits

Annual, weekly or day permits are available from:

> The Electricity Supply Board Shop
> Bishop's Quay
> Limerick
> *Telephone* 061 45599

The Mulcair is a big spate river with lots of character, some lively streams and plenty of good holding water in the form of long, deep flats. It rises north of Tipperary town and flows north west to join the Shannon downstream of Annacotty. Together with its tributaries, it drains an extensive catchment.

It is regarded primarily as a grilse river but it also gets a small run of spring fish and provides fair brown trout fishing downstream of Annacotty Bridge.

The angling season runs from 1 March to 30 September. It holds a few spring salmon by mid March and the best of the spring fishing is from mid-April onwards. The run is small. It is as a grilse fishery that the river excels. They begin arriving in big numbers in the last week of May and the first 2 weeks of June can be excellent. With every rise in water, new fish move into the river right to the end of the season. The annual rod catch for the river and its tributary, the Newport River, in recent years is estimated to be between 2,000 and 3,000 fish.

Access to the river is at recognized entrances to the left bank and at the bridges. There is a selection from Annacotty Weir up to the railway bridge that is badly overgrown and unfishable except for a bit of fishing at Ballyclough. The other unfishable stretch is from Boher to Abington Bridge. Otherwise, in high water, the river can be fished right up to Cappamore, giving at least 17 miles of fishing.

All fishing methods are allowed. Baits favoured by local anglers include the Orkla and a copper and silver spoon. Favourite fly patterns include Hairy Mary, Black Goldfinch, Garry Dog and 2 local patterns, the Michaelangelo and Silver Shrimp.

In low water, the Long Field and the Haunt hold a lot of fish. In good water you can expect to meet a fish anywhere, but many favour Walsh's Streams and Scart.

A statutory regulation prohibits fishing immediately above and below Annacotty Weir after 1 May and below Ballyclough Weir at all times.

THE DEAD RIVER   R 80 47

The Dead River is an extension of the Mulcair from Old Bridge up towards Oola. It is overgrown and nearly impossible to fish. It is best to give it a miss.

SLIEVENOHERA RIVER   R 68 54

NEWPORT RIVER   R 70 62

ANNAGH (CLARE) RIVER   R 70 59

These three rivers converge and join the Mulcair on the north bank 2 miles upstream of Ballyclough. The Newport River is an extension of the Slievenohera River and the Annagh is a tributary. This system gets an excellent run of grilse on a flood from late June at the same time as the Mulcair. The fishing can be really good. Fishing is best on a falling spate because the fish become very nervous as a result of poaching in low water. There is a nice pool-stream sequence up to Barrington's Bridge. Barrington's Bridge to Killeenagarriff Bridge is deep and slow flowing, then there are more streams and pools followed by a deep stretch up to Annagh Bridge. In all, it can be fished up to Martin Hearn's bar on the road to Newport and as far as Killoscully in high water. There is about 200 yards of fishing at the bottom of the Clare River. In addition to the flies for the Mulcair, try a Thunder and Lightning.

Beware of hog-weed on all these rivers in summer.

For gillies on the Mulcair River and on all these rivers, contact:

Mr Michael Doherty   Mr Jim Robinson
56, Pineview Gardens   Fishing Tackle Shop
Moyross   Thomond Shopping Centre
Limerick   Limerick
Telephone 061 327770   *Telephone* 061 44900

KILMASTULLA RIVER   R 75 70

Season

Brown trout: 1 March to 30 September.

The Kilmastulla River is 14 miles long. It rises south of Nenagh and empties into the Shannon at Parteen Weir. It is a river that has been drained and is maintained fairly regularly. The banks are very high in places – up to 10 feet – and much of the channel is shallow and featureless. It holds some good trout – 2 lb plus – at Shalee and a moderate stock of trout to 1 lb upstream of Kilmastulla Bridge on the N7 Nenagh–Limerick road.

NENAGH RIVER   R 86 83

Season

Brown trout: 1 March to 30 September.

Permits

Whelan's Tackle Shop
Summerhill
Nenagh
Co. Tipperary

The Nenagh and Ollatrim Rivers are leased by the Ormond Anglers Association from the Electricity Supply Board. The Nenagh River is 28 miles long. It rises in the Silvermine Mountains in Co. Tipperary and flows north west through the town of Nenagh to join Lough Derg at Dromineer. It has two main tributaries, the Ollatrim River (described below), itself no mean trout fishery and the Ballintotty River, which is really a spawning stream. This is a spring-fed system so the rivers maintain quite good flows in periods of low rainfall, except in periods of prolonged drought.

These rivers are primarily brown trout fisheries and hold a few grilse in the autumn. A fish stock survey, sponsored by Shannon Development Ltd, was carried out in 1988 and this confirmed that the rivers hold really excellent stocks of trout. The majority were in the 6 oz – 12 oz range, but trout up to 5 lb were encountered.

The system holds 2 distinct kinds of trout: a very big stock of indigenous river trout and migratory lake trout from Lough Derg. The

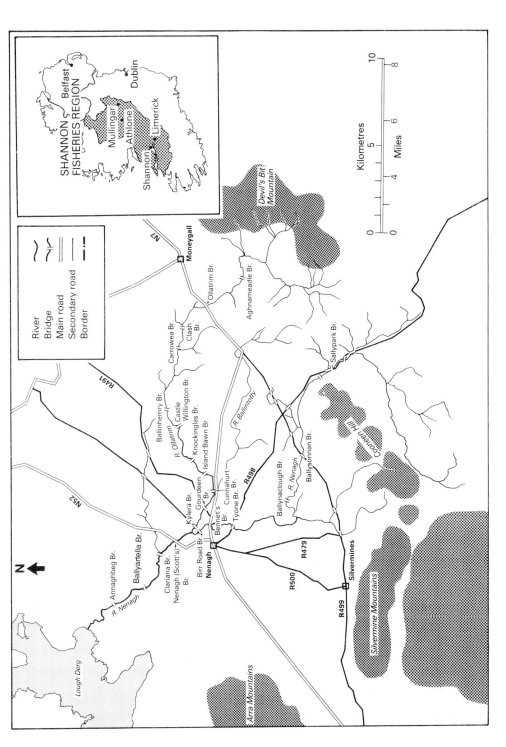

The Nenagh River

latter begin to run the river with the first summer flood in June or July.

Access to the river bank is mostly at the bridges and is very good. Stiles and footbridges have been erected all along the angling water by a Foras Aiseanne Soathair social employment scheme under the sponsorship of the Shannon Regional Fisheries Board.

The river was the subject of an arterial drainage scheme in the past and while the banks are of normal height in the upper reaches, they are very high in the lower parts – up to 15 feet. Wading with body waders is essential for fishing these stretches and even then only the athletic should attempt it. Barbed wire fences are a nuisance in many places, too.

All legitimate fishing methods are allowed, including the despicable practice of fishing for trout with maggots.

The river has hatches of dark olives, iron blues, simulium and various diptera, mayfly, pale wateries, pale evening duns, blue-winged olives, yellow May duns and a prolific sedge hatch in summer evenings. The mayfly hatch can sometimes begin in late April. In July, the big evening hatches of sedges – locally known as 'rails' – give excellent sport at dusk.

Trout Stock Distribution – Nenagh River.

The angling water on the Nenagh River begins approximately opposite Young's bar on the Nenagh – Thurles road. This stretch holds good stocks up to ½ lb.

The 2-mile stretch Ballysonnan Bridge to Ballynaclough Bridge holds good stocks of 10 oz trout. The bank conditions vary – good in places, terribly high in places and badly overgrown in places.

The stretch from Ballynaclough Bridge downstream to Tyone Bridge is 5 miles long – but permission for access to fish downstream on the right bank can be obtained at Bayly Farm. A beautiful stretch, with lovely pools and nice holding water for trout it holds excellent stocks of 8–10 oz of trout with some to 2 lb The fishing here involves a long walk.

Between Tyone Bridge and Bennett's Bridge there is an excellent stock of trout from 8 oz to 2½ lb in the stretch immediately above the railway bridge, but it is slow flowing and the trout are hard to tempt.

Between Bennett's Bridge and the Birr Road Bridge the river is not worth fishing.

From Birr Road Bridge to Scott's Bridge there are excellent stocks of trout from 9 to 11 inches and is an especially good area for the lake trout after the first summer floods.

From Scott's Bridge to Clarianna Bridge trout stocks are no more than poor or moderate. A few salmon lie in the 400 yard stretch above Clarianna bridge.

The stretch between Clarianna Bridge and Ballyartella Bridge is a lovely one with big stocks of 8–14 inch trout. The renowned Violet Banks water is in this stretch. The stretch holds lake trout in summer. Approach the upper section by the left bank and use body waders.

Between Ballyartella Bridge and Annaghbeg Bridge the river consists of fast, streamy water, deep glides, pools and flats. It holds excellent trout stocks from 10 to 15 inches and is one of the best stretches for lake trout. The banks are very high and covered with tall foliage in summer.

From Annaghbeg Bridge to Lough Derg the river is deep and sluggish. It holds virtually no trout and occasional salmon at the bends.

OLLATRIM RIVER   R 90 79

The Ollatrim River joins the Nenagh River downstream of the town of Nenagh. The gravel nature of its channel has enabled it to recover well from the effects of arterial drainage. It offers what can best be described as small stream fishing with a channel that is only 3 yards wide in the upper reaches and 15 yards wide at the confluence. The majority of the trout are in the 8 – 10 inch size range but there are some to 18 inches or 2 $\frac{1}{2}$ lb.

From Carrowea Bridge to Ballinhemry Bridge the river is 3–5 yards wide with lovely water in the middle reaches and plenty of trout to $\frac{3}{4}$ lb. Stay on the left bank.

The stretch from Ballinahemry Bridge to Castlewillington Bridge is about 1 mile long with riffles and small pools and a fair stock of $\frac{1}{2}$ lb trout.

The stretch from Castlewillington Bridge to Knockinglas Bridge offers fair prospects for wet-fly in spring but runs too low in summer. The same holds for the next stretch to Islandbawn Bridge.

At the top of the stretch from Islandbawn Bridge to Cullahurt Bridge there are a few pools which hold fair stocks of 8–10 inch trout. Approach it from Islandbawn Bridge.

Between Cunnahurst Bridge and Gurdeen Bridge the river is about 12 yards wide. There is a good pool above the confluence of the Ballintotty River and from Lisbunny Castle downstream there are nice glides and pools. The trout average $\frac{1}{2}$ lb with some to $\frac{3}{4}$ lb.

From Gurdeen Bridge to Kylera Bridge the Ollatrim holds excellent stocks of $\frac{1}{2}$ lb trout with some to $1\frac{1}{2}$ lb This is attractive water, best fished off the left bank. The railway embankment is high and difficult to climb.

There is excellent accommodation at Ballyartella Farmhouse, close by Ballyartella Bridge and the proprietors, Mr and Mrs. Frank Lewis, can give good advice on the fishing (*telephone* 067 24219).

BALLYFINBOY RIVER   R 89 94

This once lovely prolific little trout river has been badly damaged by an arterial drainage scheme and I fear it will be a long time before it recovers.

LITTLE BROSNA RIVER   M 99 10

CAMCOR RIVER   N 10 04

Season

Salmon and Brown trout: 1 March to 30 September

Permits

Trout (excluding Birr Castle grounds)
Regional Fisheries Board permits available from:

The Fish Farm	Mr Michael Madden
Fanure	Tackle Shop
Roscrea	Main Street
Co. Tipperary	Birr, Co. Offaly
Mr Michael Davis	
Emmett Street	
Birr, Co. Offaly	

Permits

Salmon

The Fisheries Office	The Electricity Supply Board Shop
Electricity Supply Board	Birr
Hydro Group	Co. Offaly
Ardnacrusha	
Nr. Limerick	

Regulations

There is a 9-inch size limit and a 6-trout bag limit. Artificial fly only is permitted from Milltown Bridge to Monastery Bridge, from Brosna Bridge to Shanavogue Bridge and from Purcell's Drain to Riverstown.

The Little Brosna rises near Roscrea and flows north west past the town of Birr to join the Shannon at Meelick. It is a limestone river and holds good stocks of ½ lb and fair-to-good stocks of salmon in summer in the lower reaches.

The grilse arrive in late June or early July, depending on water and a few nice fish arrive with every flood to the end of the season. The salmon fishing is confined to the deep water downstream of the Angler's Rest bar at New Bridge. It is fished mainly by local anglers and worm, shrimp and spinner are the usual fishing methods.

The brown trout range in size from 6 oz to 1¼ lb. In summer, the river gets a run of lake trout, locally known as 'croneen'.

The trout fishing is in 2 sections, from Milltown Bridge to Sharavogue Bridge and from Purcell's Drain – one mile above Riverstown – downstream to Derrinsallow Bridge at Bunrevan House. The river has all the usual fly hatches associated with a limestone river. There are good hatches of iron blues in early May in the vicinity of Sharavogue Bridge and the best mayfly hatches occur at Ballyeighan after mid May. Reed smut, grey flag sedges and blue-winged olives are also important in season.

Weed growth can be a problem from late June.

The Camcor River

The Camcor River is an acid spate stream with a loose gravel bottom. It flows down from the Slieve Bloom Mountains and joins the Little Brosna at Birr.

The fishing on this river depends entirely on runs of 'croneen' from Lough Derg and only begins with a flood after mid August. When conditions are right, there is about 4–5 miles of good fishing upstream of the Red Bridge. Most of the fishing is done with a worm.

The fishing on both rivers inside the grounds of Birr Castle is private and permits are not let.

RIVER BROSNA   N 11 24

Season

Salmon and trout: 1 March to 30 September.

Permits

Salmon

> The Electricity Supply Board Shop
> Athlone, Co. Westmeath

> The Electricity Supply Board Shop
> Tullamore, Co. Offaly.

> The Electricity Supply Board Shop
> Birr, Co. Offaly

Trout

> Mr Jim Griffin
> The Tackle Shop
> Rahan, Co. Offaly
> *Telephone* 0506 55979

> Mr Joe Finlay
> William Street
> Tullamore, Co. Offaly

> Mr Al Conroy
> Stella Press
> Tullamore, Co. Offaly

> Mr J. Rabbitt
> The Supermarket
> Clara, Co. Offaly

> Mr M.F. Kenny
> River Street
> Clara, Co. Offaly

> Nannery's Grocery
> Kilbeggan
> Co. Westmeath

The River Brosna rises in Lough Ennell and flows south west through Kilbeggan, Clare, Ballycumber and Ferbane to join the Shannon at Shannon Harbour. It has a number of important angling tributaries and together they provide extensive opportunities for brown trout fishing and some important salmon fishing stretches.

The river was the subject of an arterial drainage scheme in the late 1960s which has left the banks very high. It also flows through one of the biggest areas of bog and active peat harvesting in the country and consequently there can be a lot of problems from peat silt and sediment.

The grilse run depends on water but the first salmon of the season begin showing at the end of May and the run increases through June. The peak of the run is in the first 2 weeks of July. The river usually runs low in summer and a rise in water in September generally brings out renewed interest in both salmon and the anglers. Probably over 200 salmon are caught annually.

Local knowledge of the best stretches is all important and Jim Griffin of the Tackle Shop in Rahan, Co. Offaly, has a lot of information on hot spots and is very helpful.

Basically, there are four areas to concentrate on: downstream of

Clonony Bridge where there are some nice runs, pools and glides but the banks are high and overgrown; the streams and pools for a mile below Belmont Weir; a short stretch downstream of Ferbane; and at a place called the Rock a mile below Pollagh Bridge.

Some of the runs would suit a fly but worm, float-fished shrimp and spinner are the usual methods. A brass spoon is very good, as is a copper and silver spoon and a No. 3 red-spotted Mepps.

The River Brosna and its tributaries offers quite good wet and dry-fly fishing for trout in many areas. It is a limestone system and the trout grow big – to 3 lb plus – and in addition it gets a large run of 'croneen' from the Shannon in late July and August on rising water.

Distribution of Trout Stocks

The following is a breakdown of the kind of trout stocks to expect on the Brosna at present, starting at the bottom of the river and working upstream.

The river is wide and swift at Clonony and the best trout fishing is immediately above and below the bridge.

From Clonony to Ferbane the access is bad, banks difficult to negotiate and trout stocks poor. Give it a miss.

From Ferbane up to Pollagh is not very attractive, with a lot of spoil and bog, but the banks are reasonably good and so too is the fishing for $3/4$ lb trout over a 6-mile stretch. Weed is a problem in summer.

From Ballycumber up to Clara the access is fair-to-good, the banks are not great, but the stocks are good and $3/4$ lb trout are fairly plentiful.

Between Clara and Lismoyny Bridge the river has been drained recently. It has a lot of weed and should be given a miss.

From Lismoyny Bridge to Kilbeggan is about 4 miles by river. There are excellent stocks of $3/4$ lb trout in the 2-mile stretch downstream of Kilbeggan and even some to $1 1/2$ lb.

The trout average 6–8 oz between Split Hill and Ballynagore Bridge between Ballynagore Bridge and Lough Ennell there are few trout except in high water in March.

It is always possible to find a place to fish the Brosna, but it has to be said that the best of the fishing is in spring and early summer before the weed comes up in June.

KILCORMAC SILVER RIVER   N 14 20

Season and Permits

As for the River Brosna, above.

The Kilcormac Silver River is a tributary of the Brosna. It rises in the Slieve Bloom Mountains and flows north for 24 miles through Kilcormac in Co. Offaly to join the main river just east of Ferbane.

It flows almost entirely through bog and this presents the angler with many problems for the angler regarding access, difficult banks and dangerous wading conditions. For all that, it is a limestone river and holds fair stocks of brown trout.

The river can be divided in four sections for angling purposes. Starting at the bottom, there are fair stocks of $\frac{1}{2}$ lb trout, including some nice trout to $1\frac{1}{4}$ lb from Coole Castle upstream to Lumcloon Bridge. Access is at Lumcloon power station but the banks are difficult and the water is discoloured by peat sediment. There are some nice streamy sections here where it is possible to wade.

From Lumcloon Bridge up to Millbrook Bridge the stocks are much as in the last section, but the banks are high. Do not attempt to wade.

From Millbrook Bridge upstream to Broughal Bridge is nearly 3 miles. There is a good stock of trout here averaging $\frac{1}{2}$ lb. Again, the bottom is soft, so do not wade. Weed becomes a problem here from June. Sedges are important and there is a mayfly hatch in the Broughal area.

Finally, there is some fast water between the village of Kilcormac and Broughal Bridge. It holds a good stock of trout, especially at the Broughal end. Wading is possible. There are some who claim that this stretch is overfished.

CLODIAGH RIVER   N 25 25

Season and Permits

As for River Brosna, above.

The Clodiagh River is 25 miles long. It rises in the Slieve Bloom Mountains and flows north through Clonaslee and Rahan to the River Brosna. It is another drained river with high, steep banks in places.

The Clodiagh holds some good trout stocks and gets a good run of salmon.

The fishing can be divided in four sections.

The stretch from the confluence with the Brosna up to Rahan is nearly 5 miles long. The river is deep (no wading) and 20 feet wide and the banks are high. This stretch holds a very good stock of $\frac{3}{4}$ lb trout with many to 2 lb. This stretch is renowned for holding a good head of croneen which run up from the Shannon after a mid-summer flood.

The river gets a great run of salmon from July if the water is high enough to take them up. The best of the salmon fishing is in this stretch up as far as Rahan.

From Rahan to the junction of the Tullamore River the Clodiagh gives some of the best brown trout fishing in the whole of the River Brosna catchment. The banks are high, the water is fast and for the most part, you cannot wade. The trout average 1 lb. The best access is along the left bank.

The short stretch from the Tullamore River confluence up to the aquaduct is overgrown but has fair stocks.

The rest of the river is mainly spawning water, except for a short stretch above and below Charleville Bridge on the N52.

TULLAMORE RIVER   N 28 28

The lower section of this river above the confluence holds good trout but it is not possible to recommend it because of a chronic pollution problem.

TULLAMORE SILVER RIVER   N 28 28

Season and Permits

As for River Brosna, above.

The Tullamore Silver River flows west to join the Clodiagh River downstream of Rahan. It holds plentiful stocks of trout averaging 6 oz with some up to 1 lb. It can be fished, early in the season, from its confluence with the Clodiagh up as far as Aharney Bridge. It is a limestone stream with a very good mayfly hatch. Unfortunately, weed takes over at the end of May and brings the fishing to an end. Access is fairly good along the banks.

GAGEBOROUGH RIVER   N 24 35

Season and Permits

As for River Brosna, above.

The Gageborough River is a small stream which flows south from Horseleap and joins the River Brosna a mile downstream of Clara in Co. Offaly. It can be fished for about 3 miles up from the confluence and the trout stocks and conditions are on a par with the Tullamore Silver River, above.

RIVER INNY   N 17 56

Season

Salmon and Trout: 1 March to 30 September.

Permits

Sammy Smith	David O'Malley
Tackle Shop	Tackle Shop
Castle Street	Dominic Street
Mullingar, Co. Westmeath	Mullingar, Co. Westmeath

The Inny is over 55 miles long and drains a catchment of 486 square miles. It rises near Oldcastle in Co. Meath and drains several midland lakes. It then flows west, through Ballymahon in south Longford, into Lough Ree. An arterial drainage scheme in the 1960s left the banks very high.

At present it is best described as a mixed fishery. It has a big head of coarse fish and presently holds large stocks of roach. Some areas hold pike.

A small number of salmon are taken around Ballymahon every season and there are still a few pockets of trout left.

There is a small stock of trout above and below Ballynacarrow Bridge on the R393 Ballynacarrigy–Ardagh road. The banks are good here and I have been told it fishes well in low water.

The next stretch worth fishing is the streamy water extending about 1 mile above and below Abbeyshrule Bridge. This stretch holds a fair stock of $^3/_4$ lb trout. The banks are very high. Keep to the left bank.

Downstream of Abbeyshrule there is 1 mile of trout fishing above Clynan (Tenalick) Bridge and about 2 miles below it at Taghshinny. Stay on the right bank above the bridge and try to find a patch under the bushes on the left bank below the bridge.

There are reported to be some large trout below Newcastle Bridge and a fair stock of $^3/_4$ lb trout from Newcastle Bridge downstream through Ballymahon to the confluence of the Tang River. The most popular flies on the river are Greenwell's Glory, Iron Blue Dun, Ginger Quill and a small brown sedge – indicative that olives and sedges are the most common fly hatches. The mayfly hatch has disappeared.

TANG RIVER   N 15 54

Season and Permits

As for River Inny, above.

The Tang River joins the Inny from the south between Ballymahon and Lough Ree.   Like the main river, a drainage scheme has left high banks which are wild and uncared for and well nigh impassable.   The Tang holds trout up as far as Ballymore but after June it runs low and weeds up.

RATH RIVER   N20 56

Season and Permits

As for River Inny, above.

The Rath River joins the Inny just over 2 miles upstream of Ballymahon. It has a stock of trout up to about 8 inches and a very occasional trout to $3/4$ lb.   Most of these fish are concentrated in the $1\frac{1}{2}$ mile stretch from the confluence upstream to the first bridge at Newcastle.   It is best fished in high water in March and April because thereafter it runs very low.   It is very overgrown and difficult to fish.   Stay on the right bank.

CAMLIN RIVER

Trout fishing on Longford's Camlin River is now but a memory.

THE YELLOW RIVER

Season

1 March to 30 September.

Permit

Free.

The Yellow River enters the northern end of Lough Allen from the east. It is a mountain river and holds a small stock of resident brown trout in the deep pools on the lower reaches.

OWENNAYLE RIVER

Season

Trout: 1 March to 30 September.

Permit

Free.

The Owennayle is a mountain river which enters Lough Allen from the north. It is reputed to hold some of the best stocks of trout in the Lough Allen catchment. There are plenty to $\frac{1}{2}$ lb and occasional bigger trout in the pools.

The banks are partly clear and partly overgrown and the pools are always likely to give up a trout or two, especially after a spate.

ARIGNA RIVER   G 90 16

Season

Trout: 1 March to 30 September.

Permit

Free.

The Arigna River drains a steep valley in a mountain range of the same name into Lough Allen. It is reputed to hold good stocks of small trout in the pools in the lower reaches, downstream of the Iron Bridge. It is occasionally stocked by the Lough Allen Conservation Association. The banks are mainly clear and easy to fish.

FEORISH RIVER

Season

Trout: 1 March to 30 September.

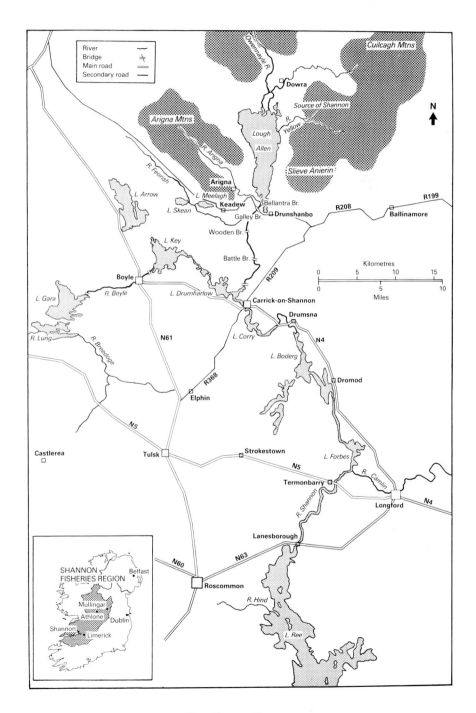

The Upper Shannon

Permit

Free.

This small limestone river comes down from Lough Na Bo past Geevagh and Ballyfarnan and joins the Shannon upstream of the Wooden bridge. It is a fair sized stream and the pools are well worth fishing for trout. Stocks are fair to good, with trout to 1 lb. It has good hatches of olives, sedges and mayfly.

BOYLE RIVER   G 80 02

Season

Trout: 1 March to 30 September.

Permit

Free.

The Boyle River rises in Lough Gara and the stretch of interest to trout anglers is between Lough Gara and Lough Key, from a point 2 miles above the town of Boyle and 1½ miles below it.

The trout average ½ lb, with fish to 2 lb and there are plenty of small fish. Access is reasonably good off the roads to the right bank and the best fishing is said to be upstream of Boyle. This is a limestone river, with some nice streamy water. The fly hatches are prolific. It has a mayfly hatch and sedges are very important.

HIND RiVER   M 88 61

Season

Trout: 1 March to 30 September.

The Hind River flows through the town of Roscommon into Lough Ree. It was a marvellous brown trout fishery and if it ever recovers from its present pollution problems it will be worth a visit. It is leased from the ESB by Roscommon Rod and Gun Club. Inquiries to Mr Gabriel Finn, Main Street, Roscommon, or Mr Barney Lunt, *Telephone* 0903-62735

LUNG RIVER   M 65 95

BREEDOGE RIVER   M 74 95

Both of these rivers have been drained recently and cannot be recommended.

RIVER SUCK   M 60 80

Season

Salmon and Trout: 1 March to 30 September.

Permits

Salmon

> The Electricity Supply Board Office
> Market Square
> Ballinasloe
> Co. Galway
> *Telephone* 095 42340

Trout

> Mr Padraig Campbell
> Lough O'Flyn Bar
> Ballinlough
> Co. Roscommon
>
> Mr John Hunt
> Patrick Street
> Castlereagh, Co. Roscommon

> Mr Patrick Keogh
> The Square
> Ballinasloe, Co.Galway

The River Suck is an extensive tributary system of the Shannon and drains large areas of Counties Galway and Roscommon. Upstream of Ballymoe it is mainly fast-flowing, streamy water and best suited to trout production. Downstream of Ballymoe, to the confluence, it is mostly deep and slow and more suited to coarse fishing, except for a few streamy sections at the fords. Most of the tributaries hold trout and some have marvellous potential as trout rivers.

Practically all of the Suck catchment is on limestone and fly hatches are prolific, including mayfly in certain areas.

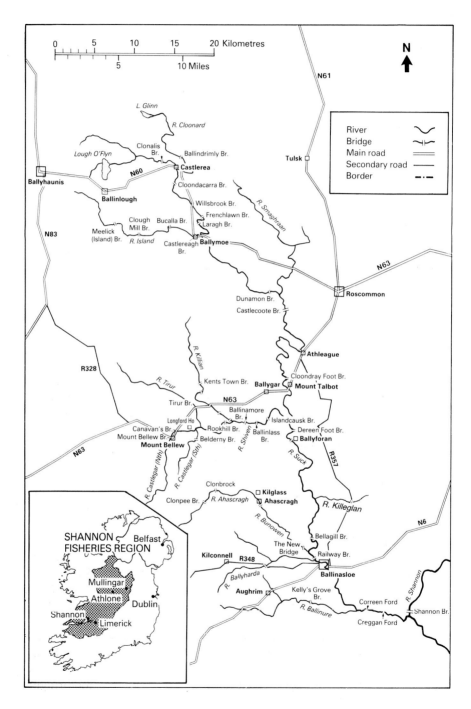

River Suck system

Salmon

The river gets a small run of spring salmon from April and a big run of grilse and summer fish from mid-June. Up to 1990 the salmon fishing took place at 5 distinct locations along the river – Creggan Ford, Coreen Ford, Pollock's Ford, Reilly's Ford and the Cuts at the Bunowen river confluence. At the time of writing (December 1990) two of the fords have been dredged and there are plans to dredge the remaining two to allow river cruisers upstream to Ballinasloe. To compensate for the loss of the angling at the fords, the Office of Public Works proposes to construct a new salmon fishery 600 metres long at Pollboy Mill, downstream of Ballinasloe.

It will be interesting to see how successful this venture is. Coreen Ford alone used yield approximately 70 salmon per season. Worm, shrimp and copper and silver spoons were the most common baits used. For fly fishing, Blue Charm and Dunkeld were said to work best.

Up to date information on the fishing is always available from the local fishery inspector, Mr Brian Connaughton, Harbour Road, Ballinasloe, Co. Galway, (*telephone* 0905 42367).

Brown trout

There is about seven miles of trout fishing in spring and early summer from the bridge on the Castlerea–Kilkelly road (near Clonalis House) downstream past Castlerea, Cloondacarra Bridge, Willsbrook Bridge, Frenchlawn Bridge and on to a point $\frac{1}{2}$ mile downstream of Laragh Bridge. The River here is 7–9 yards wide, was drained, but also successfully rehabilitated and is mostly fast-flowing. The banks are high and stiles and footbridges are provided by the Shannon Fisheries Board.

The trout range from $\frac{1}{2}$ lb to $\frac{3}{4}$ lb and the better fish are downstream of Frenchlawn Bridge. This is an early season fishery and weeds up after May. It is fairly heavily fished by local anglers, using all methods. There is a good mayfly hatch.

Information on the fishing is available from Mr John Ryan, Fisheries Inspector, Ballinlough, Co. Roscommon, (*telephone* 0907 40063/40103).

The next piece of trout fishing downstream is at Dunamon Bridge. Then there is a mile of fishing at Castlecoote. Most of it is upstream of the bridge and access is on the left bank.

There is another mile of trout water at Cloondray footbridge. This footbridge is about $1\frac{1}{2}$ miles upstream of Mount Talbot with access off the Mount Talbot–Athleague road.

At Ballyforan there is a stretch of trout water at Deereen footbridge upstream of the village.

In the Ballinasloe area there is trout fishing at Bellagill Bridge and the

Railway Bridge above the town and at Pollboy downstream.

CLOONARD RIVER   M 67 82

Season and Permits (trout)

As for the River Suck, above.

This fast-flowing rich little river comes down from Lough Glinn and joins the River Suck at Castlerea. It is a river for the active fisherman, for it involves a lot of walking and there are no stiles or footbridges. Stay on the left bank. It holds a lot of trout up to ½ lb. It fishes best in March, April and in a wet September. It runs very low in summer. Concentrate on it from Clonree downstream to Ballindrimly Bridge and downstream to the confluence.

THE ISLAND RIVER   M 68 72

Season and Permits

As for the River Suck, above.

The Island River rises south of Ballinlough in Co. Roscommon and flows east to the River Suck at Ballymoe. It is a rich limestone river, slow flowing in many parts but with a few lively sections. It weeds up badly in summer. The peak season is from March to May. It holds a huge stock of trout to ½ lb, a fair stock to 1½ lb and the deep pools hold trout to 3 lb These are beautiful deep trout. It can be fished all the way from Island Bridge, past the mill of Clough and on to Buchalla. Try a wet-fly in spring down to the Mill of Clough. There are some nice pools for dry fly from the Mill of Clough to Buchalla Bridge. There is another good stretch at Ballymoe from a point one mile upstream of Castlereagh Bridge down to the confluence.

There are no stiles or footbridges on this river. The banks are mostly clear. It has all the usual fly hatches, including mayfly.

Keep mostly to the right bank. Up to date information on the fishing can be had from Mr John Ryan, Fishery Inspector, Ballinlough, Co. Roscommon, (*telephone* 0907 40063/40103).

SMAGHRAAN RIVER   M 80 65

Season and Permits

As for River Suck, above.

The Smaghraan River rises 6 miles west of Roscommon town and joins the River Suck from the north a mile downstream of Dunamon Castle. It was famous for its big fat trout until drained and now holds a small stock of trout to 1½ lb in the last mile between the Railway bridge and the river Suck confluence. Access to the right bank is by a small lane a short distance north of Dunamon Bridge.

RIVER SHIVEN   M 78 48

KILLIAN RIVER   M 72 50

TIRUR RIVER   M 70 49

CASTLEGAR RIVER (NORTH)   M 70 48

CASTLEGAR RIVER (SOUTH)   M 70 47

Season

Trout: 1 March to 30 September.

Permits

> Mr Patrick Keogh
> The Square
> Ballinasloe, Co. Galway

The River Shiven receives a number of tributaries and drains into the River Suck from the west between Ballygar, Co. Galway, and Ballyforan in Co. Roscommon. It flows over limestone, is very rich in fly life and at one time was regarded as one of the leading trout fisheries in the country. It has the potential to achieve that status again. No development work has taken place for nearly twenty years, stiles and footbridges are neglected and this makes negotiating the banks difficult. Some stretches have a serious peat silt problem. It has also been drained and runs low in summer. The best of the fishing is early in the season – up to mid-June.

The trout average $\frac{3}{4}$ lb and the river holds fish up to 4 lb.

It is only a short river but there are some especially productive areas. These are – starting at the confluence with the Suck and working upstream – a half-mile stretch at Nolan's Ford at Muckanagh Timber Bridge, a half-mile stretch either side of Islandcausk Bridge, a half-mile either side of Ballinlass Bridge, a quarter mile below and a mile above Ballinamore Bridge, a half-mile at Rookhill Bridge and a half-mile down from the Tirur confluence.

The best of the mayfly hatch is from Rookhill downstream and there is an excellent hatch of olives at the Tirur River confluence.

Access is very difficult to the Castlegar Rivers, North and South, with no stiles or footbridges. The best of the fishing is from early April to mid-May. The trout average $\frac{3}{4}$ lb with fish to $3\frac{1}{2}$ lb. The best fishing stretches are downstream of Mount Bellew Bridge, a 1 mile stretch below Canavan's Bridge and from Longford House down to the Tirur River confluence.

The best of the fishing water on the Castlegar River (South) is from Beldermy Bridge (on the Ballyforan–Mount Bellew Bridge road) downstream to the confluence.

The Tirur River is another early season trout stream and the best stocks are from a point $\frac{1}{2}$ mile upstream of Tirur Bridge down to the confluence. Access is difficult.

The Killian River is reported to still have an excellent mayfly hatch. Access is difficult. The trout average $\frac{1}{2} - \frac{3}{4}$ lb and it can be fished at the various bridges downstream from Kentstown Bridge.

KILLEGLAN RIVER   M 86 39

Season and Permits

As for the River Shiven, above.

The Killeglan stream joins the River Suck from the east 3 miles north of Ballinasloe. It is a spring-fed river with gin clear water over limestone and is very rich in insect life. It holds moderate stocks of $\frac{1}{2}$ lb fish with occasional trout to $1\frac{1}{2}$ lb and fishes best in the spring of the year. The upper limit of the fishing is at Finneron's Bar on the R357 Ballinasloe–Thomas Street road and access is at the bridges downstream.

BUNOWEN RIVER (AHASCRAGH RIVER)   M 80 36

Season and Permits

As for River Shiven, above.

The Bunowen River flows through Clonbrock and Ahascragh in east Galway and joins the River Suck 2 miles north of Ballinasloe. It is a medium-sized river, flows over limestone and has the potential to be one of the finest trout rivers in the country. It flows mainly through pastureland, there is no silt problem and it has some stiles and footbridges. The trout average ³/₄ lb and the lower reaches can hold trout to 5 lb. The best stretches are from a point ¹/₂ mile upstream of Clonpee Bridge downstream for nearly 3 miles past Clonbrock House (in ruins); a 1-mile stretch downstream of Ahascragh Bridge; and a 2-mile stretch from Sonnagh down past Killure Castle.

The town of Ballinasloe has a big angling population and the river is heavily fished. The Inland Fisheries Trust has a fly-only rule upstream of Ahascragh Bridge. There are excellent hatches of fly and a good mayfly hatch downstream of Sonnagh.

BALLYHARDA RIVER   M 82 32

This little river joins the River Suck from the west a short distance upstream of Ballinasloe. It flows east from Kilconnell and has trout from ¹/₂ to 3 lb in the last 4 miles. Access is at the bridges.

BALLINURE RIVER   M 86 26

The Ballinure River drains the Bloody Hollow and the site of the Battle of Aughrim east into the River Suck downstream of Correen Ford. It is a limestone river holding moderate stocks of ³/₄ – 1 lb trout. There are no stiles or footbridges. The best fishing areas are for 2 miles upstream of Kelly's Grove Bridge and downstream as far as Whyte's sandpit at Cloonascragh. Access is at the bridges.

KILCROW RIVER (KILLIMOR RIVER)   M 79 10

Season

Trout: 15 February to 30 September.

Permission

Free.

The Killimor River, as it is best known, flows south from Kiltormer, through Killimor into the top of Lough Derg. It is a medium sized fast-flowing limestone river in spring, winding through rich pastureland, and can provide exciting trout fishing early in the season. It becomes difficult to fish in summer when the weed comes up. It holds a good stock of trout, averaging about 1 lb. The fishing water is in a stretch from Oxford Bridge downstream for 10 miles approximately to Ballyshrule Bridge on the R352 Portumna–Gort road. Access is at the bridges and off the side roads. Local anglers divide the season into three sections: the early season wet-fly fishing up to the end of March; the mayfly season, and dry-fly fishing on summer evenings.

Up to date information on the fishing is available from Mr Brian Connaughton, Harbour Road, Ballinasloe, Co. Galway, (*telephone* 0905 42367, for the Killimor River and the Lisduff, Woodford and Cappagh rivers, below.

LISDUFF RIVER   M 78 13

The Lisduff River joins the Killimor River from the west. It can provide good early season wet-fly fishing from Gortymadden downstream.

CAPPAGH RIVER   M 79 04

Season and Permission

As for the Kilcrow river, above.

The Cappagh River rises near Loughrea and flows south-east into the Killimor River less than a mile up from Lough Derg. It is a nice fast-flowing river with some nice pools and flats, good banks and a limestone base. The trout average 1 lb. There is an excellent mayfly hatch on the lower reaches. The best fishing is between Duniry Bridge and Cappagh Bridge and the season falls into much the same periods as for the Killimor River, above.

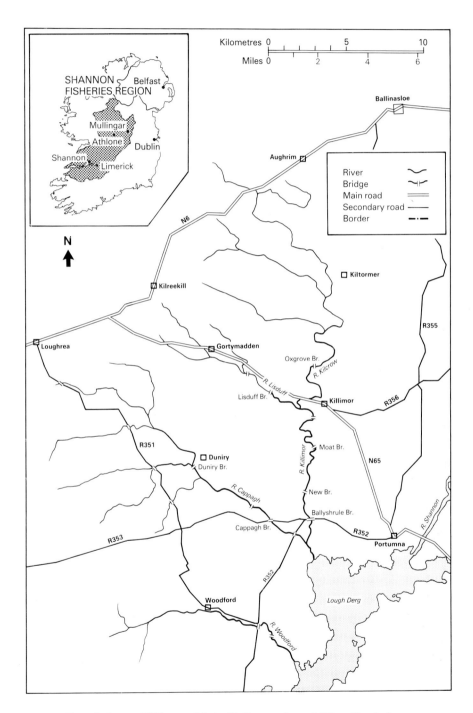

East Galway: Killimor, Lisduff, Cappagh and Woodford rivers

WOODFORD RIVER   M 77 98

Season and Permission

As for the Killimor River, above.

The Woodford River holds a moderate stock of trout. It is quite overgrown and difficult to fish with anything except a worm through the bushes.

CROSS RIVER   M 99 42

Season

Trout: 1 March to 30 September.

Permission

Free

This lovely little limestone stream has trout ranging from ½ lb to ¾ lb. It is on the Roscommon side of Athlone and enters the Shannon downstream of the town. The best of the fishing is from a point ½ a mile upstream of the R362 Athlone – Tuam road down to the bridge on the N6 Athlone–Ballinasloe road. Up to date information on the fishing can be had from Mr Niall O'Shea, The Mill Bar, Tuam Road, Athlone, Co. Roscommon, (*telephone* 0902 92927).

BREENSFORD RIVER   N 10 43

Season

Trout: 1 March to 30 September.

Permission

Free.

The Breensford (Ballykeeran) River flows into Killinure Lough, just north of Athlone. The trout average ¾ lb and this is an early-season fishery only. It is stocked by the Ballykeeran and Killeenmore Anglers' Association. For up-to-date information, contact Mr Patrick Fallon, Ballymahon, Co. Longford (*telephone* 0902 32306).

RIVER MAIGUE   R 52 41

Season

Salmon: 1 February to 30 September.
Brown trout: 15 February to 30 September.

Permits

See below.

The River Maigue rises south of Bruree and flows north through Croom and Adare in Co. Limerick into the Shannon estuary. This is a rich limestone river and together with its tributaries, the Camoge, the Morning Star and the Loobagh, it drains the lush pastures of Limerick's Golden Vale.

Writing in 1913, Grimble said of the Maigue: 'It is worthy of mention that the Maigue throughout its upper waters can hardly be surpassed as a trout river in regard to the size and quality of its fish'. It was regarded as one of Ireland's premier trout rivers up to the starting of an arterial drainage scheme in the 1970s. The drainage works ravaged and canalized the channels, destroying their natural character and it now looks like any other drained river with very high banks in some places.

A certain amount of rehabilitation work has been carried out by the Shannon Regional Fisheries Board and trout stocks have made a comeback in certain areas. Some sections hold a nice stock of trout averaging ¾ lb – 1 lb and there are trout there to 2 and even 3 lb.

The Maigue has all the fly hatches associated with a limestone river, including mayfly. The peak of the trout fishing season is in May and up to mid-June. For early season wet-fly fishing, an Orange and Grouse, Greenwell's Glory and Silver Spider are recommended.

The fishing rights are either privately owned or are controlled by angling clubs. Understandably, with their fishing now curtailed, some do not let day tickets. There is limited fishing available and inquiries should be made to:

Mr Edmond Costello
Maigue Anglers' Association
Riverfarm,
Ballycarney
Clarina
Patrickswell, Co. Limerick
Telephone 061 355116

Mrs. Eileen McDonagh
Cooleen House
Bruree
Co. Limerick
Telephone 063 90584

The Recreation Manager
Adare Manor Hotel
Adare, Co. Limerick
Telephone 061 86566

CAMOGUE RIVER   R 55 41

Permission

Inquiries to Mr Dan Quain, Secretary, Camogue Angling Club, 11 Coshma Avenue, Croom, Co.Limerick (*telephone* 061 43672).

The Camogue flows west and joins the Maigue upstream of Croom. Camogue Angling Club controls about eight miles of the river from the confluence at Cloghanduff upstream to the Iron Bridge, a short distance downstream of Glenogra Bridge. This is an exceptionally rich river and the trout grow remarkably fast. The average weight is probably close to $1\frac{1}{2}$ lb A certain amount of rehabilitation work has been carried out since the drainage. The banks have been replanted and small weirs constructed. Nevertheless, it still bears the scars of the drainage scheme.

The river is strictly fly fishing only. There is a 10 inch size rule and a six trout bag limit. The Camogue can be a difficult river to fish even when conditions seem right. The big trout are a terrific attraction and evening fishing in summer to the sedge and blue-winged olive can be very good.

The peak of the season is from mid-April to mid-June. The fly hatches are prolific. The mayfly is making a comeback and the alder is very important in May.

Access is at the bridges: Cloghanduff Bridge, Monaster Bridge, Grey's Bridge near Meanus, the Iron Bridge and Glenogra Bridge.

MORNINGSTAR RIVER   R 55 33

The Morningstar suffered badly as a result of the drainage and trout stocks are poor. Very few anglers bother to fish it any more.

RIVER LOOBAGH   R 55 27

Permission

Inquiries to: Mr Raymond Breen, Kilmallock and District Anglers' Association, Riverfield, Kilmallock, Co. Limerick, (*telephone* 063 98437).

The River Loobagh flows west from Kilmallock to join the Maigue. It has suffered badly as a result of drainage and all the good fishing in the Tankardstown area is gone. There is a bit of fishing from the confluence up to Garrvoge Bridge and upstream of Kilmallock in springtime. The trout are small, averaging ½ lb with some to ¾ lb and 1 lb.

CROAGH RIVER   R 42 43

The Croagh River joins the Maigue from the west downstream of Adare. As you cross Drehidnaman Bridge on the N21 road between Adare and Rathkeale, remember that here was a little river that could once upon a time produce a dozen trout for a father and son in an afternoon. That is the story the son gave me and I have no reason to disbelieve it.

RIVER DEEL   R 37 40

Season

Brown trout: 15 February to 30 September.

Permission

Most of the most of the fishing is controlled by the Deel Anglers Association with clubs in Newcastle West, Rathkeale and Askeaton. Newcastle West Angling Club has the fishing from Belville Bridge downstream to Reens Pike and Rathkeale Angling Club takes it from there down to Newbridge.

For permission to fish the Newcastle West water, contact:

Mr Matt Scanlan	Mr Mike Sheehy
Tackle Shop	Bridge Street
Maiden Street	Newcastle West, Co. Limerick
Newcastle West, Co. Limerick	*Telephone* 069 62620/61291

The River Deel rises near Drumina in north Cork and flows north through Co. Limerick to the tide at Askeaton on the Shannon estuary. The river is 40 miles long and its innumerable tributaries drain the hills of west Limerick around newcastle West. In 1913 Grimble wrote of a weir at Askeaton that impeded the run of salmon and the situation remains virtually the same today. Hence we are dealing with a brown trout river only, and one with a lot of potential. Unfortunately, it too has been drained and we are left with very high banks and problems associated with drainage.

The river holds a fair stock of brown trout. It is a limestone river, so growth rate is good, and the average size is around 1 lb, while trout to 5 lb are taken every season. In addition to the wild fish, the local clubs stock fry and some adult trout.

Before drainage, the local anglers' association was very proud of the river and fly fishing was very much the rule. Even now there are fly only stretches. One is from Deel Bridge downstream to the Black Bridge at Newcastle West.

The peak of the season is considered to be from mid-May to mid-June with good but difficult evening fishing to the blue-winged olive through the summer. Useful daytime flies are the Light Olive, Gold Ribbed Hare's Ear, Tup's Indispensable and Red, Orange and Ginger Quills. For night fishing the locals use a Black and Silver Spider, Black Pennell, Silver Sedge, Brown Sedge, Greenwell's Glory and Orange and Grouse.

The Newcastle West Club has 12 miles of river from Belville Bridge downstream to the Slawnaun Bridge at Reens Pike. There is some good fishing at Belville early in the season but the best of the fishing is considered to be from the confluence of the Bunoke River downstream to Castlemahon and from Deel Bridge all the way to Reens Pike. From Reens Pike, past Courtmatrix the river is deep and sluggish as far as Rathkeale, but for those who know the river there is some nice fishing below Rathkeale at the Castle, the Glen, Kilcool Bridge and Newbridge. It is a hard river to fish after May, unless you know exactly where to go.

Access is at the bridges. The road runs conveniently close to the river in the Newcastle West area and the clubs are on good terms with the local farmers.

RIVER FEALE   Q 99 33

Season

Salmon and Sea-trout: 1 March to 15 September.

In recent years, an extension of the angling season has been granted to 30 September, by ministerial order.

The River Feale and its tributaries constitute the most important salmon and sea-trout river in those parts of north Kerry and west Limerick lying south of the Shannon estuary. The Feale rises in the mountains of north Cork, near Rock Chapel, flows for 46 miles through the towns of Abbeyfeale and Listowel and enters the sea south of Ballybunnion. For the last 6 miles of its course it is known as the Cashen River. It drains a catchment of approximately 450 square miles. Even

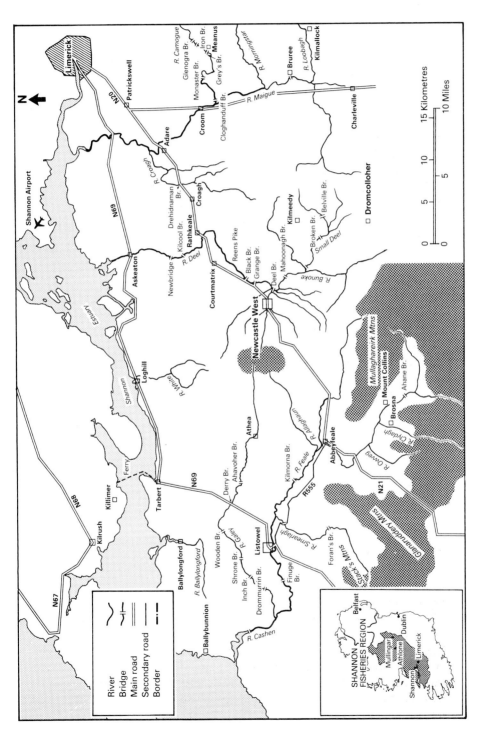

North Kerry and the Golden Vale

though it drains such a large area, it is a typical fast-flowing spate river, subject to huge floods. The lower section is dominated by large, deep fish-holding pools and an important feature of the upper river and its tributaries is the frequency with which deep holding pools occur. It is presumably this latter feature that makes it such a good fishery so far upstream. At the bottom, it is tidal almost to Finuge Bridge and rod-and-line fishing ends about 2 miles below this bridge. There is an active draft-net fishery, with approximately 56 licences operating in the Cashen River. The netting season extends from 14 March to 25 July and is sometimes extended into August by ministerial order. The rod fishing improves dramatically after the nets go off.

The custom of removing gravel from the river bed for road making still persists in the catchment and this can cause problems for anglers.

In times of low flow the water runs clear but takes on a dark, peat stained appearance in a spate.

This is a big river and wading is necessary at times. Body waders would be a great help and a wading staff is essential.

Most of the fishing is controlled by 5 angling clubs, some is let to rods yearly by private owners and there are a few short stretches that are regarded as free fishing.

The Feale gets equally good runs of salmon and sea-trout. In a good season – with frequent spates to bring the fish up and high winds to hamper the netting – it is estimated to produce at least 1,500 salmon and grilse and well over 2,000 sea-trout to rod and line. In a season with low rainfall levels the catch would be much reduced.

The best of the salmon fishing is from the tide up to Abbeyfeale. The sea-trout tend to run quickly through the middle reaches and the best fishing is considered to be either below Listowel or above Abbeyfeale in the Brosna-Mountcollins Club water.

There are fish in the river from opening day on 1 March and the best of the spring fishing is from opening day up to mid-April, depending on water levels.

Small grilse begin showing in the river about mid-June and there is always a dramatic improvement after the draft nets go off in mid-July with very good fishing for bigger fish from mid-August in suitable weather conditions. The spring fish average about 9 lb and the grilse 6 lb.

All legitimate fishing methods are allowed, with spinning, worm and fly being most popular for salmon. The Feale is the home of the Lane minnow spinning bait and the most popular colours are brown and gold, grey and gold, and blue and silver. They are available in all local tackle shops and the most useful sizes are 3 inches for high water and 2½ and 2 inches for medium to low water. Toby spoons are useful as well. The popular salmon flies are Garry Dog, Black Goldfinch, Fiery Brown,

Thunder and Lightning, Hairy Mary, Blue Charm, Curry's Red Shrimp, Wilkinson (for a bright day) and a local dressing known as The Halpin, which is said to be an excellent fly on the river late in the season. The dressing of The Halpin is:

Hook	Size 6 or 8
Tag	Fine oval silver
Tail	Golden Pheasant Crest
Butt	Red wool
Rib	Oval silver
Body	Black floss silk
Body Hackle	Dyed red cock
Hackle	Pale blue dun
Wing	Grey squirrel tail with a topping over
Head	Red varnish

Sea-trout

Sea-trout enter the system from early May and provide sport right through to September. The bigger fish arrive early and the peak of the season is from mid-June into August. They range from $\frac{1}{2}$ lb to 7 lb. Most of the sea-trout are taken by spinning downstream of Listowel. Mepps spoons and small Lane minnows are preferred. The best of the fly fishing is said to be above Abbeyfeale. Dark flies are best for daytime fishing – Zulu, Connemara Black, Black Pennell, Bibio, Mallard and Claret – size 10 to 14. A small dry fly can get results too, for example a Grey Duster or a Black Gnat, size 18 or 20. At night, try silver-bodied flies, such as a Bloody Butcher, a Silver Doctor, a Teal, Blue and Silver, a Priest or a Jungle Cock and Silver.

The Clubs

The Killocrim-Finuge Club has 3 miles of water downstream of Listowel. Good salmon and grilse fishing and fair sea-trout fishing as the fish run through. Day tickets from:

Mr Dan Joy   Mr George Gaine
Killocrim   Greenville
Listowel, Co. Kerry   Listowel, Co. Kerry

The North Kerry Anglers' Association has access to about 9 miles of fishing in the vicinity of Listowel on both the main river and its tributary, the Smearlagh. There is salmon and grilse fishing with occasional sea-trout. Day tickets from:

Mr Jack Sheehan
23 Church Street
Listowel, Co. Kerry
Telephone 068 21298

Tom Walsh
Tackle Dealer
Upper Church Street
Listowel, Co. Kerry

Tralee and District Anglers' Association has over 2 miles of fishing located downstream of Kilmorna Bridge. This is nice salmon water with fifteen named pools.

Day tickets are available from:

Arthur Drugan
114 St. Brendan's Park
Tralee, Co. Kerry
Telephone 066-27618

Matt Doody
Colbert's Terrace
Abbeyfeale, Co. Limerick.
Telephone (office) 068 31241 (home) 068 45189

Tim Landers
Landers Leisure Lines
Courthouse Lane
Tralee, Co. Kerry
Telephone 066 24378

Joe O'Keeffe
Glenview
Kilmorna
Co. Kerry
Telephone 068 45189

Abbeyfeale Anglers' Association has about 5 miles of fishing, the greater part of which is located downstream of Abbeyfeale. It offers good spring-salmon fishing, very good salmon fishing from July and sea-trout from June. The stretch at the town provides the best sea-trout fishing.
Day tickets from:

Ryan's Tackle Shop
New Street
Abbeyfeale, Co. Limerick

Paddy Sullivan
Knocknasna Upper
Abbeyfeale, Co. Limerick
Telephone 068 31453

Brosna-Mountcollins Angling Club controls approximately 8 miles of double-bank fishing from a point a $\frac{1}{4}$ mile below the Owveg River confluence up past Mountcollins to within $\frac{1}{2}$ mile of Ahane Bridge. This stretch produces a small catch of grilse but excels as a sea-trout fishery. The sea-trout fishing here is from mid-May to September. There is a 10 inch size limit, and maggots and clear-water worming are not allowed.

Day tickets from:

Lou Murphy
Brosna Village
Co. Kerry
Telephone 068 44148

Kevin Barry
Mountcollins
Co. Limerick

Gillies and Guides

All of the above clubs can arrange gillies if given notice in advance.

Regulations

There is a statutory ban on fishing or carrying a rod on the bank of the river for 60 metres above and below Scartleigh Weir which is located downstream of Listowel.

Fly only is the rule on a stretch of the Killocrim-Finuge Club water at the tide. Brosna-Mountcollins Angling Club has regulations for its own water. Elsewhere, all legitimate methods are allowed.

RIVER SMEARLAGH   R 02 33

The River Smearlagh flows in from the south about 3 miles north of Listowel. North Kerry Anglers' Association (above) controls most of the fishing up to Foran's Bridge - about 5 miles in all. It is a fast-flowing, boulder strewn, overgrown river and can give good fishing on a falling spate. The best taking places are said to be just above the confluence (but this is regarded by many as being too long a walk) and at a small falls known locally as 'the rock'. There are also a few good pools above Foran's Bridge.

CLYDAGH RIVER   R 13 18

This is a small spate stream which flows down through Brosna. It can give a bit of sea-trout fishing on a falling spate to a worm by day or a fly at night.

ALLAGHAUN RIVER   R 12 28

The Allaghaun River is 16 miles long and flows from the east to join the Feale downstream of Abbeyfeale. The fishing is regarded as free. It can give good sea-trout fishing and produces an occasional grilse too when water conditions are right. The fishing extends up as far as Barber's Bridge.

UPPER RIVER FEALE   R 17 16

There are two locations upstream of Ahane Bridge where the fishing is regarded as free. They are Walsh's Flat and Nookra and sea-trout can be taken there on high water.

RIVER GALEY   Q 99 37

Permission

Anglers fish with the goodwill of the riparian owners.

The Galey River (pronounced locally as 'Gale' river) is the longest of the River Feale tributaries – 27 miles. It flows west through Athea in west Co. Limerick and enters the River Feale 5 miles west of Listowel. It flows over flagstone, sandstone and limestone in its lower reaches. It is regarded primarily as a brown trout river and is fished mainly by local anglers using small spinners and worms. It is a lovely wild river with a gravel bottom and nice streams and pools. The majority of the trout range from $\frac{1}{2}$ to $\frac{3}{4}$ lb with the occasional one to 3 lb and better. Access is from bridge to bridge and it can be fished all the way down from Ahavoher Bridge. Some anglers claim to have had nice trout fishing upstream of Athea. It gets a run of estuary trout up as far as Shrone Bridge from February to April and these average $\frac{1}{2}$ lb. There is also a run of sea-trout in August and September.

Familiar faces at Ballynahinch (see page 102)

·8· Southern Fisheries Region

The Southern Fisheries Region stretches from Clammers Point, at the mouth of Bannow Bay, to the southern tip of Ballycotton Bay. It comprises the catchments of four major rivers, the Barrow, Nore, Suir and Munster Blackwater, and a number of smaller streams which can be productive in season. The head office of the Southern Regional Fisheries Board is at Anglesea Street, Clonmel, Co. Tipperary, (*telephone* 052 23624).

RIVER BARROW   S 71 44

Season

Salmon: 1 February to 30 September.
Sea-trout: 1 February to 30 September.
Brown trout: 1 March to 30 September.

These opening and closing dates apply also to all tributaries of the Barrow.

The River Barrow rises in the Slieve Bloom Mountains in Co. Laois and flows north and then east through the Bog of Allen towards Portarlington. At Monasterevin it turns southwards and makes its way through the rich tillage and pasturelands of Counties Kildare, Carlow and Kilkenny. From the town of Borris, the adjoining landscape changes to a scenic wooded valley as the river makes its way to the tide in Waterford Harbour, where it shares a common estuary with the River Nore and River Suir. In all, it is 120 miles long and drains a catchment of 1,185 square miles.

A lot of uncertainty appears to exist over the ownership of fishing rights on the river. Ownership has only been established in a few cases. In fact, most of the fishing on the Barrow is probably free. However, arrangements about access have to be made with riparian owners.

The river has been developed as a navigable waterway from Athy downstream and the locks and weirs on that 35-mile stretch have greatly altered the character of the river, making it more suitable for coarse fish

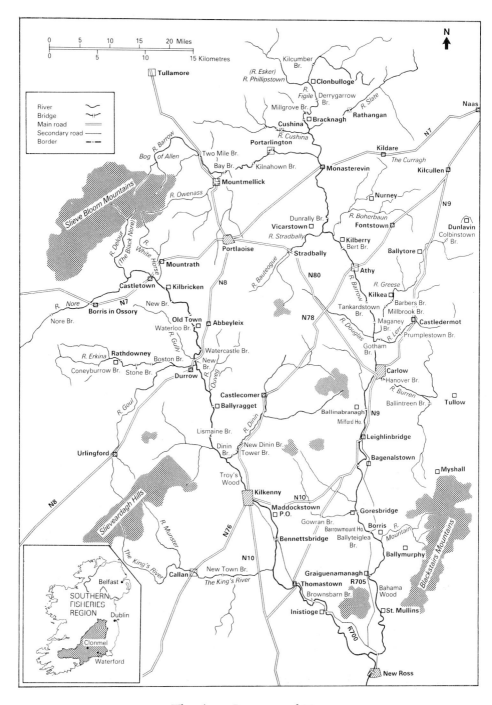

The rivers Barrow and Nore

and pike than for trout and salmon. It has heavy cruiser-type traffic.

At present it is not a noted salmon river. A number of fish are taken every year below the weir at St Mullins and a few at Borris. Many reasons are given for the poor run of salmon. Included among them are the extensive coastal drift-net fishery and the obstacles the weirs create for fish.

The trout fishing is described as fair to good with the average size of the trout probably reaching $3/4$ lb. The best trout fishing is considered to be upstream of Monasterevin and on the tributaries, where fishing was excellent in the past and can still be so. There are plenty of smaller trout downstream, too, as far as St Mullins.

To see what the river has to offer, let us begin at the tide and work upstream.

St Mullins Angling Club has about 4 miles of water extending downstream from St Mullins Weir, past the island, to St Mullins Lock. This is very much a mixed fishery with trout, salmon and coarse fish – mainly bream and pike.

The trout are small – averaging $1/2$ lb – but fairly plentiful.

There are said to be salmon in the river from April but the best salmon fishing is considered to be in September. Occasionally, June can produce good grilse fishing – referred to locally as 'gilleen'. Try the tidal pool by Odlum's Old Mill.

A feature of the river at St Mullins is the run of shad which comes every year in May. Anglers come from far and wide to fish them and they will take many baits, including a fly.

Permits for the fishing at St Mullins are available from:

Mr Nicholas Blanchfield
St Mullins
Co. Carlow
Telephone 051 24745

Graignamanagh Angling Club has about 4 miles of water on the left bank, extending downstream from Clashganna past the town of Graignamanagh to Bahana Wood, and a further $1/2$-mile stretch on the right bank about 600 yards downstream of Ballyteiglea Bridge. The brown trout average about 10oz and the fishing can be very good in May and June. Anglers with local knowledge do very well indeed and can take trout to 2 lb on the evening rise.

The grilse fishing is best in June and worm fishing is the most used method.

Inquiries about the fishing and fishing permits to:

Mr Liam Foley
Turf Market
Graignamanagh, Co. Carlow
Telephone 0503 24341

Borris Angling Club has about 3 miles of fishing on the left bank, extending downstream from Ballyteiglea Bridge to below the weir at Clashganna. This is a mixture of trout, salmon and coarse fishing. The trout fishing can be very good and occasionally so too can the salmon fishing. Boats trolling up and down can be a source of great annoyance to trout fly fishers and the best tactic is to stick to the shallow water below the weirs.

Inquiries about the fishing and permits should be made to:

Mr. Frank Hynes
Cournellan
Borris, Co. Carlow
Telephone 0503 73423

The Milltown Fishery near Borris offers about ¼ mile of fair trout fishing and occasional grilse in summer. It is located below a weir. Inquiries for permission to Mr Michael Fenlon, Milltown, Borris, Co. Carlow.

Goresbridge Salmon and Trout Angling Association has the goodwill of the fishing on approximately 4 miles of water, extending from Fenniscourt, upstream of Goresbridge, on the Carlow border, downstream as far as Barrowmount House. The trout fishing can be very good in this area. There is a good stock of wild and artificially stocked trout but local knowledge is essential.

Day cards are available from:

Mr John Murphy
Barrack Street
Goresbridge, Co. Carlow
Telephone 0503 75194

Milford Angling Club has a half-mile stretch of water midway between Carlow and Leighlinbridge. The water is fast and streamy. It holds a good stock of trout, with many ranging from 10 oz to ¾ lb. It is fly fishing only.

Permits from

Mr Bobby Quinn
The Locks Guesthouse
Milford, Co. Carlow
Telephone 0503 46261

Carlow-Graigue-Cullen Angling Club has about 8 miles of fishing on the river, extending from Maganey Bridge downstream to Milford. The main trout-angling water is at two places, locally known as the Back River and Lanigan's. The trout fishing is described as fair and some artificial stocking takes place.

Fly hatches consist mainly of olives, sedges and midges.

The fishing is regarded as 'open fishing'.

Vicarstown Angling Club members fish extensively on the Stradbally River, the Killiney River and on the main river. Most of the water is better suited to coarse fish, except, perhaps, the Stradbally River. Even there, the trout fishing is said to be poor. Further information on the fishing from:

Mr James Crean
Vicarstown Inn
Vicarstown
Portlaoise
Telephone 0502 25189

There is some trout fishing available at Baganalstown. Inquiries to:

Mr D. J. Rea, The Parade, Baganalstown
Co. Carlow   *Telephone* 0503-21292

Athy and District Anglers' Club has access to an extensive stretch of the River Barrow. This water is fished for salmon late in the season and the trout fishing is regarded as being only fair. This is an active club that carries out extensive development work on its fishery.

Inquiries about fishing and club membership to: Mr Denis Whelan, 29 Graysland, Carlow Road, Athy, Co. Kildare, *Telephone* 0507-37537 or Mr Brendan Murphy, Publican, Leinster Street, Athy, Co. Kildare.

The Kilberry-Cloney and Boherbaun Angling Club has fishing on the Boherbaun River. It flows down from Nurney and it joins the Barrow near Kilberry. Despite recent drainage works and pollution, it still has the potential to be a great trout river. It is mainly a limestone river with gravel and a lovely white marl bottom. Bianconi, the legendary coachman of the 1800s, once described it as the Irish Test. The banks are good and stiles are in place.

When the river is in good condition, the trout average 1-2 lb and the fishing can be very good. Fly hatches are good and all the usual flies found on a limestone river are present, including mayfly. The peak of the fishing is in May–June but this river can produce a trout from April to September.

For permits and/or information on the river, contact:

Mr Larry Foy
553 Kilberry
Athy
Co. Kildare
Telephone 0507-38803

Mr Denis Lawlor/Mr Michael Kelly
Kilberry
Athy
Co. Kildare

Monasterevin and District Angling Club has approximately 15 miles of fishing on the Barrow upstream from Dunrally bridge. This water produces about half a dozen salmon every season, but the trout fishing is good. The average weight is ¾ lb, with some to 4 lb.

It is necessary to wade to make the most of the fishing. Stiles are in place.

The trout fishing extends from top to bottom of the stretch, varying in quality. There are good hatches of sedges and blue-winged olives and there is a mayfly hatch.

Permits are available from:

Mr K. Cullen
Main Street
Monasterevin, Co. Kildare

Mr J. Caughlan
Main Street
Monasterevin, Co. Kildare

Portarlington Angling Club Waters on the River Barrow extend from Kylenahown Bridge, which is three miles on the Mountmellick side of Portarlington, to the footbridge 4 miles downstream of the town – about 8 miles in all.

The club has access to both banks. The river is 30-40 feet wide at this point. It flows over limestone and has stretches of stony, sandy bottom. The river habitat provides good natural cover for trout. The banks are low and clear over 90 per cent of their length while the remaining 10 per cent has been damaged by a drainage scheme. A lot of work has been done providing stiles and footbridges.

Very few salmon reach this stretch in the angling season, but in the past the waters around Lea Castle provided excellent spring salmon fishing from mid-March.

The club waters presently hold decent stocks of wild brown trout and stocked trout ranging from $^3/_4$ lb to 4 lb. The fishing is fair at present. It is still recovering from a serious pollution spill in 1987, but should soon return to its former greatness. Popular trout stretches include the Pump House, the Widow's Hill, Lawnsdowne Bridge, Quinn's Sharp, Maker's Ford, the Footstick, the Mill Island and Green's Flat.

The trout-fishing season begins in early March, when the spun natural minnow is widely used and juvenile members fish a floated worm. A slow-sinking line with a team of wet flies – March Brown, Alexandra and Bloody Butcher – gets results at this time too.

The first fly hatches occur around midday in April and a wet Waterhen Bloa or a Pale Watery are suggested. The principal fly hatches are blue-winged olive/sherry spinner, alder, grey flag sedge, mayfly (limited) and black gnat.

Favourite wet flies include a Gold-ribbed Hare's Ear, Greenwell's Glory, Waterhen Bloa, Coachman, Red Spinner and Black and Peacock Spider.

Most fly-fishing activity takes place in the period from May to August.

The visiting angler would be well advised to visit Mick Finlay's Bar, Bracklane Street, Portarlington, where the proprietor will only be too glad to supply information on what 'they're on'. With the river now improving again, visiting anglers are welcome and inquiries about permits and so on should be made to:

Mr. Michael Finlay
Finlay's Bar
Bracklane Street
Portarlington, Co. Laois

Mr Dominic Ryan
Grocer
Kilmalogue
Portarlington, Co. Laois

Mr Joe Hargrove
Burrowbank
Portarlington, Co. Laois

CUSHINA RIVER   N 60 15

The Cushina River flows through Clonsast Bog north of Portarlington and joins the Figile River, a tributary of the Barrow, in the middle of Derrylea Bog about 2 miles south of Bracknagh. It flows over limestone, has a marl bottom and has excellent spawning grounds. It is mostly a wild, deep, narrow river with lots of pool area, but it also has some streamy water. The banks are generally clear but, as can be appreciated, such a remote river can have its wild, overgrown stretches. It holds trout all the way for 5 miles downstream from Cushina Bridge to the confluence. The average size is $^3/_4$ – 1 lb and there are trout there to $5^1/_2$ lb. These fish are very wild and catching them on fly is a real thrill. It is best to wait till dusk and stalk them with great care.

In a wet summer the Cushina can fish well right through the season, though from time to time it does suffer problems with bog silt.

For information and permits contact:

Mr Peter Dunne	Mr Bill Carmody
Clonsast	Tullamore Road
Rathangan, Co. Kildare	Portarlington, Co. Offaly
Telephone 0502 23020	

OWENASS RIVER   N 45 06

The Owenass River rises in the Slieve Bloom Mountains and joins the Barrow at Bay Bridge, downstream of Mountmellick. It holds a very big stock of small trout. Only downstream of the town is it worth fishing. Here the trout can reach 1 lb and they can provide pleasant evening fishing in June and July, when a Cinnamon Sedge is likely to account for a nice trout.

FIGILE RIVER   N 61 20

The Figile River rises a few miles south of Edenderry in Co. Offaly and flows in a southerly direction through the village of Clonbulloge to join the Barrow just north of Monasterevin. It flows almost entirely through bog, and peat silt can be a problem, though it may decrease shortly with the scaling down of the peat harvesting operations in that area. The Figale holds brown trout to 2 lb from Kilcumber Bridge down to Clonbulloge Bridge. This stretch runs entirely through bog. There used to be trout at Bracknagh before recent drainage. Some excellent trout have been taken on the fly at Millsgrove Bridge. This river holds large stocks of bream, perch and pike and it is free fishing.

PHILLIPSTOWN RIVER   N 55 27

The Phillipstown River joins the Figile River from the west at Clonbulloge. It is mainly a coarse fishery with a lot of peat silt problems, but there are fair numbers of trout in a half-mile stretch up and downstream of Esker Bridge.

SLATE RIVER   N 62 17

The Slate River rises near Robertstown in Co. Kildare and flows west through Rathangan to join the Figile River 2 miles south of Bracknagh. It holds good stocks of trout but is mainly an early-season river. It was drained some time in the past and consequently runs low and becomes weeded in places in summer. The banks are high. The fishing can be very good around Rathangan and the trout are of a good average size, wild and free-rising. For further information, contact the Secretary of Rathangan Angling Club Peter Dunne, Clonsast, Rathangan.

Joe Husgrove of Portarlington has devised very effective Blue-Winged Olive and Mayfly patterns for the Upper Barrow and its tributaries, and Willie Murphy ties an excellent Red Rail. The dressings are:

Blue Winged Olive

Hook	Size 12 or 14
Tail	Light-olive hackle fibres
Body	Unwaxed primrose silk
Wing	Starling primary
Hackle	Light-olive

Mayfly

Hook	Size 8 longshank
Tail	None
Body	Natural raffia
Hackle	Ginger cock, palmered
Front hackle	French partridge

Red Rail

Hook	Size 10 or 12
Silk	Brown
Body	Ginger floss lacquered
Hackle	Ginger cock, palmered, and ginger cock in front of wing
Wing	Hen pheasant

RIVER GREESE   S 79 96

The River Greese rises near Dunlavin, Co. Wicklow, and joins the Barrow north of Carlow. It is a clear, fast-flowing limestone stream with some deeper, slow stretches, ideal for holding trout. It holds a very good stock of trout from $\frac{1}{2}$ to $1\frac{1}{2}$ lb and in recent years has produced trout to $6\frac{1}{2}$ lb.

The River Greese Anglers Association is active on the river, developing the banks and protecting the trout stocks. The club water stretches for about 10 miles, from Colbinstown Bridge down through Ballytore Village to Barber's Bridge near Kilkee Castle.

Visiting anglers are catered for and they should contact Mr Patrick Leigh, Woodhill, Narraghmore, Ballytore, Co. Kildare (telephone 0507 26611), or Mr Michael Lawlor, Corner House, Ballytore, Co. Kildare.

Further downstream on the River Greese, the Barrow Angling Club members fish with the permission of the riparian owners. The stretch extends downstream for about 4 miles from Millbrook Bridge to the confluence. It holds a nice stock of trout and visitors can fish it by getting in touch with riparian owners or Barrow Angling Club's Mr Eamon A. Moore, Chapelstown, Carlow (*telephone* 0503 42225).

J. R. Harris notes in *An Angler's Entomology* (1952) that purple duns occur on the Greese and hatch between May and August. They still do and a visiting angler would be well advised to have a few patterns ready. A larger version of the dressing of the Iron Blue Dun will do at a pinch.

RIVER BURREN   S 74 75

The River Burren rises near Myshall in Co. Carlow and flows in a semicircle to the Barrow at the town of Carlow. It was a brilliant trout river and can still be quite good. The Barrow Angling Club leases 8 miles of the river from the Southern Regional Fisheries Board. This stretch reaches from Hanover Bridge in Carlow town up to Ballintrean Bridge at Rathtoe near Tullow. A lot of the trout range from ¾ lb to 1 lb and they are lovely, slim specimens. The banks are generally low and a drainage committee carried out weed cutting. This is a limestone river and has all the usual flies, including mayfly.

Membership of the club is open and permits can be obtained at JB Motor & Sport, Castlehill Centre, Carlow, or from Mr Eamon A. Moore, Chapelstown, Carlow (*telephone* 0503 42225).

RIVER LERR   S 72 82

The River Lerr is a small stream which comes down from Castledermot and joins the Barrow 3 miles upstream of Carlow. It holds beautiful deep, heavily spotted pink-fleshed trout. Stocks are not as numerous as in the Burren but the average size is bigger. They take a wet fly, some would say in preference to the dry fly, though the latter too has its days. The Lerr has an especially good hatch of iron blues and plenty of sedges. The banks are artificially built and overgrown in places.

The fishing is leased in sections up to Prumplestown by Barrow Angling

Club and permission to fish can be obtained as for the River Burren above.

RIVER NORE   S 51 56

Season

Salmon: 1 February to 30 September.
Sea-trout: 1 February to 30 September.
Brown trout: 1 March to 30 September.

The River Nore rises on the eastern slopes of the Devil's Bit Mountain in Co. Tipperary and, at first, flows east through Borris in Ossory and then turns south through Co. Kilkenny, passing through Durrow, Ballyragget, Kilkenny City, Bennettsbridge, and Thomastown before meeting the tide at the lovely village of Inistioge. It is 87 miles long and drains a total catchment of 977 square miles. It rises on a sandstone base but the catchment soon turns to limestone and remains so to the sea. The countryside is one of mixed farming, with some tillage, quite a bit of pasture and dairying and some bloodstock. The river has a fairly steep gradient but the flow is checked by innumerable weirs and it is probably true to say that shallow glides are the predominant feature.

Wading is quite safe, and necessary in many areas (body waders) for the trout fishing. The banks are lined with trees in many places. Aquatic vegetation is less than its sister rivers, the Barrow and Suir.

The best of the salmon fishing is said to extend up as far as the confluence of the River Dinin and the best trout fishing is upstream of Thomastown, though there is some below it too.

This was once one of the finest salmon rivers in the country, but has declined dramatically recently. It now gets very few spring salmon. The grilse run fluctuates and so too does the autumn run. The peak of the grilse fishing is from mid-June till early July and the autumn run arrives some time after mid-August. These fish can be big – from 12 to 20 lb – but the run is uncertain. The last good autumn run was in 1988.

As far as the brown trout are concerned, a recent (1990) survey carried out by the Central Fisheries Board revealed an excellent stock. The survey team reported huge numbers in some areas. The average size is 10–12 oz, with few fish over 1 lb.

The best of the trout fishing is from early season to mid-June on the tributaries and throughout season on the main river.

I do not have a great deal of information on fly hatches. There are some olives' and stoneflies appear to be important early in the season. There are big numbers of various sedges. It is definitely a river where the visiting trout angler could usefully bring his fly-tying kit along.

The ownership of the fisheries is well defined and the fishing rights are either exercised by the individual owners or leased to clubs and angling associations.

The Fisheries

Inistioge Anglers' Association has the first fishery up from the tide at the village of Inistioge. There is a ³/₄ mile of fresh water – both banks – and a tidal stretch. This is primarily a salmon fishery. It is at its best in low water and anglers expect to take spring fish from the first day of the season (1 February) when conditions are right.

Permits are available from:

> The Castle Inn
> The Square
> Inistioge, Co. Kilkenny
> *Telephone* 056 58483

The Cotterell Fishery is the next fishery on the right bank up river. It begins a short distance downstream of Brownsbarn Bridge and extends for ²/₃ mile. This is a lovely stretch with a nice mix of pool and stream. It is mainly a low-water fishery and fish can reach this fishery when water conditions prevent them from travelling further up river. It quite often produces the first fish of the season.

Season tickets and day tickets are available from:

> Mr Andy Cotterell
> Kilmacshane
> Inistioge, Co. Kilkenny
> *Telephone* 056 58403

Kilkenny Angling Club has extensive fishing rights on the River Nore and its tributary, the Dinin River. The club water on the Nore begins at Ballyragget Bridge and extends downstream on the left bank to Lismaine Bridge (3 miles approximately); from the Dinin confluence downstream on the left bank to the Bleach Green (3 miles approximately); from Maddockstown Post Office on the left bank downstream (2½ miles) to a point about a mile upstream of Bennetts Bridge; a short stretch on the left bank at Holden's; and both banks at Brownsbarn Bridge.

The club water on the River Dinin extends upstream from the confluence for 1½ miles on the left bank and there is about ½ mile on the right bank downstream of the New Dinin Bridge.

These waters hold salmon and brown trout.

One can expect to meet a salmon on any of the stretches from March to September. The spring fishing is poor – some would say that the spring fish are virtually gone. The June run of grilse is fair, but not nearly as good as in the past, and some seasons see a great run of big fish in late August and September. This run virtually collapsed in 1989 and 1990.

A lot of the club water is fast and streamy and ideal for the fly. In fact, the club hopes to make some stretches fly only. Shrimp fishing is frowned upon and is forbidden on certain stretches.

The best of the brown trout fishing is on the waters from Bennetsbridge upstream to Ballyragget. The trout average $3/4$ lb, with some to $1^1/_4$ lb and occasional fish to 4 lb. There is very good trout fishing downstream of Maddockstown and the water downstream of the Dinin confluence holds some of the best stocks of trout on the entire river.

There is a bag limit of five trout and an 8-inch size limit. Maggot fishing is strictly prohibited.

Membership of the club is limited. Trout day permits are available in local hotels or from Mr Paul Campion, Dean Street, Kilkenny, or The Sports Shop, High Street, Kilkenny. Salmon day tickets are limited to twenty per day and are available from Mr Ed Stack, Bleach Road, Kilkenny (*telephone* 056 65220). Gillies are available by prior arrangement. Contact Mr Ed Stack, above.

Thomastown Angling Club has 4 miles of double bank fishing upstream and downstream of the town. This stretch is said to have some of the nicest pools and some of the best salmon fishing on the River Nore. There is a lot of streamy water and it is an especially nice spring-salmon fishery and fishes well throughout the season when there is a rise in the water. Fly fishing, worming and spinning are the fishing methods allowed.

This water also holds excellent stocks of brown trout. There is a club regulation which does not permit trout fishing till April and only fly fishing and worming are allowed for trout.

Ten salmon permits and ten trout permits are available per day. They can be obtained at :

John Synnott's Shop
The Quay
Thomastown, Co. Kilkenny
Telephone 056 24196

Kilkenny Corporation has some kind of ancient riparian rights on the Nore, extending upstream on the right bank from opposite Maddockstown to Talbots Inch, a distance of about 7 miles, and there are rights on the left bank too. The fishing is regarded as free.

Mount Juliet House has 3 miles of double-bank fishing on the Nore upstream of Thomastown and a further mile of fishing on the right bank of the King's River, extending upstream from the confluence. The fishing is divided into ten beats and both trout and salmon fishers are catered for.

The salmon fishing is mostly grilse and autumn fishing and can be very good. In 1988 this stretch produced 271 fish but the 1989–90 figures were only a small fraction of the 1988 catch. All fishing methods are allowed.

The brown trout fishing is very good on this stretch in April and the evening fishing can be magic through July and August.

Salmon rods are let by the day and there are evening permits for the trout fishing. Gillies are available by prior arrangement and fishing tackle can be hired. The fishing can be booked through:

The Fishery Manager
Mount Juliet House
Thomastown, Co. Kilkenny
Telephone 056 24455.

Durrow and District Anglers' Association has extensive fishing on the River Nore, extending from Watercastle Bridge downstream to the confluence of the Ouveg River; on the Erkina River from Boston Bridge downstream to the old mill at Durrow; on the River Goul from Boden's Hole to the confluence with the Erkina River; and on the lower reaches of the Ouveg River.

The River Nore is about 18 yards wide at this point. It has deep pools and fast streamy water with a good gravel bottom. The trout stocks are very good.

The Erkina River is about 16 feet wide and is slow-moving, with a silt bottom and occasional gravel-bottomed streams. It holds good stocks of trout to $3\frac{1}{2}$ lb. The best fishing is early in the season.

The River Goul joins the Erkina River. It is a fast-flowing deep stream and holds lots of trout from $\frac{1}{2}$ lb to $\frac{3}{4}$ lb.

The Ouveg River is a feeder stream of the Nore. It is a fast-flowing gravel stream and fishes especially well for trout to the wet fly in high water. The banks are relatively clear but there is a lot of natural woodland in the Durrow area and fishing is difficult where the river flows through the wood. Any angler fishing this river would be well advised to take along body waders.

There was great spring and grilse fishing on the Nore in the Durrow district from 1950 to 1965. Famous 'throws' included the Mossy Rock, the Sandy Walk, Anker, Commons Hole and Hastings. At present not more than ten fish are taken each season.

Permits from:

William B. Lawlor
The Square
Durrow, Co. Laois
Telephone 0502 36234

Rathdowney Angling Club has fishing on the Erkina River, extending downstream from Coneyborow Bridge to Boston Bridge, a distance of about 2½ miles. Access is good, the banks are relatively clean and the river at this point has a nice sequence of pool, riffle and glide. There are good stocks of trout in this stretch. The average weight is between 10 and 12 oz, with trout to 3 lb, and it fishes best early in the season.

Permits from:

Mr Michael White
Moorville
Rathdowney, Co Laois

Abbeyleix Angling Club has about 4 miles of water on the River Nore, extending downstream from the New Bridge at Donore House to Waterloo Bridge at Old Town. The river holds good stocks of trout ranging in size from ½ to 1¼ lb. Access to the banks is quite difficult, especially on the upper stretches.

Permits from:

Mr Victor Bowell
Sandymount
Abbeyleix, Co. Laois

Mountrath and District Anglers' Club has fishing on the River Nore, the Delour River (known locally as the Black Nore) and the Mountrath River (known locally as the White Horse River). The trout in the Black Nore tend to be small. On the main River Nore the best trout fishing extends from Kilbricken downstream to New Bridge. The White Horse River has substantial numbers of trout averaging 10 oz downstream of the town of Mountrath. Body waders would help greatly for fly fishing.

For permits and information on the fishing, contact:

Mr Thomas Watkins
6 St Finan's Terrace
Mountrath, Co. Laois
Telephone 0502 32540

Callan and District Anglers' Association has approximately 5 miles of
fishing on the Kings River. This river – like its tributary, the Munster
River – rises in the Slieveardagh Hill in Co. Tipperary and flows east
through Callan in Co. Kilkenny to join the Nore north west of
Thomastown. This is a rich limestone river, 15–20 yards wide with a
gravel bottom and occasional 'swallow holes' which cause stretches to go
dry in summer. The Callan and District Anglers' Association fishing
extends from the Metal Bridge which is located about $2\frac{1}{2}$ miles upstream
of the town. There is a lot of nice streamy water, especially early in the
season, and some of the best fishing is from April to June. This river was
drained and the banks are high in places. The trout average $\frac{3}{4}$ lb, with
trout to $3\frac{1}{2}$ lb and better. Wet fly is most popular from March to May
and there is good evening dry-fly fishing in summer. Fly hatches include
various olives, mayflies, stoneflies, black gnats, midges and various sedges.

For permits and information, contact:

Mr Chris Vaughan
Green Street
Callan, Co. Kilkenny

RIVER SUIR AND TRIBUTARIES   S 20 22

Season

Salmon: 1 February to 30 September.
Sea-trout: 1 February to 30 September.
Brown trout: 1 March to 30 September.

The River Suir (pronounce 'sure') rises in the Devil's Bit Mountain in Co.
Tipperary and flows south and then north and east to join the Barrow
and the Nore in Waterford Harbour. It is 115 miles long and together
with its tributaries it drains a total catchment of 1,394 square miles.
   The main river lies entirely on limestone except for a few miles at the
source and all the tributaries are on limestone, with the exception of the

Nire, the Clodiagh and the upper reaches of the Multeen, which comes in from the west near Cashel.

The flow in the main river is characterized by deep and shallow glides interrupted by shallow riffles.   Its width increases as it proceeds downstream and the sequence of relatively shallow glide and riffle is maintained.

This combination of a rich limestone base and huge areas of relatively shallow glides makes the Suir ideal for the production of brown trout. There is massive recruitment of young trout from the extensive system of tributaries and the trout survive and grow in what is a near-perfect environment.   They have few predators in the form of pike, and coarse fish are almost entirely absent.

The Suir is one of Ireland's premier brown trout fisheries.   Only a handful of rivers can compare with it in terms of numbers of trout produced per square yard and I doubt if any river can equal it in terms of the overall numbers of trout that it produces and that are available to the angler.

The average size of the trout ranges from ¾ to 2 lb in different areas, depending on the habitat.   Their lifespan is relatively short and few trout exceed 4 years of age.

Fly Life

The relative uniformity of the nature of the riverbed type means that the dominant fly hatches are more or less similar over the entire length of the river, with the exception of the mayfly, which is found only between Camus Bridge and Golden, and stoneflies, which are confined to fast shallow sections.   Otherwise, from March to late April, there are large dark olives around midday.   From late April to mid-May, there are medium olives, iron blues and stoneflies – early brown. From mid-May to mid-June, there are alders, medium olives, reed smuts and midges, mayfly, pale wateries, blue-winged olives, caenis, hawthorn, black gnat, yellow stoneflies and various sedges, including murroughs and grey flags. From mid-June to the end of July sees blue-winged olives, pale wateries and pale evening duns, small dark olives, a variety of sedges (including murrough, cinnamon sedge, red sedge and silverhorns) and ants on occasions.   August has similar hatches.   The blue-winged olive is very important in the evening, as are various sedges, and trout take small black and green midges by day.   In September the trout take blue-winged olives during the day and on mild evenings. Midges, olives and small sedges and the cinnamon sedge are also important.

The peak of the trout fishing is from early May to mid-June for day-long fishing, at dusk for the rest of the summer and during the day and evening in September.   At these times, there is usually no shortage of

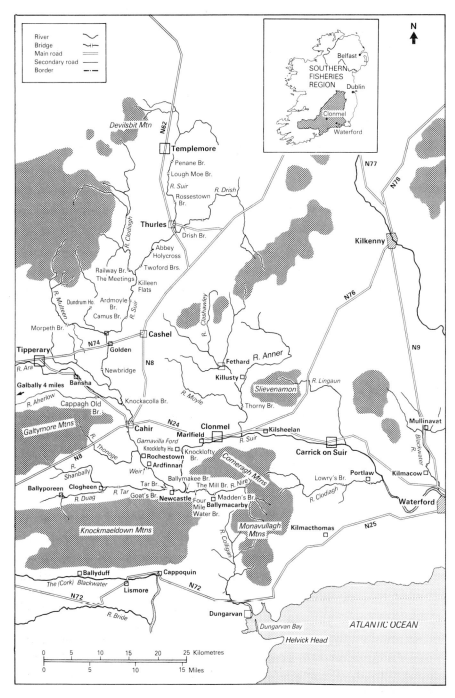

River Suir

feeding trout.

Body waders and a wading staff are practically essential for an angler when fishing the main channel of the Suir. In most areas, the bottom is firm and consists of stone, gravel or sand. This is a big river with a strong current and anglers should take due care when wading.

Salmon Fishing

The best of the salmon fishing on the River Suir is said to extend downstream from Ardfinnan towards Carrick-on-Suir. The fishing is controlled mainly by either angling clubs or syndicates and very little information is available on the quality of the fishing. The river still produces occasional spring salmon and is thought to get a fair run of grilse. In some seasons, when conditions are right, it gets a good run of 12–18 lb salmon. The Suir has the distinction of producing Ireland's record rod-caught salmon. It weighed 57 lb and was taken on a fly by Michael Maher in 1874. There is very little salmon fishing available to the general public and the best fishing on what is available is in June and September.

The Fisheries

This description of the fisheries starts at the bottom of the river and, as far as is practical, they are dealt with in sequence moving upstream.

The Portlaw Clodiagh River joins the Suir east of Portlaw. The fishing rights are owned by the Marquis of Waterford, but trout fishing is available outside the boundary of Carraghmore Estate – upstream of Lowry's Bridge and downstream of Portlaw. It is a sandstone river and has moderate stocks of trout averaging 10 inches.

RIVER BLACKWATER

The River Blackwater enters the Suir from the north a short distance upstream of Waterford City. It has good stocks of trout to 10 inches between Kilmacow and Mullinavat. Much of the river is overgrown and difficult to fish. There is some fishing available with the consent of riparian owners and inquiries should be made locally.

The Lingaun River rises on the eastern slopes of Slievenamon and joins the Suir two miles downstream of Carrick-on-Suir. It holds good stocks of trout up to 10 inches. The fishing is with the permission of the riparian owners.

RIVER SUIR – KILSHEELAN TO CARRICK-ON-SUIR

The river is tidal up to Carrick-on-Suir. From Carrick-on-Suir up to Kilsheelan the river is characterized by long glides, 5–7 feet deep, and occasional deep pools. There are moderate stocks of trout from Kilsheelan to Duffcastle and good stocks from Duffcastle to Carrick-on-Suir. The average size is 10-12 ozs. Twaite shad come into this area to spawn during May and can provide good sport.

There is free fishing downstream of Kilsheelan on the left bank.

The Glencastle Fishery consists of 2 miles of salmon and trout fishing on the right bank, downstream of Kilsheelan. Information on permits and fishing from:

> Mrs Maura Long
> Glencastle
> Kilsheelan, Co. Tipperary
> *Telephone* 052 33787

Carrick-on-Suir Angling Club has approximately 1½ miles of fishing on the left bank from Duffcastle downstream to Miloko. Information on fishing and permits from:

> Mr John O'Keefe
> O.K. Cycles and Sports
> New Street
> Carrick-on-Suir, Co. Tipperary
> *Telephone* 051 40626

The fishing is free on the tidal water downstream of Miloko but the trout are very small.

A Clonmel-based angling club has fishing on the left bank downstream of Kilsheelan but membership is over-subscribed.

Finally, Mrs Eileen Ryan has access to some three miles of good trout and salmon fishing, all of which is on the left bank, opposite Glencastle. There are salmon in this water from 1 May. For details, contact:

> Mrs Eileen Ryan
> Clonanav Farmhouse
> Ballymacarbry
> via Clonmel
> Co. Waterford
> *Telephone* 052 36141

RIVER SUIR – CLONMEL TO KILSHEELAN

Clonmel and District Anglers' Association has extensive fishing on the Suir downstream of Clonmel. Inquiries for permits to fish for trout and salmon should be made to:

Mr John Kavanagh
The Sports Shop
West Gate, Clonmel,
Co. Tipperary

Kilsheelan Angling Club has leased the trout fishing on a mile of the river on the left bank upstream of Kilsheelan. Permits from Mr J. Moriarty, Kilsheelan, Co. Tipperary.

RIVER ANNER   S 24 24

The Anner is a limestone stream which comes down from Slievenamon and joins the Suir just east of Clonmel. It has a nice glide–riffle–pool sequence. Fethard and Killusty Angling Club has reserved the fishing from Thorny Bridge upstream. There are moderate stocks of trout from Thorny Bridge downstream to the confluence and the fishing is available to visitors with the permission of the riparian owners – except the Anner Castle Fishery.

RIVER SUIR – NEWCASTLE BRIDGE TO CLONMEL

From Newcastle Bridge downstream to Clonmel the river is over 40 yards wide and is characterized by long glides and fast-flowing shallow stretches. It holds really good stocks of trout to 2 lb and can provide excellent dry-fly and wet-fly fishing. There are a number of good salmon fisheries on this stretch, including Suir Mount, where Michael Maher took his famous 57 lb Irish record rod-caught salmon on fly. All of the fisheries are either controlled privately or leased by angling clubs which are already over-subscribed and have no room for visitors.

Mrs Eileen Ryan, Clonanav Farmhouse, Ballymacarbry, via Clonmel, Co. Waterford, (telephone 052 36141), runs an excellent angling centre at Clonanav and gives a good service to anglers. Up-to-date information on both trout and salmon fishing is always available. There is a gillie service and tackle can be hired. She can take bookings for fishing on some of the best trout fishing and salmon beats on the river, including a 2 mile stretch downstream of Knocklofty Bridge. The Marlfield Fishery is about 1 mile of single bank trout and salmon fishing. Permits from Marlfield Lodge, Clonmel, Co. Tipperary, *Telephone* 052-25234.

Knocklofty House Hotel, the former home of Lord Donoughmore, has approximately 1 mile of double-bank fishing upstream of Knocklofty Bridge. The trout fishing is excellent and there are occasional salmon. The situation regarding the letting of the fishing is unclear at the time of writing. *Telephone* 052-38222.

RIVER NIRE   S 20 13

The River Nire (16 miles long) is a fast-flowing mountain river which flows through farmland and a scenic wooded valley. It has good stocks of $3/4$ lb trout, with some to 3 lb or better. The water is sparkling clear and, while the best of the fishing is from Madden's Bridge downstream, the rocky pools hold sizeable trout away up into the Comeragh Mountains.

Information on the fishing and permits from Mrs E. Ryan, Clonanav Farmhouse (p265).

RIVER TAR   S 03 14

The River Tar is 19 miles long. It joins the Suir from the west just over a mile upstream of Newcastle Bridge. The main Tar itself from Clogheen downstream flows over a limestone base while its two tributaries, the Shanbally and the Duag, which flows down from Ballyporeen, drain areas of sandstone. All three rivers hold good stocks of trout averaging $1/2$ lb and there are some good ones there too to 3 lb and better. The fishing is with the consent of the riparian owners. The stretch downstream of Goats Bridge by the public road is regarded as free fishing. Further information on the fishing from Mrs Eileen Ryan, Clonanav Farmhouse, (*telephone* 052 36141).

RIVER SUIR – ARDFINNAN TO NEWCASTLE BRIDGE

From Ardfinnan to Newcastle is about 4 miles. From Ardfinnan Bridge downstream to Clocully you have a big, fast flowing, meandering river which holds good numbers of trout. At the confluence of the River Tar and upstream of Newcastle the river is shallow and holds only moderate stocks of trout. Much of the fishing in this area is controlled by Ardfinnan Angling Club. In fact, the club waters start at Rochestown, nearly 2 miles upstream of Ardfinnan. This section of the river consists of long, shallow glides which hold excellent stocks of trout averaging $3/4$–1 lb. The stretch upstream of the weir at Ardfinnan holds only moderate stocks and is best fished on summer evenings. In all, the Ardfinnan Angling Club water extends for nearly 4 miles on both banks from Rochestown to Cloncully, but excluding the left bank for 550 yards upstream of Ardfinnan Weir, the stretch between the weir and Ardfinnan Bridge and the Cloghardeen Fishery. Permits for Ardfinnan Angling Club water are available from:

Mr John Maher
Green View
Ardfinnan, Co. Tipperary
Telephone 052 66242

A limited number of rods are available on the Cloghardeen Fishery from:

Mr P.F. Mason
Cloghardeen
Ardfinnan, Co. Tipperary
Telephone 052 66236

RIVER SUIR – CAHIR AREA

The greater part of the fishing in the vicinity of Cahir (pronounce 'care') that is available by permit to the visitor is controlled by Cahir and District Angling Club. The club controls the fishing on the right bank from Suir Castle (upstream of New Bridge) to the Bakery Weir upstream of Cahir and downstream of the town from the Swiss Cottage to Carrigatuha on the right bank and from the Swiss Cottage to Garnavilla Ford on the left bank.

The character of the river varies here, as do the trout stocks.

From Suir Castle to Knockacalla the river is broad and meandering, with glides, riffles and occasional pools. It holds a very good stock of ³/₄ lb trout.

From Knockacalla to Cahir the river is deep and lazy, with limited stocks, and best suited to evening fishing in summer. From the Swiss Cottage to Carrigatuha there are fast, shallow glides and streams and the river holds an excellent stock of trout.

The trout fishing is strictly fly-only. Gillies are available. For information on gillies and permits, contact:

Morrissey's Bar
Castle Street
Cahir, Co. Tipperary
Telephone 052 41516

The Shamrock Lodge Fishery is on the left bank, just upstream of Rochestown. It has ¼ mile of good trout fishing.

Permits

> Mr Joe O'Connor
> Shamrock Lodge
> Cahir, Co. Tipperary
> *Telephone* 052 66202

RIVER ARA   R 95 33

RIVER AHERLOW   R 95 29

The River Ara and River Aherlow are two tributaries that join and enter the Suir from the west 4 miles north of Cahir.

The Ara comes down from Limerick Junction and Tipperary town. It lies mainly on limestone and provides good angling from Kilshane downstream to the confluence. It is about 10 yards wide and holds good stocks of trout to ¾ lb and some trout to 1¾ lb. From Bansha upstream to Kilshane it consists of a series of ripples, glides and pools and from Bansha downstream it is a continuous deep glide with some short riffles and a few pools. It can provide some excellent dry-fly fishing. The water is controlled by Ara Angling Club.

Permits from

> W.G. Evans
> Tackle Shop
> Main Street
> Tipperary Town

The Aherlow River is more acid than the Ara and drains off old red sandstone. It holds big numbers of small trout up to a maximum of ¾ lb. The fishing on the upper reaches is regarded as free. The best fishing water is in the Galbally area and in the lower reaches downstream of Cappa Old Bridge. There is an angling club on this stretch and permits can be obtained at Morrissey's Bar, Castle Street, Cahir, Co. Tipperary, (*telephone* 052 41516).

MULTEEN RIVER   R 99 40

The Multeen River joins the Suir from the west near Cashel. It flows off old red sandstone onto limestone and holds a big stock of trout averaging about ¹/₂ lb in the middle and lower reaches. The fishing is with the permission of the riparian owners and the best of it is from Dundrum House on the north channel and from Morpeth Bridge on the south channel.

RIVER SUIR – CASHEL-GOLDEN AREA

This stretch is nearly 8 miles long and extends from Camus Bridge, downstream past Golden to New Bridge.

The river is wide and shallow in the vicinity of Camus Bridge and holds good stocks of trout. The next section at Castle Lake, 2 miles downstream, is a continuous deep glide and holds relatively poor trout stocks. It is best suited to evening dry-fly fishing in summer. From Mantlehill downstream through Golden and on to Athassel Abbey the river meanders attractively with pools and glides. This is prime trout water with the exception of one deep stretch between the confluence of the Multeen River and Golden Bridge which is best suited to summer-evening dry-fly fishing.

From Athassel Abbey to New Bridge (nearly 2 miles) the river is characterized by fast-flowing shallow glides and has an excellent stock of trout from ¹/₂ lb to 1¹/₂ lb, and some much better ones. This stretch has a number of weirs, downstream of which some daytime fishing may be had even in mid summer. It is the only stretch of the Suir with a mayfly hatch.

The Cashel-Golden-Tipperary Angling Association controls extensive stretches on both banks downstream from Camus Bridge to Suir Castle and also shares the right bank with the Cahir and District Angling Club from Suir Castle downstream to New Bridge.

Permits from

Mr Myles O'Keeffe
Golden
Co. Tipperary

Mrs Ryan's Shop
Friar Street
Cashel
Co. Tipperary

Mr Leo Glynn
The Bridge House
Golden, Co. Tipperary

O'Rahilly's Sports Wear
Main Street
Tipperary Town
Co. Tipperary

Columb Furniture Store   Drumm's Sports
Tipperary Town   Tipperary Town
Co. Tipperary   Co. Tipperary

RIVER SUIR – THURLES TO ARDMOYLE BRIDGE

The Suir between Thurles and Holycross is a big, deep, slow-flowing river with only limited shallows in the vicinity of the bridges. This is a 5 mile stretch in which the trout stocks are very limited and one which cannot be highly recommended. It also holds pike. The fishing is free with the permission of the riparian owners.

The Thurles-Holycross-Ballycamus Angling Association has access to extensive fishing on the River Drish, The Clodiagh River and on the main river from Holycross Weir for 4 miles downstream to Kileen Flats.

The stretch between Thurles and Holycross is mainly deep and cannot be recommended for trout fishing.

Trout stocks are limited in the section between the weir at Holycross and Agent's Flats. The weir diverts the water to a hydrohead race and this results in low summer flows and excessive aquatic vegetation.

From Agents Flats to Twoford Bridge the river has a nice mix of glide and pool suitable for either wet or dry fly. It holds moderate stocks of trout to $1^3/_4$ lb.

From Twoford Bridge to the confluence of the Clodiagh River is not worth fishing; but from the confluence downstream to Ballycamus Ford is excellent dry-fly water and can hold plenty of trout, though their numbers seem to fluctuate at times.

Fly fishing only is allowed. There is a size limit of 25 cm (10 inches approximately) and a daily bag limit of six trout.

Permits

The Reception Desk   Mr William O'Gorman
Hayes Hotel   Publican
The Square   Bohernacrusha Cross Road
Thurles, Co. Tipperary   Holycross, Co. Tipperary.

Mr Michael Mockler
Ballycahill
Thurles, Co. Tipperary

Visitors to Ardmayle House can enjoy a mile of excellent trout fishing on private water just upstream of Ardmayle Bridge. Ardmayle House, Cashel, Co. Tipperary, (*telephone* 0504 42399) is a comfortable ITB approved farmhouse which specializes in catering for anglers. So also does Holycross House, Holycross, Co. Tipperary (*telephone* 0504 43278), and Bridge View Farmhouse, Holycross, Co. Tipperary, (*telephone* 0504 43152).

RIVER DRISH S 14 56

The River Drish is a rich limestone stream which joins the Suir about a mile south of Thurles. It drains large areas of peat bog. In its lower reaches it is a typical clean, slow-flowing, lowland limestone stream, its banks laden with bush vegetation. It holds excellent stocks of trout up to 4 lb in the middle and lower sections. From Drish Bridge downstream the river is usually fishable throughout the summer and can provide lovely dry-fly fishing on summer evenings. The middle reaches of the river, near Athlummen and upstream become very weeded in summer.

The fishing is controlled by Thurles-Holycross-Ballycamus Angling Club and permits are as for the Suir, (previous pages).

The same club controls the fishing on the Clodiagh River which joins the Suir from the west, downstream of Twoford Bridge. There is a nice bit of trout fishing on the Clodiagh for 1 mile from the Railway Bridge downstream to the confluence.

The upper reaches of the Suir, from Templemore downstream to Rossestown Bridge, are controlled by Templemore Angling Club. Drainage works have been carried out recently and the fishing is not recommended.

COLLIGAN RIVER X 23 95

Season

Salmon: 1 February to 30 September.
Sea-trout: 1 February to 30 September.
Brown trout: 1 March to 30 September.

The Colligan River rises in the Monavallagh Mountains of south Waterford and flows south for 15 miles into Dungarvan Bay. The upper reaches tumble through a wooded valley and the last 2 miles are more slow-flowing, with some lovely pools. It is strictly a spate river and is reputed to be one of the fastest-flowing rivers in Ireland. Its catchment is 40 square miles.

It is a brilliant little river when in condition for both salmon and sea trout. The first sea-trout run in early May and June, and July can see large shoals enter the river – if they succeed in escaping the nets. The average size is 2 lb and the Colligan is said to hold sea-trout to 10 lb or better. In terms of the quality of its sea-trout, it is very close to a Welsh sewin river, and small wonder, for Wales is only a short distance across the Celtic sea.

The sea-trout can be fished on a falling spate, but the best sport is with the fly at night. Local favourites include Mallard and Red, Silver Doctor and Mallard and Claret.

There is good grilse fishing to be had too in summer and the river gets a good run of big autumn salmon – many 15-17 lb – in September.

The local club controls the fishing and has done a lot of work clearing the banks. There is about 7 miles of fishing in all, but local knowledge is important.

Permits

    Boumann Jewellers
    Main Street
    Dungarvan
    Co. Waterford

MUNSTER (CORK) BLACKWATER   X 04 98

Season

Salmon and sea-trout: 1 February to 30 September
Brown trout: 15 February to 30 September

The Munster Blackwater rises in east Co. Kerry near the source of the Brown Flesk River and flows for 105 miles east through the counties of Cork and Waterford to the tide at Cappoquin. Its entire catchment is more than 1,200 square miles. It has a long, narrow estuary, some 15 miles long. It dominates the southern province, draining five ranges of mountains, and in times of heavy rainfall the levels can fluctuate wildly by more than 12 feet on the gauge at Careysville. The peaty nature of the terrain in the upper reaches and of some of the tributaries gives the water a pronounced dark colour. It is indeed 'black' water. The geology of the catchment is divided roughly into old red sandstone and limestone and lower limestone shales.

The river is noted for its enormous run of salmon over the years. The average size of the brown trout is rather small and it is not a noted sea-trout fishery. A distinguishing feature of the Blackwater is that it probably holds more species of fish than any other Irish river. It is the

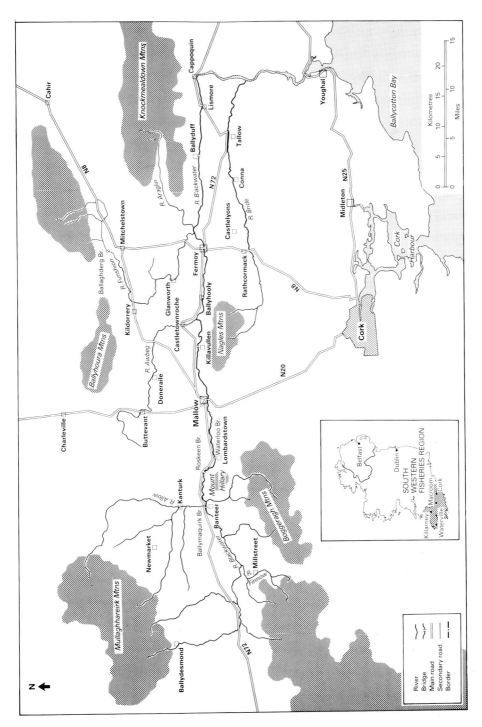

Cork Blackwater

only one to have dace, and roach were introduced to Ireland via the Blackwater in the late 1800s.

It is important for salmon anglers to note that the water condition can fall into about four different categories, depending on the amount of colour: in a flood, when the river carries a lot of suspended solids, it will be heavily coloured and unfishable; it is known as 'dark water' when it has a lot of colour but no suspended solids, and then spinning is more likely to succeed; in slightly coloured water a fly, spinner or worm will take fish; it is said that the Blackwater does not run really clear till July and some then maintain that the fly or the natural shrimp give best results for salmon.

The river is characterized by mighty pools, lovely streams, glides and, generally, a good push of water coming through except in very low water.

Careysville Weir, downstream of Fermoy, is one of the dominant features on the river. It controls the run of fish in low, cold water conditions. A lot of fish lie back and refuse to run, but when the water rises, or in high water, they will run the weir. Consequently, fishermen on the river often remark that 'you can get a spring fish at Millstreet on opening day', meaning that there are always fish upstream of Fermoy from early in the season.

Fishing methods

The Blackwater has to be regarded as a great multi-method salmon river. Spinning and fly fishing are allowed on all fisheries, but on some the use of worm and shrimp is prohibited. It is probably true that no one method is completely effective in all water conditions. If there is one method more effective than all the others, it is probably fly fishing. For those who blindly place all their hopes in the natural shrimp, it is well worth noting that it is not always effective and fishermen would be well advised to wait for clear water in July before fishing it.

Tube flies, Esmond Drury trebles or even big single hooks, up to size 4/0, are used for spring fishing.

In summer, smaller flies – size 6–12 – are called for. Flies with a touch of yellow or lemon work well and favoured patterns include Lemon and Grey, Garry Dog, Munro Killer, Thunder and Lightning, Curry's Shrimp, Stoat's Tail, Blue Charm, Hairy Mary and Silver Stoat's Tail.

Since this is a river with a lot of streamy water, it is not surprising to find that the spun shrimp is a frequently used method for summer fish, but one that requires correct tackle and not a little skill.

For the spring and back end, large spoons (up to 28 grams), spinners and Devons up to 3 inches are used. Smaller brown-and-gold Devons and Lane minnows are favoured by some in summer.

The Fisheries

CAREYSVILLE FISHERY

The Duke of Devonshire's Careysville Fishery is probably the best-known on the river. It consists of $1^3/_4$ miles of double-bank fishing with well-defined pools for fly fishing and bait fishing, depending on the height and colour of the water. It takes four rods in February and March, three rods from April to July and two rods in August and September. There is a comfortable fishing hut where lunch is served every day and accommodation is at Careysville House.

The spring salmon fishing is very highly regarded, with February being the most productive month. June is best for grilse.

CAREYSVILLE SALMON ROD CATCH 1985–90

	1985	1986	1987	1988	1989	1990
Salmon	254	367	356	394	649	274

Bookings

> The Manager
> Careysville Fishery
> Fermoy
> Co. Cork
> *Telephone* 025 31094/31712

THE DEMPSTER FISHERIES

Peter Dempster has been booking and letting fishing on the Blackwater for 16 years. At present he has ten beats in the section of river between Ballyduff and Ballyhooly. He has one rotating beat on the three-beat Ballyhooly Castle water and this is fly and spinning only. The number of rods per beat is restricted so that each fisherman can enjoy a substantial stretch of water and there is no crowding. Neither are parties mixed on the same beat. Gillies can be arranged, with prior notice. There is a tackle shop and accommodation can be arranged for clients.

PETER DEMPSTER LTD ROD CATCH 1986–90

	1986	1987	1988	1989	1990
Salmon	205	141	358	358	164

Bookings

Peter Dempster Ltd
Carrigeen Hill
Conna, Co. Cork
Telephone 058 56248

BLACKWATER LODGE HOTEL FISHERIES

Blackwater Lodge Hotel has eighteen beats, spread from the lowest beat, which is only 3 miles above the tide, to Mallow, some 40 miles upstream. The hotel is located 1 mile west of the village of Ballyduff in Co. Waterford. It caters especially for angling parties and its facilities include a tackle shop, a drying room and smoking and freezing facilities. All legal fishing methods are allowed.

The beats are rotated daily and each is about $3/4$ mile long. Up to four rods per beat are allowed.

In addition to the salmon fishing, the hotel has exclusive beats for brown trout fishing on the Awbeg River, a major spring-fed tributary of the River Blackwater, and sea-trout fishing can be arranged on the River Bride. There are self-catering facilities as well as accommodation at the hotel.

BLACKWATER LODGE HOTEL ROD CATCH 1986–90

	1986	1987	1988	1989	1990
Salmon	750	379	1,488	1,156	355

Bookings

Blackwater Lodge Hotel
Upper Ballyduff, Co. Waterford
Telephone 058 60235 / *Fax* 058 60162

FOX'S FISHERY, KILLAVULLEN

This very productive fishery is about ¾ mile long, left bank only, and is situated about a mile downstream of Killavullen Bridge – 10 miles west of Fermoy. It has a nice mix of streams and pools, including the famous Poul Caum, and is noted for both spring fish and grilse. By all accounts, this is an excellent stretch of water and it is thought to have produced over 100 fish per season in recent times. A maximum of four rods is allowed. A gillie can be arranged and all legitimate methods are permitted.

The fishing is let in conjunction with three beats on the River Lee and accommodation at Woodview House, near Blarney, one of Cork's leading restaurants.

Bookings

Mr Dan O'Donovan
32 Woodlands
Kerry Pike
Cork
Telephone 021 872322

BALLYMAQUIRK FISHERY AND LODGE

This fishery is located at Ballymaquirk Bridge on the road between Kanturk and Banteer. It consists of ¾ mile on the left bank of the Blackwater and ¼ mile on the Allow River. It was first let in 1991. It is let as one beat with three rods. It has some nice fly water which can be fished in summer with a single handed rod.

The Allow River holds some good-quality trout and grilse on a spate in June and July.

The fishing is let with a self-catering lodge which sleeps five, but only three may fish.

Bookings

Mr B. Murphy O'Connor
Greybrook House
Waterfall
Co. Cork
Telephone 021 502555
Fax 021 502376

BALLYVOLANE HOUSE

Ballyvolane House has access to one rotating beat on the Ballyhooley Castle Fishery. It takes three rods. The house is a period Georgian House, offering excellent accommodation and registered with the Irish Tourist Board.

Bookings

> The Manageress
> Ballyvolane House
> Castlelyons
> Co. Cork
> *Telephone* 025 36349

LOMARDSTOWN AND DISTRICT TROUT ANGLERS' CLUB

This club has access to about 4 miles of trout fishing only on the Blackwater between Waterloo Bridge and Roskeen Bridge. A private syndicate has the salmon fishing rights. The trout average ¹/₂ lb and the fishing can be classed as fair to good.

Permits

> The Secretary
> Lombardstown & District Trout Anglers' Club
> Lombardstown
> Mallow
> Co. Cork

MILLSTREET ANGLERS' ASSOCIATION

The association has about 10 miles of mainly trout fishing – with occasional salmon late in season – on the Blackwater and its tributaries, the Finnow River and Aubane River. The trout average ¹/₄–¹/₂ lb, with occasional fish to 1¹/₂ lb. The fishing is very good, especially in the months of April, May and June. Useful patterns for this – and, indeed, all the trout water on the Blackwater – are Greenwell's Glory, Dark Olive Quill, Pheasant Tail, Blue Black, Orange Partridge, Green Partridge, Wickham's Fancy, Black Palmer, Snipe and Purple and Snipe and Yellow.

Permits

> Dermot O'Keeffe
> Main Street
> Millstreet
> Co. Cork

RIVER FUNSHION   R 80 02

The River Funshion is a good little trout river which comes down from Mitchelstown, Glanworth and Kilworth to join the Blackwater just downstream of Fermoy. There are four angling clubs on the river – Mitchelstown, Kildorrery, Glenworth and Kilworth. Membership is open. The river is signposted stating where permits are available. It is fly fishing only.

Knocklofty Bridge on the Suir

·9· South-Western Fisheries Region

The Southern-Western Fisheries Region extends from Kerry Head south and then east to Ballycotton and covers the greater part of Counties Kerry and Cork. The headquarters of the South-Western Regional Fisheries Board is at 1 Nevilles Terrace, Masseytown, Macroom, Co. Cork, (*telephone* 026 41222).

In addition to being a region endowed with great natural beauty, its rivers are especially rich in salmon and sea-trout. Spring salmon enter some of the river systems from early January, grilse – locally referred to as 'peal' – are plentiful and large early season sea-trout are a special feature of the south-west. A few systems hold good-quality brown trout.

OWENNACURRA RIVER   W 87 74

Season

Salmon: 1 February to 30 September.
Sea-trout: 1 February to 12 October.
Brown trout: 15 February to 12 October.

Permission

Midleton and District Anglers' Association has the goodwill of the fishing. The Hon. Secretary is Mr Edward Reck, Rocky Road, Midleton, Co. Cork. Up-to-date information and membership cards are available from T.H. Sport, Main Street, Midleton, Co. Cork.

The Owennacurra River flows for 14 miles in a southerly direction through Midleton into Cork Harbour. It drains a catchment of 66 square miles. Much of the land along the river is under tillage.

It is regarded primarily as a sea-trout fishery. It gets a few grilse in July and August, but the numbers are so small they are not worth fishing for specifically. Strangely enough, the river gets a good run of salmon outside the season from November to January. It holds big stocks of very small brown trout.

Access is good, with the R626 Midleton–Rathcormack road running

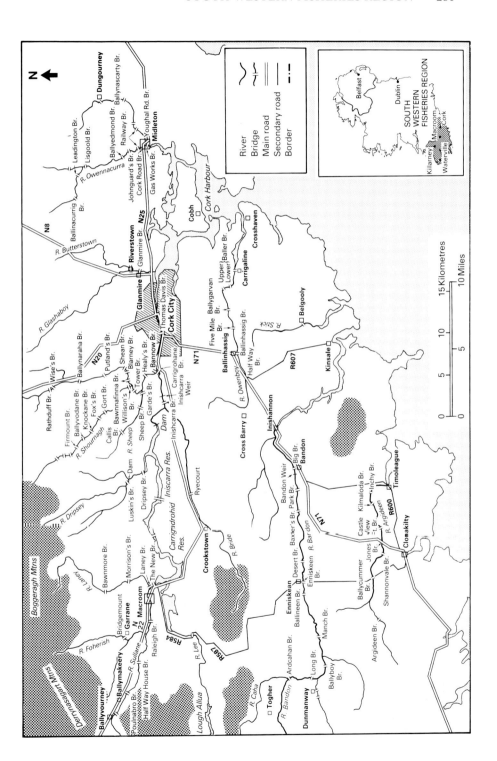

Rivers Owennacurra, Lee, Bandon and Argideen

close to the bank and bridges at about 1-mile intervals.

A small number of big sea-trout come in May but the peak of the run is in July and through August and September.

In low water, fishing is confined to the lower section – downstream from the Gas Works Bridge. After a spate, it is worth fishing up as far as Ballyedmond Bridge and there are five or six good pools in the vicinity of John Guard's Bridge. The majority of the sea-trout are small ($\frac{3}{4}$ lb) and the annual catch is said to be about 1,000 fish. The numbers have declined in recent years.

The majority of local anglers fish a fly at night – some persist from dusk to dawn. The favourite patterns are Peter Ross, Teal Blue and Silver, Watson's Fancy and Silver Jungle Cock. Visiting anglers are welcome.

The river holds a big stock of free-taking brown trout averaging 7 inches, with better fish up to 1 lb. It is stocked annually with 1,000 1-lb. brown trout to improve the fishing. The best of the fishing is from Cork Road Bridge up to Lisgoold Bridge – a distance of about 4 miles – and after a spate the river can be fished up to Ballincurrig Bridge. The banks are overgrown in places and there is room for a lot of development work. The best of the fishing is in late April, May and June, with evening fishing during the summer. Wet-fly and dry-fly fishing tactics both have a place and the trout can sometimes respond in a very lively fashion.

ROXBORO (DUNGOURNEY) RIVER   W 90 74

Seasons and permission:

As for the Owennacurra River, above.

The Roxboro River rises north of Dungourney and flows south and then west before entering the same estuary as the Owennacurra River. It is a small stream, about 9 miles long, and the fishable stretches are about 4 yards wide. It flows through countryside dominated by tillage and pastureland. It holds some good brown trout and gets a small run of sea-trout. About 200 sea-trout are taken annually.

The sea-trout fishing stretch is about $\frac{1}{2}$ mile long and is situated immediately upstream of Youghal Road Bridge as far as the distillery (Irish Distillers). The access is through the town park at a place called 'The Baby's Walk'. The banks are clear and there is room for about six anglers. The best of the fishing is usually in July and August.

The best of the brown trout fishing is from Ballynascarty up as far as Dungourney. Midway along this stretch there are some nice pools at Ballynacole. There are trout here up to 1 lb. It is lightly fished and said to be well worth a visit. A basket of half a dozen trout is a distinct possibility. Access is off the R627 Midleton–Dungourney road.

GLASHABOY RIVER   W 72 75

Season

Salmon: 1 February to 30 September.
Sea-trout: 1 February to 12 October.

Permission

Bobby Seward, Hon. Secretary, Glanmire and District Salmon and Trout
Anglers' Association.

The Glashaboy River (15 miles long), with its main tributary, the
Butterstown River, drains a 38 square mile catchment and flows through
a heavily wooded valley through the village of Glanmire into the Lee
estuary. It is a spate river, noted in the past for its huge runs of sea-trout,
which began about the third week of June every year. The angling
stretch is from Glanmire village up to the confluence at Riverstown, a
distance of about a mile. The pools are deep and slow-moving –
Poulcaum, the Rocky Hole, the Long Reach and the Barleycorn Pool.
The fishing has deteriorated greatly recently, allegedly due to water
abstraction and the construction of an almost impassable weir. Over
1,000 sea-trout were taken in 1988 but only about 250 in 1989.   Night
fishing with a fly (Silver Rail) and maggot is the traditional method and
there is a four-trout bag limit. Poulcaum is heavily fished.
    Access to the river bank is quite easy, with steps in the riverside wall at
Glanmire, at the country park further up and at Riverstown village
opposite the John Barleycorn Hotel.
    The Butterstown River is fast flowing and rocky. The banks are
wooded and overgrown. The pools in the lower reaches hold fish but are
not fished because of the difficult bankside conditions.

RIVER LEE   W 60 71

Season

Salmon: 1 February to 30 September.
Brown trout: 15 February to 12 October.

Permission

This is dealt with in detail below.

The River Lee rises in a wild and lovely mountainous region near Gauganebarra in west Cork and flows 56 miles due east and through the city of Cork. It and its tributaries drain a catchment of 484 square miles. The Lee and some of the tributaries rise high in the mountains before reaching a terrain of alternating moorland and small farms. The valleys are now flooded as a result of the erection of two dams for hydroelectric power stations in 1956. The resulting elongated reservoirs stretch for a distance of approximately 16 miles and have destroyed miles of river fishing from Inniscarra Dam to Macroom and above.

The erection of the dams appears to have interfered greatly with the free passage of fish, particularly salmon, and it is alleged that while some salmon make it through the fish pass very few smolts survive to go back to sea. In order to supplement the smolt run, the Electricity Supply Board built a hatchery at Carrigadrohid and is committed to stocking 136,000 smolts annually into the river.

Salmon fishing is now confined to an 8-mile stretch of river, reaching from Inniscarra Dam to the centre of Cork City. The progeny of the generous stocking programme together with the escapement of wild smolts ensures a very substantial run of both spring salmon and grilse to the river. Those who have access to this stretch enjoy some of the best salmon fishing in Ireland. It is difficult to get accurate statistics for the various fisheries, but a figure of 800 salmon per season may well be a gross underestimate of the rod-and-line catch in a good season. Of these, 200 or more would be spring fish.

Permission

The best fishing is all controlled and the only free fishing is a stretch of dead water immediately above Cork Weir. The controlling parties are: Cork Salmon Anglers' Association Ltd; the Lee Salmon Anglers' Club; the Electricity Supply Board ; and private interests.

Cork Salmon Anglers' Association is a limited company with 50 shareholders and it grants 30 annual permits. It also welcomes bone fide tourist anglers and salmon-fishing day tickets are available at £10 per day from Mr John Buckley, Raheen House, Carrigrohane, Co. Cork, (*telephone* 021 872137). Day tickets are also available for trout fishing at a nominal fee, but anglers must seek permission.

The association's fisheries are in three sections: the left bank above and below Inishcarra Bridge; the right bank below the same bridge; and up near the dam on the left bank.

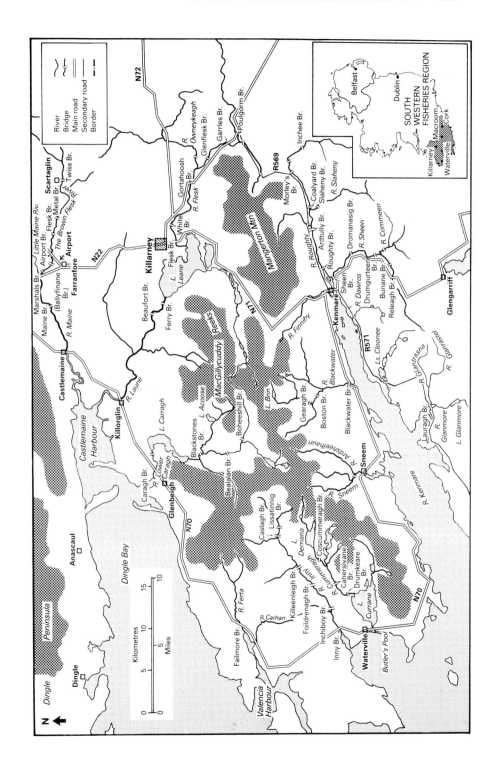

The Ring of Kerry

The Lee Salmon Anglers' Club limits membership to 70 and issues 70 annual permits. Day tickets for tourists, costing £10, are available for fishing, Monday to Friday, from Percy Cole, Auto Factor, Douglas Street, Cork.

The ESB fisheries are located at the top and bottom of the stretch below the Iniscarra Dam and at Fitzgerald Park. They are leased to the South-Western Regional Fisheries Board (head office, Macroom, *telephone* 026 41222) and the board lets rods on a daily basis.

The free fishing is at a place called the Lee Fields, upstream of Thomas Davis Bridge. This is slow, deep water and is not considered productive.

The fisheries are located in an environment of woodlands, pasture lands and finally an urban setting. The level of the water is artificially controlled and the flow depends on how many turbines are in operation. Local anglers actually talk in terms of 'megawatt flows' – 1½ megawatts is low flow, 4 megawatts is nice fly water, 15 megawatts is for spinning and 19 megawatts is a 'full load'. As is the case on all rivers, the period just before the water rises and after it drops is considered the best taking time.

In spring, the fishing is also influenced greatly by Inishcarra Weir, which is located downstream of Inishcarra Bridge. When temperatures are low, the fish lie below it and only when the water warms up does the fishing improve above it.

It is estimated that the fisheries produce at least 200 spring salmon every season. The peak of the run is usually in the last two weeks in March and the first week in April. A lot of fish are caught then, even on high water. Fly fishers use tube flies dressed on brass tubes from 1½ to 2½ inches and fast sinking and sink tip lines, depending on the height of the water. Others spin or fish worm or shrimp. The grilse run peaks in late June and early July and the river continues to fish through August and September. Small flies (sizes 8–14) and light tackle give good sport and favourite patterns are Thunder and Lightning, Blue Charm, Lady Caroline, Hairy Mary, Shrimp patterns and Lee Blue. The dressing of the Lee Blue is as follows:

Tag	Fine oval silver and yellow floss
Tail	Golden pheasant tippets and topping
Rib	Oval silver
Body	Light blue floss or seal's fur
Body Hackle	Light blue cock
Shoulder Hackle	Yellow cock
Wing	Golden pheasant tippets, red, yellow and blue swan, golden pheasant tail, teal and bronze mallard over.
Head	Black varnish

The average weight of spring fish is 8 lb and the grilse are small, averaging about 3 lb. There is a nice mix of water on the various fisheries, with streams, pools and flats. The local angling associations have done much to improve the waters by way of constructing weirs and groynes, deepening streams and clearing bank cover.

Gillies

Contact:
John Buckley
Raheen House
Carrigrohane, Co. Cork
Telephone 021 872137

Brown trout

The river holds a fair stock of beautifully marked pink-fleshed brown trout averaging about ½ lb. As with all rivers where salmon are the primary attraction, the trout fishing is virtually ignored. The best of the day fishing is in May and June and there is good evening fishing during the summer. Both angling associations accommodate genuine fly-fishing trout anglers.

RIVER MARTIN   W 60 80

Season

Brown trout: 15 February to 12 October.

Permission

Free.

The Martin is a small brown-trout river, 11 miles long and about 15 yards at its widest point. It rises north-north-west of Cork City and flows in a southerly direction through Blarney to join the River Shournagh, a tributary of the Lee. Access to the river is easy, with roads running close to the river banks. The banks are wooded and very overgrown and fishing can be difficult.

The average size of the trout is about 6 oz though some grow to about 2 lb in the stretch at Blarney Bridge and again up between Wise's Bridge and Rathduff Bridge. This latter section is very overgrown. From Blarney Bridge up to Wise's Bridge has a lot of fishable water.

Local anglers claim that the size of the trout has declined since the dam for Blarney Woollen Mills was removed in the early 1970s.

Wet-fly fishing and spinning are the most widely practised fishing methods and the most common flies used are Black Palmer (always on the point), Fenian (a Greenwell's Glory dressed with an emerald green body), March Brown Spider, Hare's Ear, Olive Quill, Red Quill, Orange Grouse, the Hawthorn in April–May, small sedge patterns with variously coloured bodies in sizes 14 and 16 and the natural 'wood bee', a fly of the order Diptera which is found in the woods in early June. It is usually found around the droppings of animals and is captured and stored in a box, bottle or cow's horn. One or two flies are mounted on a hook and cast into the pools and streams. On warm summer days it is reckoned to be one of the deadliest methods of trout fishing on all the rivers in these parts.

RIVER SHOURNAGH   W 60 74

Season

Brown trout: 15 February to 12 October.

Permission

Free.

The Shournagh rises at 1,000 feet and rushes and tumbles for about 17 miles, passing to the west of Blarney Castle, before entering the Lee at Leemount Bridge. It holds a large stock of brown trout up to about 9 inches, with some better fish downstream, where it is joined by the River Martin. There is a nice pool below Bannow Bridge and some nice water above it. The rest of this stretch up to Healy's Bridge is sluggish with a bit of nice water below Healy's Bridge. From Healy's Bridge to the golf course is very overgrown and suitable only for spinning but from the golf course (on the left bank) up to Tower Bridge it is possible to fly fish. There is a piece of fly water at the confluence and the rest is spinning water. A lot of the water from Willison's Bridge up to Gort Bridge is suitable for fly fishing and all is easily accessible from the road. The section below Fox's Bridge has some nice pools but is very overgrown, but there is a nice stretch of fly water for two fields above Fox's Bridge. From Knockane Bridge to Ballyvodane Bridge is a favourite stretch, suitable for fly fishing, with nice open water and a good stock of 8-9 inch trout. The river becomes very overgrown above Ballyvodane Bridge and it is not worth the effort of trying to fish any further upstream.

April, May and June are considered the best months. For flies, see the River Martin, above.

OWENNAGEARAGH (SHEEP) RIVER   W 57 74

Season

Brown trout: 15 February to 12 October.

Permission

Free.

The Owennagearagh or Sheep River is about 7 miles long and joins the River Shournagh west of Blarney. It holds a good stock of brown trout between Garde's Bridge and Ballyshoneen Bridge, but they are very small. There is a section of clear bank suitable for fly fishing upstream of Garde's Bridge and a clear section on the right bank above Sheep Bridge. The Yellow House is a well known landmark and there is a nice piece of fishing downstream from Callis Bridge for a couple of miles. The banks are reasonably clear and it is possible to wade. For flies, see the River Martin, above.

RIVER DRIPSEY   W 49 73

Season

Brown trout: 15 February to 12 October.

Permission

Free.

The River Dripsey is 14 miles long and feeds Innicarra Reservoir west of Coachford. It holds a good stock of small brown trout. It is best suited to wet-fly fishing, with the best of the fishing being in the lower reaches. A dam a couple of miles up from the reservoir possibly prevents the migration of reservoir trout upstream late in the season.

LANEY RIVER   W 36 73

Season

Brown trout: 15 February to 12 October.

Permission

Free.

The Laney River is 15 miles long and joins the Sullane River 3 miles east of Macroom. It is a fast-flowing moorland stream and has the reputation of having the best average weight of trout of all the Lee tributaries. The banks are very overgrown up to Morrison's Bridge but this stretch has some good pools. From Bawnmore Bridge downstream, the banks are reasonably clear of obstructions except for a stretch immediately above Morrison's Bridge. It is not worth fishing above Morrison's Bridge. Use the same flies as for the River Martin.

FOHERISH RIVER   W 29 76

Season

Brown trout: 15 February to 12 October.

Permission

Free.

The Foherish River, a tributary of the Sullane, is a spate stream about 9 miles long. It holds a fair stock of small brown trout and the most productive area is in the vicinity of the bridge at Bridgemount. The banks are quite overgrown.

SULLANE RIVER   W 33 73

Season

Brown trout: 15 February to 12 October.

Permission

Free.

The Sullane River and its tributaries drain the western slopes of the Derrynasaggart Mountain range. The river flows for 23 miles in an easterly direction through Ballyvourney and Macroom into Carrigadrohid Reservoir. It is mainly a moorland river flowing over sandstone.

It holds a good stock of brown trout averaging just under ½ lb but it also gets a run of larger fish up from the reservoir and 1½ lb. trout are not uncommon. For this reason it is heavily fished, especially early in the season, with the greatest angling pressure being at weekends. The good trout are generally found in localized populations. Why this should be, nobody knows. It fishes well right through the season and there can be good fly fishing there on summer evenings through July and August which can last till midnight.

The fishing extends upstream as far as Ballyvourney and the most popular stretches are from the New Bridge upstream to Macroom, a stretch upstream of Raleigh Bridge on the right bank, a ½ mile stretch on the right bank downstream of the Half-Way House Bridge and a stretch on the right bank upstream of Poul na Bro Bridge.

The Sullane has hatches of various olives, the iron blue, the blue-winged olives, stoneflies and sedges. The popular fly patterns for wet-fly fishing include Greenwell's Glory (with emerald green body), Orange Grouse, Red Spinner and small Sedges.

RIVER BRIDE (SOUTH)   W 55 70

Season

Brown trout: 15 February to 12 October.

Permission

Riparian owners. Much of it is considered free.

The River Bride (South) rises in west Cork and meanders for nearly 20 miles through Crookstown, Ryecourt and Ovens, to join the River Lee upstream of Inishcarra Bridge. The upper reaches flow over sandstone and the middle and lower stretches lie on limestone. It is a very productive river and holds a really excellent stock of small fat brown trout. The average size is probably just under ½ lb, but it can produce some to 1 lb and even a few to $1\frac{1}{4}$ lb and $1\frac{1}{2}$ lb. It is one lovely trout stream, with pools and riffles and meanders, and it can be fished to well above Crookstown. Indeed, some of the best fishing on summer evenings is from there down to Ryecourt. The rise of trout can be spectacular. Access is mainly from the bridges. It can get heavy angling pressure at weekends, particularly in spring, but it is not usually overcrowded for the evening rise on weekdays during the summer. It has all the usual fly hatches found on a limestone river, except mayfly.

The Bride gets a big run of salmon but sadly, they don't arrive till after the season closes.

OWENBOY RIVER   W 70 62

Season

Salmon: 1 February to 30 September.
Sea-trout: 1 February to 12 October.
Brown trout: 15 February to 12 October.

Permission

The fishing is strictly with the permission of the riparian owners.

The Owenboy is located 5 miles south of Cork City. It is about 14 miles long and mostly slow-flowing and sluggish. It flows eastwards through Ballinhassig and Carrigaline and empties into Cork Harbour at Crosshaven through a narrow $4\frac{1}{2}$ mile estuary.

It is primarily regarded as a sea-trout fishery up to Ballinhassig and produces over 1,000 sea-trout annually and about 40 salmon. The best of the fishing is from mid June, through July, August and September.

The sea-trout are fished for mainly at night and fly fishers favour the Butcher, Silver Rail and Teal, Blue and Silver. Prime fishing locations are at the Pier Hole, the estuary and the flats below John A. Wood's gravel pit near Ballygarvan Bridge.

The salmon fishing is unpredictable and the run is small, with a good percentage of the summer fish being stray ESB fish from the Lee. Worm fishing in the lower stretches is the most popular fishing method.

The brown trout fishing has deteriorated greatly in recent years and is confined mainly to the stretch between Ballea bridges, upper and lower.

Access to the fishing is at the bridges. The banks are relatively clean and easily fished.

This river was badly damaged as a fishery by an arterial drainage scheme from Cross Barry downstream to Ballinhassig. A lot of spawning and nursery water was lost and there is now a heavy weed growth which makes fishing impossible in summer.

RIVER BANDON   W 50 55

Season

Salmon, sea-trout and brown trout: 15 February to 30 September.

Permission

While there are a few small sections of free fishing on the Bandon, the vast majority of the fishing is controlled and used either by private owners, syndicates or angling associations.

Fishing is available through the following:

Mr Chambre Good
Belmont
Innishannon, Co. Cork
Telephone 021 75261 ($\frac{1}{2}$ mile approximately)

Miss Patricia Blanchfield
Blanchfield House
Ballinhassig, Co. Cork
Telephone 021 885167 ($\frac{3}{4}$ mile approximately)

Bandon Salmon and Trout Anglers' Association
Mr Michael J. O'Regan
Oliver Plunkett Street
Bandon, Co. Cork
Telephone 023 41674 (7 miles approximately)

The above association makes day tickets available to bona fide tourists and to all who give seven days' notice of their intention to fish.

Ballineen and Enniskeane Anglers' Association
Tom Fehily
Bridge Street
Ballineen
Co. Cork (4 miles approximately)

David Lamb
Kilcoleman Park
Enniskeane, Co. Cork
Telephone 023 47279 (4 miles approximately)

Dunmanway Salmon and Trout Anglers' Association
Patrick McCarthy
Yew Tree Bar
Main Street
Dunmanway
Co. Cork (10 miles approximately)

The Bandon River rises in the Shehy Mountains in west Cork and flows for 45 miles in an easterly direction through Dunmanway, Ballineen, Enniskeane, Bandon and Innishannon. It drains an area of 235 square miles. The tide comes up to Innishannon and the narrow estuary stretches for 11 miles to Kinsale. The upper reaches drain mountain, bog and moorland before the river enters a rich, fertile and very scenic valley at Manch Bridge.

About eight draft nets work the estuary. Unsupervised arterial drainage works caused a lot of damage to the river from Dunmanway downstream to Manch Bridge and it is good to see that the situation regarding agricultural and industrial pollution has improved in recent times.

The Fishing

The Bandon River offers a great variety of fishing and its potential is vastly underestimated. It gets a very good run of salmon and has excellent sea-trout fishing and good fishing for small brown trout.

Salmon

The salmon fishing extends all the way from Innishannon upstream to Togher Castle – depending on the season and water conditions. It is estimated that the river produces 1,300 salmon to rod and line annually. About 300 of these are spring fish taken before 1 May. Bandon Weir controls the run of spring fish. When the water is cold – February to mid-March – the majority of fish are taken below the weir. This corner of the south-west is never cold for too long, being quickly warmed by the influence of the Gulf Stream and so from about mid-March the fish are moving steadily upstream. April usually sees the peak of the spring run.

The grilse run occurs at the end of June and water levels can be critical for good fishing. The river weeds up badly when the water drops, though a couple of fisheries carry out weed cutting.

The river gets a very good run of big fresh fish in August and September, and this is again dependent on good water.

According to informed local opinion, the salmon fishing is all considered to be excellent from Innishannon upstream to Desert Bridge.

It becomes more spread out further up. From Desert Bridge upstream to Enniskeane Bridge is considered fair and from Enniskeane Bridge up to the Carbry Milk Products factory, which is located upstream of Ballineeen, is not thought of highly. From the factory up to Manch Bridge is again good salmon water. There are eight pools between Manch Bridge and Ballyboy Bridge and of these McCarthy's High Bank a short distance above Manch, and the Weir Pool are best. From Ballyboy Bridge up to the Long Bridge at Dunmanway is rarely worth fishing by the salmon angler, except, perhaps, 'Poulamount', $^1/_2$ mile up from Ballyboy Bridge.

There are five pools worth the angler's attention between the Long Bridge and Ardcahan Bridge. The Turn Hole, the Fox's Hole, the Tailor's Hole and the Tinker's Hole are all worth a try and all within a mile of the Long Bridge. The middle section of this stretch is inaccessible and useless. Poulatagart is about 400 yards downstream from Ardcahan Bridge and well worth a visit. It should be approached along the left bank.

From Ardcahan Bridge to Togher Bridge is nearly 4 miles of desolate moorland and bog. There are three or four pools worth fishing a short distance above Ardcahan Bridge and the best of the fishing should be approached from Togher Bridge, where Poulgorm, which is upstream of Togher Castle, the Turn Pool, the Punch Bowl and the Ford are all worth a try.

It should be remembered that from Togher Bridge to Manch Bridge the river has been severely damaged by drainage works and the best of the fishing is on a falling spate.

The fisheries allow all methods, except David Lamb's water, which is fly only from 1 April. Favourite spring baits are brown-and-gold, blue-and-silver and yellow belly Devons. Best of all is probably a bunch of worms. The Hairy Mary is probably the most popular salmon fly, followed by the Silver Wilkinson, Silver and Blue (not unlike a Teal, Blue and Silver), Garry Dog and a very interesting locally devised shrimp pattern known as 'Yer Man'.

A 14-foot fly rod is recommended in big water, while a single-handed rod is adequate in summer.

Sea-trout

The river gets an excellent run of sea-trout. The big run commences in early July and can last till the end of August and beyond. It is estimated that thousands of sea-trout are taken every year on the free waters of the estuary and the fishing can be really good on the 4-mile stretch from Bandon to Innishannon. A smaller number of better-quality sea-trout are taken up as far as Enniskeane. Peter Ross, Teal Blue and Silver, Bloody

Butcher and Connemara Black are the most commonly used flies.

Brown trout

The river holds an excellent stock of brown trout and a number of fisheries allow fly fishing only. The average weight is about ½ lb and there is a 9-inch size limit. The best fishing months are April, May, early June and September.

The river gets good hatches of olives, sedges, black gnats, blue-winged olives and stoneflies in season as well as falls of hawthorn and woodfly. Favourite wet-fly patterns are Greenwell's Glory (with bright green body) Light and Dark Olives, Snipe and Purple, Partridge and Orange, Orange Grouse, Wickham's Fancy, Hare's Ear, Black Zulu, Bracken Clock, and Blue Dun.

Weed growth poses a big problem in summer.

CAHA RIVER   W 24 57

Permission

Free.

The Caha River is a tributary of the Bandon and joins it from the north above Ardcahan Bridge. It holds a good stock of trout up to 14 oz for about 3 miles up from the confluence. It is best fished early in the season as weed becomes a problem later and there may also be discoloration from sand washing.

ARGIDEEN RIVER

Season

Salmon: 15 February to 30 September.
Sea-trout and brown trout: 15 February to 12 October.

Permission

Two short sections are privately owned and not let. The rest of the river is jointly managed by the South Western Regional Fisheries Board and the Argideen Anglers' Association. Visitors' tickets (£5 a day) are available from:

Mr Peter Wolstenholme
Courtmacsherry Ceramics
Courtmacsherry
Co. Cork
Telephone 023 46239

The South-Western Regional Fisheries Board
Neville's Terrace
Macroom
Co. Cork
Telephone 026 41222

The Argideen River (in Irish, the little silver stream) rises north west of Clonakilty and flows due east for 18 miles, draining a catchment of 56 square miles before entering the estuary at Timoleague. It is tidal up to Inchy Bridge.

This is primarily a good sea-trout river and it produces an occasional salmon. Angling statistics are difficult to obtain but as a sample of the quality of the fishing a survey of 18 anglers in 1988 revealed 315 sea-trout. In 1989, 30 anglers reported 700 sea-trout. There are slob trout in the estuary. These are very good to eat and recognizable by five red spots along the lateral line. Local anglers fish for them in February and March using silver-bodied flies.

A maximum of six rods are allowed by day and a maximum of twenty at night.

Anglers wishing to fish at night meet at Inchy Bridge half an hour before dark and there is a draw for the pools – all very democratic. There is a size limit of 9 inches and a bag limit of ten trout.

Methods

The most successful method for daytime fishing in clear water is a single worm on light tackle. After a flood, the trout will take a small spinner or a large 1 to 2 inch blue-and-silver lure fished on a sinking line in the steady glides and at the tail of pools. For night fishing, bright flies give best results in the estuary pools and darker flies are preferred up river.

RIVER ILEN   W 12 34

Season

Salmon: 1 February to 30 September.
Sea-trout: 1 February to 12 October.

Permission

The ownership of the fishing rights is fragmented and generally held by the riparian owners. The River Ilen Anglers' club has about 4 miles of the river. The club waters stretch up to Caheragh Bridge, with some exceptions, but there is fishing to be obtained with the permission of riparian owners up as far as Inchengeragh Bridge on the R5 and 6 Drimoleague–Bantry road. Day and weekly tickets are available from:

> Tony Kelly
> Fallon's Sports Shop
> North Street
> Skibbereen, Co. Cork
> *Telephone* 028 21435

The Ilen River is a medium-sized spate river, 21 miles long, with numerous tributaries which drain an area of 117 square miles. It flows south and enters the tide at Skibbereen.

This river gets a good run of spring salmon and grilse and an excellent run of sea-trout. Rod catch statistics are difficult to obtain but local estimates put the 1989 catch of spring salmon at well over 100 as well as at least a 200 grilse on the club water alone. The first spring fish enter the river in March and it is worth fishing from the 20 March. The main run comes in April and May. There is only one draft net in the estuary and it is operated only occasionally, so the fish have a free passage. The average size of the spring fish is 10 lb and two fish over 20 lb were reported in 1989.

The first run of grilse coincides with the first flood in June and they continue to run through July and August.

A small run of good sea-trout to 5 lb, with an average weight of 2 lb, enters the system in April and May. The big runs of ¾ lb juniors arrive in July and August.

Access to the river is good. The club water is nearly all fished off the left bank, and further up it can be fished from either bank. It is relatively easy to worm or spin it all but in places overhead bushes present a problem to the fly fisher. Shrimp fishing is not permitted.

The bottom of the river can become somewhat crowded in good water conditions, but there is unlimited scope upstream for those who are prepared to make the effort to walk and explore.

Methods

Spinning and worming are the methods most commonly used for salmon and grilse. Favourite baits include bronze and copper Mepps (No 3),

Devon minnows, blue-and-silver and black-and-gold, $2^1/_4$–$2^1/_2$ inches, and blue-and-silver and copper Tobys up to 18 grams.

The Hairy Mary, Thunder and Lightning and Silver Doctor are all good salmon flies on the river.

Dark flies, like the Bibio, Teal and Black and Black Pennell are considered best for the spring sea-trout fishing, and in summer bright flies are favoured – for example, Butchers, Teal and Silver, Silver Rail and Peter Ross in sizes 8–14 and the Ilen Blue.

The dressing of the Ilen Blue is:

Tail	Red ibis
Rib	Oval gold tinsel
Body	Flat gold tinsel
Hackle	Scarlet cock
Wing	Fibres of blue peacock neck feather

MEALAGH RIVER   W 1 50

Season

Salmon: 17 March to 30 September.
Sea-trout: 17 March to 12 October.

Permission

The bottom pool – below the falls – is private and the rest of the river is with the permission of the riparian owners.

The Mealagh River is located 1 mile north of Bantry. It is 11 miles long and drains a valley of 20 square miles. It gets a run of both salmon and sea-trout – which is surprising, considering the seemingly impassable falls a short distance up river. Salmon and sea-trout are taken in the falls pool and there are some nice deep pools upstream which are worth exploring after a spate.

OWVANE RIVER   W 1 53

Season

Salmon: 17 March to 30 September.
Sea-trout: 17 March to 12 October.

Permission

Riparian owners.

This little spate river is 12 miles long and drains a catchment of 31 square miles comprising pastureland, moorland and mountains. It gets a fair run of grilse and produces about 70 annually to rod and line. The spring run has declined greatly in recent years. The sea-trout run has also declined and the catch is about 100 per season.

The best fishing is immediately after a spate. There are four good pools in the first mile of river above the tide, three more nice pools below Carriganass Falls, 3 miles up from the tide, and another good pool above the falls. Access is off the R584 leading to the Pass of Keamaneigh.

A drainage scheme did great damage to the pools below Kealkill village and at the time of writing negotiations are in progress between the South-Western Regional Fisheries Board and the Office of Public Works regarding a weir without a fish pass which has been constructed.

The best of the sea-trout fishing is at night in July on the first mile above the tide.

COOMHOLA RIVER   V 99 55

Season

Salmon: 17 March to 30 September.
Sea-trout: 17 March to 12 October.

Permission

Riparian owners.

This delightful little spate river – 12 miles long and draining a catchment of 26 square miles – tumbles down an incredibly beautiful, rough, rugged moorland valley into the top of Bantry Bay. There are netting rights in existence in the estuary but they are not exercised. Poaching is, however, a problem that the Coomhola shares with all the other rivers in this locality.

It gets a good run of grilse and produces about 150 to the rod every season. The best fishing is after a spate. Access is good, with a road running up the valley parallel to the river. The fishing extends for 5 miles up to Borlin Falls but the best of it is on the first 3 miles near Coomhola Church and Bridge. There are about twelve pools altogether and the water is gin clear, flowing over a very light coloured river bottom.

The banks are difficult to walk in parts but this all adds to the charm. Upstream spinning gives good results on a spate.

Big sea-trout are a particular feature of this river. They come in around mid-April in sufficient numbers to warrant fishing and average 4 lb. The 'juniors' run in late June and July.

GLENGARRIFF RIVER   V 92 56

Season

Salmon: 17 March to 30 September.
Sea-trout and brown trout: 17 March to 12 October.

Permission

> Mr Bernard Harrington
> The Maple Leaf
> Glengarriff, Co. Cork
> *Telephone* 027 63021

The Glengarriff River is just 7 miles long and drains a catchment of 16-square-miles. It drains a scenic mountain valley which is thickly wooded with newly planted pines and ancient oak, yew, rowan and holly. The river, though short, is characterized by nine pools – two of them huge deep holding pools. There is Brook's Pool, Poulcaum, Poulacranna and Thompson's Pool, which is by the road side; then the Otter Pool, the Crooked Hole, the Doctor's Pool, Inchaneer and Pouleen below the waterfall. Anglers are strongly advised not to stand on the slippery rock formation at the head of Pouleen.

The Glengarriff gets a good run of grilse and a very good run of sea-trout – over 1,000 sea-trout are taken in a season. Big sea-trout averaging 1½ lb come in May and the 'juniors' run in July. This is the peak of the season and it is possible to stand by a pool at night and hear sea-trout splashing all over it. Favourite flies are Dunkeld, Butcher, Jungle Cock and Alexandra.

The salmon fishing is best after a spate and spinning and worms are the popular angling methods. A 2-inch or 1½-inch blue Devon is recommended by local anglers.

The banks are difficult to negotiate with pine forest planted right down to the edge of the water.

A plus for this river is the fact that the local angling association bought out the draft net at the estuary.

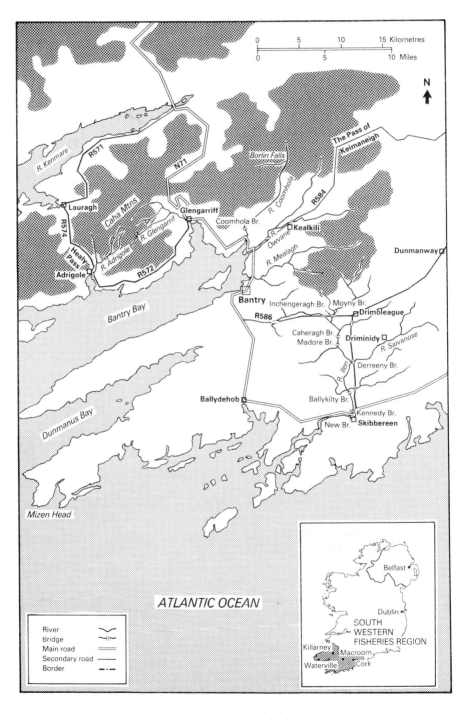

The West Cork rivers

ADRIGOLE RIVER   V 81 51

Season

Salmon: 17 March to 30 September.
Sea-trout: 17 March to 12 October.

Permission

Mrs Francis Keaney
Glenbrook
Adrigole, Co. Cork
Telephone 027 60064

This small river is about 6 miles long and drains a catchment of 12 square miles, which includes several lakes. It gets a run of grilse and sea-trout in June but, unfortunately, is reputed to be heavily poached. The best pools are in the vicinity of Adrigole Bridge. The road up to the Healy Pass in the Caha Mountains runs parallel to the right bank for about 1 mile.

SHEEN RIVER   V 93 70

Season

Salmon: 15 March to 30 September.
Sea-trout and brown trout: 15 March to 12 October.

Permission

The Manager
Sheen Falls Lodge
Kenmare, Co. Kerry
Telephone 064 41600

The Sheen River is a fast flowing spate system, 14 miles long and draining a catchment of approximately 36 square miles. It rises in the Caha Mountains and flows northwards through a magnificent scenic valley into the head of Kenmare Bay. The water runs off very quickly after a spate and prime fishing time can be of quite short duration.

It is highly regarded as a salmon fishery and is estimated to produce approximately 1,000 salmon and grilse every season. The sea-trout run is less prolific and their numbers are thought to be in decline.

It gets a fair run of spring salmon and fishing starts from opening day in March. It gets a marvellous run of grilse and these fish can arrive at the end of May or early in June, depending on water conditions.

Access to the river is relatively easy, with roads running parallel to the river for the first 7 miles and bridges at frequent intervals. The first 6 miles of fishing up from the sea are regarded as the best.

There are approximately fourteen pools up to Dromanassig bridge, ten pools to Drumgurteen Bridge, five pools to Bunane Bridge, five pools to Releagh Bridge and a big pool at Raw, above Releagh Bridge. The Comeen River is a tributary which comes in on the right bank a mile above Drumgurteen bridge and it has five pools in the first mile above the confluence.

This river has changed ownership recently and the letting arrangements are that the fishing is available to anglers who reside permanently in the locality and to the residents of Sheen Falls Lodge who will have the first option on the fishing.

The fishery owners augment the fishery's protection which is provided by the Regional Fisheries Board.

ROUGHTY RIVER   V 96 72

Season

Salmon: 15 March to 30 September.
Sea-trout and brown trout: 15 March to 12 October.

Permission

The fishing rights are fragmented among riparian owners. There is one stretch at Ardtully Castle, 4 miles from Kenmare off the R569 Kilgarvan road, which is the property of Kenmare Salmon Angling Ltd and for which day tickets can be obtained from John O'Hara, Main Street, Kenmare, Co. Kerry, (*telephone* 064 41499). The day permits allow fishing from 9 a.m. to 7 p.m. on 1 mile of double-bank fishing and there is no Sunday fishing for visitors. Otherwise the fishing is with the permission of the riparian owners.

The Roughty River is medium sized, being 19 miles long, and drains a catchment of 78 square miles. It rises in the mountains on the borders of west Cork and flows in a westerly direction through the village of Kilgarvan into the top of Kenmare Bay. Over its lower 7 miles it flows through a fertile valley over a limestone base.

It is a river beset with many problems, including poaching, land drainage and pollution. A draft net operates in the narrow estuary.

It gets a small run of spring salmon and a good run of grilse. No exact figures are available, but it is generally believed that the club's water at Ardtully produces approximately 200 salmon and grilse in a good season. The sea-trout run has declined and the best of this fishing is just above the tide, at Poultadagh, and on the Slaheny, a tributary which comes in just south of Kilgarvan. The river in its lower reaches is characterized by big slow pools. The salmon fishing, on a spate, extends all the way up to Inchee Bridge and for 2 miles of the Slaheny up to Shandrum School.

Access to the river is relatively easy, with roads running close to all the fishable water. However, the banks are very overgrown and this precludes fly fishing on much of the water. Spinning, worm and shrimp fishing are the most frequently practised methods.

FINNIHY RIVER   V 90 71

Season

Salmon: 15 March to 30 September.
Sea-trout and brown trout: 15 March to 12 October.

Permission

    The Estate Office
    The Square
    Kenmare, Co. Kerry
The river is regarded locally as free fishing.

This is a small spate river, 7 miles long, with a catchment of 12 square miles. It enters Kenmare Bay a short distance west of the town of Kenmare.

It is a neglected little river, very overgrown and unfishable except by the very determined, to whom it quietly produces quite a few grilse when the water is right in summer. There are seven pools in all – the Barrack Hole, the Crow's Dip, the Falls (Killarney Road), Lee's Weir, Two-Mile-Bridge Falls, the Turnpool and Sullivan's Falls at Rinacollee Bog.

RIVER BLACKWATER   V 79 69

Season

Salmon: 15 March to 30 September.
Sea-trout: 15 March to 12 October.

Permission

The Estate Office	Major Waller
The Square	Dromore Castle
Kenmare	Blackwater, Kenmare
Co. Kerry	Co. Kerry

The River Blackwater enters Kenmare Bay from the north 7 miles west of Kenmare. It is 10 miles long and drains a catchment of 34 square miles, including three loughs. It has several tributaries draining magnificent scenic mountain valleys. The fishable part of the river from Blackwater Bridge up to Boston Bridge is about 4 miles and this is characterized by streams and about thirty pools – including some huge holding pools.

Access is good off the road and the banks are reasonably clear.

The Blackwater gets a small run of spring fish – but sufficient to be of interest to anglers. The grilse run is really excellent and so too is the run of sea-trout. The spring fish are said to average 10 lb and the annual catch is reckoned to be in the region of 300 salmon and grilse. There are no figures for sea-trout but again the fishing is said to be excellent.

There is reported to be some nice fly fishing in good water up near Lough Brin and of course the rest of the river is all fishable as far as the rapids near the sea.

This lovely and prolific river is not without its problems, chief among them being gravel removal and severe poaching.

SNEEM RIVER   V 69 66

Season

Salmon: 15 March to 30 September.
Sea-trout: 15 March to 12 October.

Permission

Mr Henry Cooper
Sneem
Co. Kerry
The fishing is usually let together with a holiday cottage.

The Sneem River and its tributary, the Ardsheelane, drain two mountain valleys and a number of lakes. The total catchment is approximately 34 square miles.

The Sneem river gets a run of grilse and sea-trout in July and August.

The Ardsheelane is noted mainly as a sea-trout river. Both are very much spate rivers – best after a flood – and there is about 2 miles of pools and fishing on each of them.

CROANSAGHT RIVER (GLANMORE RIVER)   V 77 57

Season

Salmon: 15 March to 30 September.
Sea-trout: 15 March 12 October.

Permission

> Craigie's Hotel
> Castletown Bearhaven
> Co. Cork
> *Telephone* 027 70379

This little river is barely 2 miles long and drains Glanmore Lough and a 16-square mile catchment into Kenmare Bay. It looks so insignificant that some anglers ignore it – to their cost. It produces about 25 spring salmon a season – from March to May – and the lake produces the same again. It gets a run of big sea-trout (2–4½ lb) in April and the usual run of 'juniors' (small sea-trout) in July and August and a big run in September.

Guests in the hotel can enjoy the fishing free as part of the hotel facilities. Otherwise, there is a charge per rod and only four rods are allowed on the river.

CLOONEE RIVER   V 79 63

Permission

Private.

This river drains the Cloonee Lakes and gets a run of grilse.

DAWROS RIVER   V 89 67

Season

Salmon: 15 March to 30 September.
Sea-trout: 15 March to 12 October.

Permission

Free.

This little river lies 3 miles south of Kenmare on the R571. It was badly damaged by drainage works and is very overgrown. There is a small grilse run in August and it can hold some very nice sea-trout – but not many.

WATERVILLE RIVER   V 50 66

Season

Salmon: 17 January to 30 September.
Sea-trout: 17 January to 12 October.

Permission

> Waterville House
> Waterville
> Co. Kerry
> *Telephone* 667 4244

This is a private fishery on which rods are let occasionally. The maximum number of rods allowed is three, the letting period is for four hours, there is a bag limit of three salmon and spinning is allowed in spring but it is fly fishing only in summer.

This short fishery extends for 400 yards approximately from the bridge on the N70 at Waterville to the sea. It consists of a pool, a stream, the fish traps (which are no longer in operation), another stream and a pool – the famous Butler's Pool.

This river drains Lough Currane and the entire Waterville system and all fish entering these lakes and rivers must pass up the Waterville River.

The spring salmon tend to run through to the lough rather than rest in the river and it is as a grilse fishery, from July onwards, that it is best known. Records are not kept, but locally it is thought to produce at least

200 fish annually. It fishes best in medium to high water or with a good ripple on the pools. Favourite patterns are Hairy Mary, Silver Rat and shrimp flies.

An enormous run of sea-trout passes up the river. The water upstream of the fish traps is a noted hot spot and it can be all very good at dusk through July and August. Useful fly patterns include Jungle Cock Spider, Bibio, Bloody Butcher, Silver Doctor, Invicta and Wickham's Fancy.

CUMMERAGH RIVER   V 55 69

Season

Salmon: 17 January to 30 September.
Sea-trout: 17 January to 12 October.

Permission

Waterville House	Mr. Robert Noonan
Waterville	Dromkeare Lodge
Co. Kerry	Waterville
Telephone 0667 4244	Co. Kerry

The Cummeragh River drains a catchment of 46 square miles, including ten loughs, into Lough Currane. The fishing is approximately 5 miles long and holds its water for several days after a spate due to the slow release of water from the upper loughs.

Mr Noonan's stretch for a mile up from Lough Currane to the dam is private and the rest of the fishing is divided into three beats and let by Waterville House.

The Cummeragh meanders through a flat moorland of blanket peat and is slow-flowing, except when in spate. There are a few nice streams on each beat which can provide good fly fishing and nice spinning conditions for several days after a spate. Thereafter, a worm can get results, but so too can a fly when a breeze puts a ripple on the pools. The pools are narrow and weed is a problem in low water.

The river holds occasional spring salmon from opening day but it is as a grilse fishery that it excels through the summer to the end of September. In a good season, it will produce 150–200 fish.

The banks are rough and difficult to negotiate in places. Overfishing by unauthorized anglers can be a problem and it is advisable to organize your fishing through the local gillies in Waterville.

This is also an excellent sea-trout river from July onwards. Most of the fishing is done during the day and the trout come as a by-product of the salmon fishing. Small flies work best. The trout will take a small Shrimp Fly and Watson's Fancy and Connemara Black are especially recommended.

RIVER INNY   V 51 71

Season

Salmon: 17 January to 30 September.
Sea-trout: 17 January to 12 October.

Permission

The ownership of the fishing rights is very fragmented and claimed by several owners – some riparian and some absent. This fragmentation of ownerships gives rise to several problems, not the least of which is the right of access to the water. The following have fishing to let:

Butler Arms Hotel
Waterville, Co. Kerry
Telephone 0667-4156

Mr Frank Donnelly,
Lake Rd, Waterville, Co. Kerry
Telephone 0667-4303

Donal O'Sullivan
Inchiboy, Mastergeehy
Killarney, Co. Kerry

John O'Shea
Killenleigh, Mastergeehy
Killarney, Co. Kerry

Michael Gas,
Kylemore House,
Waterville, Co. Kerry

Jim Sugrue
Moulnahone
Mastergeehy
Killarney, Co. Kerry

James O'Connell
Foildrenagh
Mastergeehy
Killarney, Co. Kerry

Michael J. O'Sullivan
Lobster Bar
Waterville, Co. Kerry
Telephone 0667 4255

Waterville House
Waterville
Co. Kerry
Telephone 0667 4244

With its tributaries the River Inny drains a long narrow mountain valley and has a catchment of 47 square miles. It is very much a spate system, with the fishing confined to the spate conditions and rarely lasting more than eight hours. The locals advise taking a gillie if you are not to miss the best of it. There is about 8 miles of fishing up to Cuslagh Bridge.

It is regarded mainly as a grilse fishery, with fish running from mid-

June. September can be really good. It is estimated to produce 250 fish annually. Fly fishing and spinning are the usual methods and the fly can be very productive when fish are running. Useful patterns are Hairy Mary, Silver Doctor and Thunder and Lightning, sizes 6–10, single or double.

A lot of the river is flat and featureless, with short streams and long shallow pools in low water. The removal of gravel from the bed of the river has seriously disrupted its physical character and badly affects the flow regime, the bed of the river and the banks.

It gets a small run of good sea-trout in April and 'juniors' from June onwards, but is not seriously regarded as a sea-trout fishery.

CARHAN RIVER   V 50 79

Season

Salmon: 1 April to 30 September.
Sea-trout: 1 April to 12th October.

This little spate river enters Valentia Harbour north of Cahersiveen. It gets sea-trout in June and grilse from July on a flood. It is mostly overgrown with only about three fishing locations and worm is considered the best bait.

FERTA RIVER   V 51 81

Season:

As for Carhan River, above.

The Ferta enters the head of Valentia Harbour. It is a spate river with about 12 miles of fishing above and below Failmore Bridge. It gets a small run of grilse and sea-trout on summer spates.

CARAGH RIVER   V 71 87

Season

Salmon: 17 January to 30 September.
Sea-trout: 17 January to 12 October.
Brown trout: 15 February to 12 October.

Permission

> K.R.D. Fisheries Ltd   Glencar Hotel
> Salmon Exporters   Co. Kerry
> Killorglin, Co. Kerry   *Telephone* 066 60102
> *Telephone* 066 61106

The Caragh River drains the southern slopes of Macgillicuddy's Reeks and half a dozen small loughs before it enters Lough Caragh. On leaving Caragh, it flows approximately 2 miles to the tide at Rossbehy Creek on Dingle Bay. The catchment is 66 square miles.

K.R.D. Fisheries Ltd controls the river downstream of the lough and Glencar Hotel manages the upper section.

Day tickets for salmon and sea-trout fishing on the lower Caragh River can be obtained from Mr Patrick O'Grady, Hillside House, Glenbeigh, Co. Kerry, (*telephone* 066 68228).

The Caragh River is a classic spate system. It gets a very good run of spring salmon and grilse. The lower river is also a noted sea-trout fishery but, strangely, they don't run the upper river in appreciable numbers.

The lower Caragh River has about twenty pools up to the lake. There is some nice fly fishing in the middle section. The belief that the spring fish tend to run through is not altogether true and fish are taken here from February. This section has produced over twenty fish in May in recent years. The grilse begin running at the end of May and it is during the summer months, when conditions are right, that the fishing is best.

The fishing is tidal at Caragh Bridge and this stretch usually fishes best for two hours before and two hours after the high tide.

The sea-trout run late – from mid August – and the night fishing can be really excellent. The Jungle Cock and Black Pennell are two of the recommended patterns. The sea-trout will also take a fly during the day in dull conditions.

The upper Caragh is primarily a salmon and grilse fishery. The spring fish run from February to April and the grilse begin running at the end of May and the run peaks in July, depending on water conditions.

From the lake up to Blackstones Bridge is known as 'The Caol'. It is deep and sluggish, with the exception of Lickeen Pool, which has a stream and can be fished with a fly. The rest is fished from a boat – either spinning or trolling.

The stretch from Blackstones Bridge to the joinings at Boheeshil – a distance of 4 miles approximately – is divided into seven beats and has fourteen pools. The beats are rotated daily at 1.30 p.m. and there is only one rod per beat, though a child under 16 years or a wife or husband can also share the beat.

All legitimate methods are allowed except natural shrimp or prawn.

An orange tube fly (orange hair and black body) is good in spring and on dropping water. The Lemon and Grey is considered the fly for the Caragh River and after it comes the Blue Charm and Silver Doctor in sizes 6 and 8 single and 10 double.

GLENCAR HOTEL RECORDS

	1984	1985	1986	1987	1988	1989
Salmon	315	286	368	168	460	372

The spring salmon average 10½ lb and nearly every year sees a couple over 20 lb. Grilse average 4 lb.

RIVER LAUNE   V 89 91

Season

Salmon: 17 January to 30 September.
Sea-trout: 17 January to 12 October.
Brown trout: 15 February to 12 October.

Permission

The ownership of fishing rights on the River Laune is fragmented among disparate groups and private owners.

River Laune Fishery (Muckross)

Permits from the Park Superintendent, Knockneer Estate Office (near cathedral), Killarney, Co. Kerry (*telephone* 064 31246).

Land Commission Fishery at Meanus, Tubrid and Mweelcaha townlands

Inquiries to the Park Superintendent, above, or The SW Regional Fisheries Board, Macroom, Co. Cork, *Telephone* 026-41222.

Laune Salmon Anglers' Association

Secretary: Mr Ted O'Riordan, 50 Oak Park Demesne, Tralee, Co. Kerry, *Telephone* 066-24690

Daily and weekly permits available at reasonable prices from fishing tackle shops in Killarney, the shop at Beaufort Bridge and Pat O'Grady, Hillside House, Glenbeigh, Co. Kerry.

Mr John Mangan, Ardlahas, Killorglin, Co. Kerry (*telephone* 066 61393), has approximately 5½ miles of fishing to let by the day or by the week, downstream of Beaufort Bridge.

The River Laune is approximately 14 miles long and drains the lakes of Killarney and a catchment of some 320 square miles into Castlemaine Harbour at the head of Dingle Bay. It is 10 miles from the lake to the tide – the river is tidal for nearly 2 miles above Killorglin – and has at least sixty named pools. The extensive loughs ensure good fishing water for lengthy periods after a flood.

The river gets an excellent run of spring salmon and grilse. It is not unusual to see ten spring fish on the bank by 10 a.m. on the opening day at the top section of the Muckross Fishery. Catches of twenty spring salmon in one day are not unknown.

The best spring fishing, early in the season, is at the top of the river. As the season progresses, the fish tend to slow down and populate the pools downstream. The good fishing extends all over the river by May and this is probably the best month of all for spring fish. A feature of the May fishing is the number of big fish the river produces (17 and 18 lb) and it is generally accepted that the bigger fish don't run till May.

The first grilse begin appearing in May but the peak of the run takes place in June and salmon fishing lasts right through the summer, with September being regarded as a particularly good month for fly fishing.

All legitimate methods are allowed and some of the fisheries are heavily fished when the fish are running.

The river used also to get an excellent run of sea-trout but this has declined in recent times. The Laune sea-trout run early – May and June – and I have heard of anglers who took over thirty to the rod for a day's fishing. These sea-trout would average 1½ lb. The night fishing can be very good but it can be equally good during the day when conditions are right. The best of the fishing is in the tidal water above Killorglin, Poulnahalla and the Bridge stream below Beaufort Bridge. The river also holds a marvellous stock of brown trout, with quite a good percentage of them ranging from ¾ to 1 lb. Worm fishers catch up to thirty in a day in the spring. It is a river with a great variety of fly life – olives, sedges, stoneflies and terrestrials, including the hawthorn. On summer evenings the number of trout taking the blue-winged olive and its spinner has to be seen to be appreciated but they can be difficult to tempt in the clear water and the best chance is at dusk with a dry fly and fine tippet.

The Laune Fisheries (Muckross) let evening trout fishing at a reduced charge from 3 p.m. till midnight and the other fisheries charge the same as for salmon fishing.

This is a quite exceptional river and fishery. It has fish, it has character and it is in a beautiful location.

RIVER FLESK   V 98 90

Season

Salmon: 17 January to 30 September.
Brown trout: 15 February to 12 October.

Permission

Cahernane Hotel
Killarney, Co. Kerry
Telephone 064 31895

Lough Leane Anglers' Association

Permits available from:
The Handy Shop   O'Neill's Tackle Shop
Kenmare Place   Plunkett Street
Killarney, Co. Kerry   Killarney, Co. Kerry

Cloonkeen Anglers' Association
Inquiries to Cloonkeen PO, Co. Kerry

The River Flesk, 28 miles long, is a medium-to-large spate river. It drains the west Cork Mountains and flows in a north westerly direction into Lough Leane at Killarney. The lower reaches are deep, but with enough flow to carry a fly, the middle is well endowed with holding pools and fishing, and in the upper reaches, it is a fast-flowing boulder-strewn stream with occasional holding pools.

It gets a run of spring salmon, but their numbers have declined. It still gets an excellent run of grilse. The first of these fish arrive late May or early June, depending on water. The spring run may have declined, but this river has nevertheless usually produced thirty springers by the end of February every season. In all, there is over 12 miles of fishing. Water levels rise very quickly and drop just as fast. The angler who knows the river or has a good guide will know which section to fish, depending on the height of water.

A feature of this river is the amount of free fishing that is available for the angler who is prepared to inquire about it. From whom to inquire is the problem and the services of a guide are invaluable. One such is Michael O'Brien, 'Anglers' Paradise', Loreto Road, Muckross, Killarney, Co. Kerry, (*telephone* 064 33818).

The following is a rough guide to the various stretches, taking the river bridge to bridge.

From Lough Leane up to Flesh Bridge on the left bank is the Cahernane Hotel water. The right bank up to Flesh Bridge is leased by Lough Leane Anglers' Association and this association has the fishing leased also on the right bank from Flesh Bridge to White Bridge and again on the right bank from White Bridge to Gartahoosh Bridge. The left bank from Flesk Bridge to White Bridge to Gartahoosh Bridge is controlled by the riparian owners and there is a lot of good fishing available to the angler who is prepared to inquire. A lot of the fishing may even be free. Finding it is where the cost arises, for to do so you must employ a guide or gillie. Lough Leane Anglers' Association has most of the right bank from Gortahoosh Bridge to Glenflesk and the left bank is held by the riparian owners. Upstream of Glenflesh, the ownership becomes very confused. Cloonkeen Anglers' Association has a stretch and the visitor is likely to find very heavy angling pressure on the good pools when the water is right.

There is good brown trout fishing at various points from Flesk Bridge down to the lake. Wet fly is best. The trout average $\frac{1}{2}$ lb or better and there is a lot of night fishing done in the summer months when the stocks of river trout are augmented by a run of trout up from the lough. Once again, local knowledge is the key to success.

OWNEYKEAGH RIVER   W 87 06

Season

As for River Flesk, above.

Permission

Riparian owners.

The Owneykeagh River joins the Flesk from the north midway between Gortahoosh Bridge and Glenflesk. It is narrow and deep, with a reputation for holding good stocks of brown trout. Fly hatches are sparse and worm gives best results. Access is difficult, with soft undercut banks and a lot of virtually impassable marshland on either side.

RIVER MAINE   Q 90 06

LITTLE RIVER MAINE   Q 94 06

BROWN FLESK RIVER   Q 98 04

Season

Salmon: 17 January to 30 September.
Sea-trout: 17 January to 12 October.
Brown trout: 15 February to 12 October.

Permission

Free.

The River Maine is of medium size. It has two tributaries of interest to anglers and its entire catchment is 154 square miles. The Maine and the Little River Maine drain flat countryside from Castleisland to Castlemaine and on into Castlemaine Harbour at the head of Dingle Bay. The Brown Flesk River is 20 miles long and is a much swifter stream as it flows westwards through Scartaglin and Farranfore.

This river system had an arterial drainage scheme carried out in the 1950s. Consequently, many of the famous old salmon pools are no more and the banks are very high in some places. It has, however, recovered quite well and the Brown Flesk River has at least thirty-five holding pools.

Being a free fishery, it is badly maintained and is completely overgrown in places. It also has its problems with poaching and pollution.

It gets a prolific run of salmon and sea-trout and has five draft nets operating at the mouth. One, in fact, operates above Castlemaine. It is highly regarded as a grilse (end of June) and autumn salmon river. Fish average 8–9 lb. It still gets a good run of spring sea-trout – 2–4½ lb in April and smaller fish from July.

The River Maine is best fished in medium to low water. Much of it is overgrown and it is necessary to wade. The best water is from Marshall's Bridge right down to, and below Ballyfinane Bridge. It gets a great run of grilse in June and the September fishing can be really good. Favourite flies are Claret and Olive, Claret and Blue and Peter Ross, even in such large sizes as 6 and 4. A small blue-and-silver Mepps is also effective.

There is good brown trout fishing in this area. They average ½ lb. April can be an especially good month and some very big baskets are

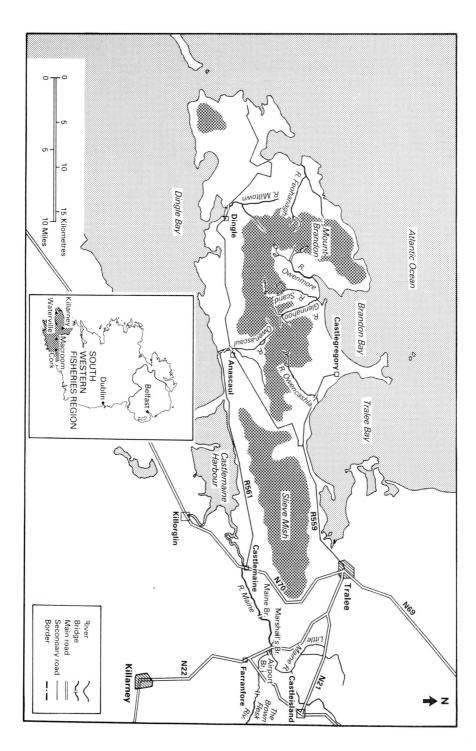

The Dingle Peninsula

taken here. Try a Greenwell's Glory, a Red Spinner or a Bloody Butcher in the evening.

The Little Maine is better known as a brown trout and sea-trout river and the best salmon fishing is in seven or eight pools up as far as the Riverside Inn at Curranes. The brown trout come four to the pound with some to ½ lb. The best of the sea-trout fishing is at night. The banks are quite open and the water runs low and very clear in summer.

The Brown Flesk River is a typical spate river and can give really excellent fishing for salmon and sea-trout after a spate. It produces well over 200 fish to rod and line every season and it is quite common for an angler who knows the river to take three or four salmon and up to two dozen sea-trout in a day's fishing. The best of it is from the Metal Bridge down to the Airport Bridge at Currow – a stretch that has at least thirty good holding pools. A lot of it is overgrown and hard to fish. On the other hand, it is this cover that helps the fish to survive.

These three rivers have a lot of potential and it is a great pity that they have no management plan. Inquiries to the SW Fisheries Board, Nevilles Terrace, Macroom, Co. Cork, *Telephone* 026-41222.

OWENMORE RIVER   Q 51 10

Season

Salmon: 1 April to 30 September.
Sea-trout: 1 April to 30 September.

Permission

Gerry Connor   Bertie Brosnan
Bridge Cottage   Mitchell's Road
Cloghane, Co. Kerry   Tralee, Co. Kerry

This is a small spate river on the Dingle Peninsula, draining nine loughs and a 17 square mile catchment on the eastern slopes of Mount Brandon into Brandon Bay. It is surrounded by bog and mountain and is totally undeveloped. It has a number of good holding pools and access is off the main road or via bog roads. It gets a run of big sea-trout in April, grilse in June and small sea-trout from July onwards. In 1988, it produced 90 salmon and 590 sea-trout and in 1989, 26 salmon and 259 sea-trout to 5 lb.

SCARID RIVER   Q 54 11

GLENNAHOO RIVER   Q 54 11

Season

Salmon and sea-trout: 1 March to 30 September.

Permission

Inquire locally.

These two small rivers flow into Brandon Bay and get a run of sea-trout from April and grilse from June. They are worth fishing on a spate.

OWENCASHLA RIVER   Q 65 11

Season

Salmon and sea-trout: 1 March to 30 September.

Permission

Inquire locally.

The Owencashla flows north into Tralee Bay. It is overgrown but well worth fishing for sea-trout and grilse as the spate runs off.

FEOHANAGH RIVER   Q 41 10

Season

Salmon and sea-trout: 1 March to 30 September.

Permission

Inquire locally.

The Feohanagh River, 7 miles long, drains a catchment of 11 square miles on the western slopes of Mount Brandon into Smerwick Harbour – which is west of Dingle. It used be a really good river for sea-trout and grilse from June onwards after a spate but, sadly, the nets have taken their toll and few fish now run it. If you get one, just remember that you have taken your fish on the most westerly river in Europe.

THE MILLTOWN RIVER   Q 43 02

Season

Salmon: 17 March to 30 September.
Sea-trout: 17 March to 12 October.

Permission

Inquire locally.

This small spate river drains southwards into Dingle Harbour, 1 mile west of Dingle. It gets occasional grilse and a few sea-trout on the spate.

OWENASCAUL RIVER   Q 59 01

Season

Salmon: 17 March to 30 September.
Sea-trout: 17 March to 12 October.

Permission

Inquire locally.

The Owenascaul River drains a number of small loughs into the northern end of Dingle Bay. It is generally regarded as free fishing and even though it may be small – 6 miles long, with a 6 square mile catchment – it is well worth fishing on the spate for both grilse and sea-trout. The fish usually arrive on the first flood in June and it gets some fish on every flood thereafter through the summer.

Index